Joseph H. Shorthouse

A Teacher of the Violin

And other Tales

Joseph H. Shorthouse

A Teacher of the Violin
And other Tales

ISBN/EAN: 9783337074548

Printed in Europe, USA, Canada, Australia, Japan

Cover: Foto ©ninafisch / pixelio.de

More available books at **www.hansebooks.com**

A TEACHER OF THE VIOLIN

AND OTHER TALES

BY

J. H. SHORTHOUSE

AUTHOR OF 'JOHN INGLESANT,' 'SIR PERCIVAL,' ETC.

London

MACMILLAN AND CO.

AND NEW YORK

1891

All rights reserved

First Edition 1888. *Reprinted* 1891

TO

THE HON. HALLAM TENNYSON

THIS VOLUME IS DEDICATED,

WITH SINCERE REGARD.

The first three stories in this volume have appeared in 'Macmillan's Magazine'; *the last, 'An Apologue,' is reprinted, by permission, from the* 'Nineteenth Century.'

CONTENTS

	PAGE
A Teacher of the Violin	1
The Marquis Jeanne Hyacinthe de St. Palaye	117
The Baroness Helena von Saarfeld	185
Ellie: a Story of a Boy and Girl	281
An Apologue	307

I

A TEACHER OF THE VIOLIN

A TEACHER OF THE VIOLIN

I

AUTOBIOGRAPHICAL.

WHEN, in the year 1787, I entered, at the age of nineteen, the university of the kingly city of Wenigstaat, I was, no doubt, a very foolish young man, but I am perfectly certain that I was not a fool. I suffered not only from that necessary disease which from the very nature of existence it is impossible for a young man to escape, the regarding of life from his own standpoint, as a man on first coming into a brilliantly lighted and crowded room must of necessity, for a few moments, be conscious of the varied scene only as it strikes himself;

but I was also to some extent subject to that fatuity which haunts some young men, the forming of opinions and the giving audible expression to them. Notwithstanding all this, I was at the same time conscious of such a crowd of ideas, actuated by such ideas, and stirred to the depths of my being by the emotions and results which these ideas wrought upon me, that looking back with the impartiality which the lapse of thirty years gives even to the review of one's self, I feel perfectly confident that I was not a fool. I shall, I fear, have to describe at some length how I came to be what I was, but I will be as short as I can. My history would be worth nothing in itself, but it is interwoven closely with that of some others whose personality seems to me well worthy of record.

I was the eldest son of the pastor of the little village of Waldreich in the wooded mountains of Bavaria. Though my father had a large family, and his cure was only a village one, he was not so poor as most of his order, for he had a little private income derived from houses in Bayreuth : my mother had also some little money of her own. My father was a man of a singular patience and quietude of conduct. He divided his time between cultivating his little garden and orchard, and preparing his sermons with elaborate care. When, in after years, I became possessed of many of these beautifully written discourses, I was amazed at the patience, care, and scholarship expended upon these addresses to a few peasants, most of whom fell asleep during the time of hearing. I believe that my father's sole relaxation and indulgence consisted in poring over an old folio Terence which he possessed, and which, shielded amidst the mysteries of a dead language, he could read in perfect security, without fear of scandalising his flock. Indeed it is possible that they regarded it as a work of deep theology, and perhaps they were right.

The little village of Waldreich lies immediately at the foot of the wooded hills. We ascended from the garden and croft of the pastor's house straight into the fir-woods and the oak-dingles that led up into the mysterious and wild heights above—into the mists and cloud-shadows—into a land of green mountain-woods rising against blue skies—a land of mist and rain-showers, of the tints of rainbows spanning the village, and of coloured prisms of light stealing down crag and forest-dingle—a land of rushing streams and still, solemn, dark lakes—a land of castles upon distant peaks and of the faint smoke of charcoal-burners on the hillsides. Through all the varied changes of the day in this romantic land, from the cheerful dawn, loud with the song of birds and the lowing of cattle, to the solemn evening stillness, I passed the first few years of my life. The scenes around him penetrated into the boy's being and formed his nature. However, I have no wish to become wearisome in describing all these influences and these results minutely. There is one influence, however, which must be dwelt upon if the story is to be told at all, for it was the leading influence of my life—the influence of sound. From a very little child I was profoundly impressed by the sounds of nature: the rushing water, the rustling oaks, the sighing and moaning wind down the mountain-valleys spoke to me with distinct utterance, and with a sense of meaning and even of speech. These sounds were more even than this: they became a passion, a fascination, a haunting presence, and even a dread.

I can give one instance of this. Below the village and parsonage house, where we lived, was a beautiful meadow on the banks of the swift winding river. This meadow was my greatest delight as a little child. At the lower end was a mill, and a mill-pool and race; and around the edges of the pool beds of flags had planted themselves for ages, forming a thick phalanx of waving pointed leaves. Nothing could exceed the fascination this sight had for me, not only when the yellow flowers mingled with the green stately leaves, but at other times of the year when I listened hour after hour to the whispering murmur through the innumerable lances of the reeds. But to reach this meadow it was necessary to pass a row of vast, lofty, straggling trees (I suppose some species of poplar), and no words can describe the terror which the same wind, which delighted me so much in the gentle murmur of its reed-music, inspired me with when heard through these lofty swaying branches. I often, even in those early days, wondered why the music of the wind through the green rushes on the water's edge should have thrilled me with cheerfulness and joy, while the same wind wailing through the branches of the great trees high above my head crushed me with an unspeakable horror and dread. Doubtless in this latter was the sense of vastness and unapproachable height, infinite as it seemed to a little child—the touch, even, of the infinite must ever, it would seem, be appalling to man.

It was in this way and by these experimental methods that I began so early to recognise the mysterious connection that exists between sound and human feeling.

Down the long winding oak-dingles, between the high cliffs and the wooded slopes of the hills, there came to me as a little child whispers and murmurs of dreams and stories of which at that time I knew nothing, and to which I could give in those early days no intelligent voice or meaning. But, as I grew in years and listened to the talk of nurse and peasant, and of village lads and children, and heard from them the legends of elf-kings and maidens and wild hunters of the forest, weird and fantastic indeed, yet still strangely instinct with human wants and hopes, I began to connect such sympathy, felt then, as it seemed, for the first time, with human life in all its varied aspects, and stories of human loves and joys and terrors, with these sounds of nature, the sweeping wind through wood.

I use these last words advisedly because, even in those earliest days, it seemed to me that all sound that was of spiritual import was in some hidden sense the product of the wind and of wood. There was a wailing of the wind at night through the crevices of the high-pitched roof and the panelled walls of the old parsonage that thrilled me as with a message from on high, but this was still wind and wood. But where the wind had no part, where it was not sound so much as noise, in the clanging of metal upon metal, in the inarticulate screaming of senseless creatures, the terror that I had felt in the wailing wood,—that terror that had still something in it of the higher life and hope,—was turned into the mere panic of despair.

I distinctly remember that I had these feelings as a child; but, since those days, I have pleased myself in finding that the great Goethe shared with me my dislike to the continuous barking of a dog. 'Annihilation,' he said one day, in conversation with the *Legationsrath* Falk, 'is utterly out of the question; but the possibility of being caught on the way by some more powerful, and yet baser monas, and subordinated to it—that is unquestionably a very serious consideration; and I, for my part, have never been able entirely to divest myself of the fear of it. At this moment a dog was heard repeatedly barking in the street. Goethe sprang hastily to the window and called out to it: 'Take what form you will, vile larva, you shall not subjugate me.' A gallant boast but an ineffectual one! Noise, especially if continued on one note, deadens and destroys the soul, the life of the mind within the brain. The constant reiteration of one note will drive a man mad, just as the continual fall of a drop of water upon the same spot of the head will cause madness and death. You may prove this on the violin. Whereas if you laid your head down in the meadow by the river on the long grass, there came to you in the whispering wind something like the sea-murmurs that live within the shell—tidings of a delicate life, news of a world beyond the thought of those who merely haunt the palaces of earth.

These two, the murmur of the wind

through grass and the whisper within the shell, are perhaps the most delicate sounds that Nature can produce: was it possible that I should find in art something more perfect still? In this passion for sound, in which I lived as in a paradise, it may be asked, Where did music find a place? The music that I heard in my childhood was not of the best class; and perhaps this might be the reason that musical sound rather than music seemed to haunt those hours of childhood, for among the untutored sounds of Nature there are, now and again, musical notes of surpassing beauty. Among the wailing sounds of the wind that haunted the high-pitched roof above the boarded ceiling of our bedroom, there was one perfect and regular note. It never varied, except in loudness according to the force of the wind. This note, in its monotony, had an enthralling effect upon my imagination. I had once associated certain thoughts with its message: no doubt the continued association of ideas of recollected imagery would explain the rest.

The wandering musicians that played in the court-yard on summer evenings upon hautboys and fiddles no doubt reached me with a strange message from afar, especially in the shrill high notes; and on Sunday, in the village church, the organist thundered out fugues and fantasias, but it was the final cadences only that touched me: somehow the organ seemed wanting in that supreme searching power of wind and wood.

But one day, it was a summer evening, there came into the court-yard four zither-players from the South. I say zither-players, but their instruments were more like the old Italian lutes for size and the number of strings. They were regulated each at a certain interval, including only the notes of the middle octaves.

They played a singular rapid music with little tune. It was like a rippling mænad dance: apparently reckless and untrained, yet in reality perfectly regulated in step and figure, every note true to its corresponding note in the higher or lower octave, and now and again all united in one sudden consonant harmony, by which the wild lawless music vindicated its perception of unison and the moral perfection of pure sound ; but even in this there seemed to me nothing that spoke in just the same voice as did the gentle whisper of that teaching wind through grass and wood.

On the organ in the parish church, written in faded gold letters, were the words from Luther's Bible : 'The wind bloweth where it will, and thou hearest the sound of it well, so is every one that is of the spirit born.' When, as a child, I sat during long sermons in the little grated seat of the pastor's children,

I pondered over these words, and for a long time could find no reason or congruity in them. What had the wind blowing where it listeth to do with the birth of the spirit? But on one hot summer afternoon, when I had fallen asleep during my father's discourse, I was suddenly aroused by the cessation of the preacher's voice and by the murmuring fall of harmony, for the organist probably had been asleep too, and was playing unconsciously such simple notes as came first to hand. I say I awoke suddenly into life and sense, and saw the rich mellow tints of the organ-wood, and these mystic letters all lighted up with the gilding rays; and an inward consciousness came like a flash of lightning from heaven into the child's mind that the wandering, seeking wind through reed or organ-pipe or flute, or over strings of violin or grassy hill, spoke to the spirit and to the spirit-born, and to such only, with a sufficient and adequate voice. This conception came to me like a message from above. It raised my thoughts of Nature and harmonised her voices with the needs and desires of my own soul. I pondered over it day and night; but before long an event occurred which was in the end the means of leading me beyond this half truth, and of more fully opening to me the gates of the mystical city of sound, of which this organ-text had already given me some fairy glimpses, and of revealing to me at last the true music which is not only heard by the spirit-born but is born of the spirit itself.

My father went once every month on a kind of supernatural mission, as it seemed to us children, to an unknown and dimly conceived mansion or mountain-palace in the hills. That is, he was chaplain to the old Gräfin von Wetstein, and once a month he preached before her on Sundays. Sometimes, on special occasions, an ornamental or state-coach was sent for the pastor, who thus seemed rapt as in a celestial chariot from his family and the ordinary village folk.

One surprising day, when the lad was between fourteen and fifteen, the father said to him: 'Put on thy best clothes, for to-morrow thou shalt go with me to the Gräfin.'

It may well be imagined that there was not much sleep for the boy that night.

It would take too long to tell of the wonders of that journey in the state-coach, of the foolish, but perhaps natural pride of sitting there above the common folk, and observing through the windows the respect paid by all to the magnificent and symbolic vehicle, if not to those who sat therein.

When we reached the *schloss*, which stood high up on the hills amid woodland meadows and cow-pastures, then indeed the boy's expectation and excitement grew too painful almost to be borne. He passed through the gardens, with terraces and urns and statues, and the cascades of water that came down from great ponds, formed in the summits of the hills by building high stone walls and dams across the ravines. Later on he was even presented to the Gräfin, who, herself a wizened, faded old woman, stood beneath the portraits of her ancestors, by a great window in the gallery of the *schloss*, overlooking the valleys and the champaign country beyond.

For some unknown reason this old woman, who scarcely spoke to any one and seemed to take no interest in the present world, looking, as it were, constantly out of the high windows into the driving cloudland, as though she saw there all her past life and the figures of all those who had alone made it dear to her, and who were themselves all gone into the cloudland of the Infinite Unseen,—this old woman, not at the first interview, but at the second or third, in the fresh mornings over the early coffee, took a strange liking for the little village lad. As this ill-assorted pair sat at the open window on the quiet summer evenings, far above the distant woodland and the forest meadows, face to face with the long streaks of solemn light along the horizon, an almost imperceptible murmur, so soft and gentle was it, passed up through the branches of the sycamore and chestnut trees and of the lower growing pines, and, mingling with the distant *Ranz des Vaches*, brought up as it seemed the life and struggles and sorrows of the plain and of the people into the ears of this worn-out, old, feeble aristocrat of the hills. She would say to the boy: 'And what do you do, you children, in the winter nights, when you steal back in your night-dresses to the great fire, and the father is reading Terence? Tell it to me all again.'

Finally, she insisted upon my staying with her for weeks at a time, and she bound herself to the pastor, by a written paper, to provide for my future career. The boy led mostly a wild life, for his interviews with his patroness took place at odd times and hours, but he had some lessons from a resident cleric who superintended the household, and had other teachers more than perhaps any one knew.

My father had often told his listening family of the great nobles who would from time to time stay at the *schloss*, and how he would be invited, being of a witty and conversational habit, derived probably from his reading in Terence, to dine with them. Some of these great noblemen I also saw at a distance in the garden or elsewhere; but on one occasion a young Graf came to stay some days with his great-aunt, having returned quite lately from the Italian tour with his tutor. This tutor, an Italian, performed wonderfully, it was said, on the violin. He was invited to play before the Gräfin, and the boy was admitted among the domestics of the *schloss*.

Then, on a sudden, was revealed to him the secret which had escaped him so long, the consciousness of the existence of which had haunted him in the wind-swept meadow and amid the awful, swaying branches of the lofty trees.

I am not going to describe this playing. Attempts have been sometimes made to describe violin-playing in words, but rarely, I think, with much success. I shall only say that almost as soon as he began to play what seemed to me then a singularly strange idea occurred to me. This man, I thought, is not playing on his instrument: he is playing on my brain. His violin is only as it were the bow, or rather, every note of his violin vibrates with the according note of the brain-fibre. I do not say that I put the thought exactly into these words; but these are the words into which, at the present time, I put the recollection of my thought. I need not point out how my ignorance erred in detail, how the brain has no extended strings corresponding to the strings of a violin; but I have since thought that there was more truth in this wild idea of a child's ignorance than would at first appear, and it seemed to lead the way to a second thought, which crossed my mind in the transport of ecstasy produced by this, the first violin-playing worthy of the name, which I had ever heard.

I knew the secret now, both of the entrancing whisper of the wind-music and also why, at a certain point, it had failed. The blind, senseless wind, blowing merely where it listed, had aroused the human spirit through the medium of grass and reed and rock and forest, and called it through the fairy gate into cloud and dreamland; but when, instead of the blind, senseless wind the instructed human spirit itself touched the strings, music, born of cultured harmony, through all the long scale of accordant sound, won for the listening, rapt, ecstatic spirit an insight and an entrance into realms which the outward eye had not seen, the secrets of which it is not lawful or possible to utter to any save to the spirit-born.

'You seem absorbed in the music, my boy,' said this gentleman to me: 'do you play the violin, perchance?'

I said that I had played on no instrument save picking out harmonious thirds on an old harpsichord at the parsonage house. My father was perfectly an amateur: he loved music so much that he refused to play himself, or to allow any one else to play in his hearing save those who could play well: 'playing a little' was his dread.

The gentleman shut up his precious violin in its case and produced another, on which he showed me the possibility of varying the note through every shade of pitch by the position of the finger on the vibrating string. It is impossible to describe the delight I felt when I was able to feel out a chord of three notes.

'I am violating your father's instructions perhaps,' said the gentleman, smiling; 'but every one must have a beginning. Nevertheless he has much on his side. It has been said, rather cynically, "The moment a man touches an instrument he ceases to be a musician."'

I did not understand this then, but I understood it well afterwards.

The gentleman left one of his less cherished instruments behind him, with some simple exercises which he enjoined me to practise only, and to attempt nothing else, but I blush to say that I did not follow his advice. I played the chords he left me now and again, but I was absorbed in the one idea that his playing had left with me—the thought of the human spirit informing the senseless wind. I delighted only in the fancy that I was a mere automaton, and that the pervading spirit—the spirit that inspires man and breathes in Nature—was playing through my spirit upon the obedient vibrating strings. In this way I played fantasias of the most striking and original character, and at the same time destroyed all my chances, or ran a serious risk of doing so, of ever becoming a violinist.

Three quiet years passed in this manner, during which I lived almost constantly at Geiselwind with the Gräfin, who, in fact, treated me as her own son. At the end of that time she informed me that she intended to send me to the university of Wenigstaat. She chose this university for me, she told me, because it was near, but above all because it was not famous, but was, in fact, a mere appanage to a kingly city, and was therefore less likely to pervert from the correct and decorous habits in which they had been brought up, the ideas and habits of young men. She would provide me with a sufficient income, and would take care that my wardrobe and appointments were those of a gentleman, a station which she wished me to occupy and to maintain without disgrace.

The habits of society in the universities and elsewhere were very different in those days from what they have since become. The old society of the days before the revolution existed in its full strength. French taste in costume and amusements was universal; and the fashion of philosophic inquiry which was copied from the French was a mere intellectual toy, and had no effect upon the practical conclusions of those who amused themselves with it. The merits of republican institutions and the inviolability of the rights of man were discussed as abstract questions, without a thought that the conclusions would ever be applied to modern life, or to the daily relationships of nobles and peasants and townspeople. Before the bursting of the torrent which was to sweep it out of existence, the old world slumbered in a rainbow-tinted evening light of delicately fancied culture and repose.

The habits and appearance of university students have changed more completely than those of any other class. In the most advanced cities even in those days they dressed completely in the French manner, in embroidered suits and powdered hair, fluttering from toilette to toilette, and caring little for lectures or professors. In the old stately city of Wenigstaat, it may be easily understood, the ideas and habits of the past existed with a peculiar unchangeableness.

I regretted leaving the life of hill and forest and dreamy phantasy in which I had found so much to delight me, but the natural love of youth for change and adventure consoled me. One great advantage I derived from the choice the Gräfin had made for me was, that I did not change the character of my outward surroundings. I was nearly nineteen when I left Geiselwind and arrived one evening in a postchaise at Wenigstaat.

The city lay in a wooded valley surrounded by hills covered to their summits with woods of beech and oak and fir: through these woods running streams and cascades forced their way now through the green mountain-meadows, now over rocky steeps and dingles: a soft blue sky brooded over this green world of leaf and grass and song birds, and sunlit showers swept over the woodland and deepened the verdure into fresher green. In the centre of this plain, almost encircled by a winding river, the city was built upon a hill which divided itself into two summist, upon one of which stood the cathedral and upon the other the King's palace. Between these summits the old town wound its way up, past gates and towers and market-place and *rathhaus* and the buildings of the university, with masses of old gabled houses of an oppressive height and of immemorial antiquity, with huge overhanging stories and tiers of rooms wandering on, apparently without plan or guide, from house to house and street to street—a human hive of intricate workmanship, of carpentry-work and stonework and brickwork, all crowded together in the little space of the rising hill-street above the rushing stream, a space small in itself but infinite in its thronged stories of centuries of life—a vast grave, not only of generations of the dead, themselves lying not far from the foundations of their homes, but of buried hopes, of faded beauty, of beaten courage and stricken faith and patience crushed and lost at last in the unequal fight with fate. The dim cathedral, full of storied windows of deep blood-stained glass and of colossal figures of mailed heroes guarding emblazoned tombs, faced the King's palace, a massive ivy-covered fortress relieved here and there with façades of carved work of the later Renaissance.

The tired horses of my postchaise struggled up over the stone pavement of this steep street amid the crowd of loiterers and traffickers and gay pleasure-seekers that thronged it and drew up before the Three Roses in the Peterstrasse, where a room had been provided for me. Here I slept, and here I dined every day at an ordinary frequented by many of the principal citizens, by some of the wealthier students, and by some officials and courtiers, when it was not the turn of the latter in waiting at the palace. This table was one at least of the centres of life and interest in the little kingly city.

To a boy reared in a country parsonage and an old half-deserted manor-house, all this, it may be conceived, was strange enough; but somehow it did not seem to me wholly strange. I had been trained at the table of the Gräfin to the usages of polite life, and the whispering wind and the solemn forests of my childhood had seemed to lift me above a sense of embarrassment, as though the passing scenes before me were but the shadows and visions of a dream. I looked down the long table at the varied faces, at the talkers and showy ones, at the grave citizens, at the quiet humorous students, who now and then said a few words that turned the laugh against the talkers, at the courtiers affecting some special knowledge of affairs of state about which the King probably troubled himself little; and I remember that it all seemed to me like turning the pages of a story-book, or like the shifting scenes of a play, about which latter, though I had never seen one, I had read and heard much.

On the second and third day I found myself seated by a little elderly man, very elaborately dressed, with powdered hair and a beautifully embroidered coat. I have always felt an attraction towards old men: they are so polite, and their conversation, when they do talk, is always worth listening to. Something of this feeling, perhaps, showed itself in my manner. On the third day he said to me on rising from dinner: 'I perceive, sir, that you are a stranger here; you seem to me to be a quiet well-bred young man, and I shall be glad if I can be of any use to you. You are doubtless come to the university, and are evidently well connected. I am a professor—a professor of *belles lettres* and music, and I have been tutor to the Crown Prince. I may possibly be of some service to you: some of the great professors are rather difficult of access.'

'I am the adopted son of the Gräfin von Wetstein, sir,' I answered. 'I have letters to several of the professors of the university, but I find them much occupied in their duties, and not very easy of approach.

'We will soon remedy all that,' he said, smiling. 'To what course of study are you most inclined, and what is the future to which your friends design you?'

'I fear, sir,' I returned, 'that my future is very undefined. I am—as you say you are a professor of music—very fond of the violin; but I am a very poor performer, and I fear I shall never be a proficient.'

'I profess music,' said the old gentleman, with his quaint smile, 'but do not teach it: I only talk about it. I will introduce you, however, to a great teacher of the violin, and, indeed, if you would like it, we can go to him now. This is about the time that we shall find him disengaged.'

We went out together into the crowded market-place and turned to the left hand, up a street of marvellous height, narrowness, and steepness which led round the eastern end of the cathedral, and indeed nearly concealed it from sight. At the top of this street, on the side farthest from the cathedral, the vast west window of which could just be seen over the gables, chimneys, and stork-nests of the opposite houses, we stopped before the common door of one of the lofty old houses, against the posts of which were attached several *affiches* or notices of differing forms and material. Among these my companion pointed out one larger and more imposing than the rest: 'Veitch, teacher of the violin.'

'I ought to tell you,' said the old gentleman, 'that my daughter is reader to the Princess, and that she comes to Herr Veitch for lessons on the violin, that she may assist her Highness. If the Graf von Wetstein should take lessons here also, he may possibly meet her.'

'I beg your pardon,' I said: 'I must correct an important mistake. I am only the adopted son of the Gräfin von Wetstein. I am not the Graf: my name is Saale.'

The old gentleman seemed rather disappointed at this, but he rallied sufficiently to say: 'You may nevertheless meet my daughter, Herr von Saale.'

It sounded so pleasantly that I had not the hardihood to correct him again.

I was accordingly introduced to every one in Wenigstaat as Herr von Saale, and I may as well say, once for all, that I did not suffer for this presumption as I deserved. Some weeks later on I received a letter from the Gräfin, in which she said: 'I have noticed that you have been mentioned to me in letters as Otto von Saale. As I have chosen to adopt you, and as Saale is the name of a river, and therefore is to a certain extent territorial, I think perhaps that this may not be amiss; and I flatter myself that I have sufficient influence at the Imperial Court to procure for you a faculty which will enable you to add the prefix *von* to your patronymic.' Accordingly, some months afterwards, I did receive a most important and wordy document; but I had by that time become so accustomed to my aristocratic title that I thought little of it, though its possession, no doubt, may have saved me from some serious consequences.

We have been standing too long on the staircase which led up to Herr Veitch's room on the second floor of the great rambling house. The room which the old gentleman led me into was one of great size, occupying the entire depth of the house. It had long deep-latticed windows at either end raised by several steps above the level of the room: the window towards the front of the house looked down the steep winding street; from the other I saw, over the roofs of the city, piled in strange confusion beneath the high-pitched windows of the upper town, a wide prospect of sky and river and valley, and the distant blue mountains and forests of the Fichtelgebirge, where my home had been.

The room was somewhat crowded with furniture, chiefly large old oaken presses or cabinets apparently full of books, a harpsichord, clavichord, and several violins. In the centre of this apartment, as he rose to receive us, stood an elderly man, rather shabbily dressed, with an absent expression in his face.

'Herr Veitch,' said my guide, 'permit me to present to you Herr von Saale, a young gentleman of distinguished family and connections, who has come to reside in our university. He is anxious to perfect himself in the violin, upon which he is already no mean performer.'

I was amazed at the glibness with which this surprising old gentleman discoursed upon that of which he knew so little.

The old violinist looked at me with a

dazed and even melancholy expression, his eyes seemed to me to say as clearly as words could have spoken: 'Here is another frivolous impostor intruded upon me.'

'Is this one of my daughter's days?' said my friend, the old gentleman.

'No; I expect her to-morrow about this time.'

'The Princess,' said my friend, 'is very shy: she dislikes taking lessons from men, and prefers to gain her knowledge of music from my daughter.'

The old master took up a violin that lay upon the table and handed it to me. I played a simple lesson that had been left me by the Italian, the only one that had taken my fancy, for it had in its few notes, as it seemed to me, something of the pleading of the whispering wind.

The old man took the violin from me without a word: then he drew the bow across the strings himself and played some bars, from, I imagine, some old forgotten Italian master. As he played the solemn chords of the sonata, in the magnetic resonance of its full smooth rich notes, there was something that seemed to fill all space, to lead and draw the nerves and brain, as over gorgeous sun-coloured pavements and broad stately terraces, with alluring sound and speech.

He laid down the violin after he had played for a few minutes, and went to the harpsichord, which stood near to the window looking down into the street.

'You know something of music,' he said to me: 'do you understand this?'

He struck a single clear note upon the harpsichord and turned towards the window, a casement of which was open towards the crowded street.

'Down there,' he said,—'where I know

not, but somewhere down there,—is a heart and brain that beats with that beat, that vibrates with the vibration of that note, that hears and recognises and is consoled. To every note struck anywhere there is an accordant note in some human brain, toiling, dying, suffering, here below.'

He looked at me, and I said: 'I have understood something of this also.'

'This is why,' he went on, 'in music all hearts are revealed to us: we sympathise with all hearts, not only with those near to us but with those afar off. It is not strange that in the notes of the higher octaves that speak of children and lark singing and heaven, you, who are young, should hear of such things; but, in the sudden drop into the solemn lower notes, why should you, who know nothing of such feelings, see and feel with the old man who returns to the streets and fields of his youth? He lives, his heart vibrates in such notes: his life, his heart, his tears exist in them, and through them in you. Just as one looks from a lofty precipitous height down into the teeming streets of a great city, full of pigmy forms, so in the majestic march of sound we get away from life and its littleness, and see the whole of life spread out before us, and feel the pathos of it with the pity of an archangel, as we could never have done in the bustle of the streets there below.'

'You are cutting the ground from under my feet, my friend,' said the old Professor, rather testily. 'It is your business to teach music, mine to talk about it.'

The old master smiled at this sally, but he went on all the same. I thought that he perceived in me a sympathetic listener.

'Have you never felt that in the shrill, clear, surging chords of the higher notes you were climbing into a loftier existence, and do you not feel that for the race itself something like this is also possible? It will be in and through music that human thought will be carried beyond the point it has hitherto reached.'

He paused a moment and then went on in a lower, less confident voice. 'This is my faith, and I shall die in it. There is one thing only which saddens me. There are men, ay, great performers, real masters of the bow—who know nothing of these things, who have no such faith. There is none whom I would sooner regard as a devil than such a one. Sometimes when I hear them they almost destroy the faith that is in me—the faith in my art.'

'Pooh! pooh! my friend,' said the Professor. 'They are not so bad as that! They have simply the divine gift of the perception of harmony—the instinctive harmonic touch. They know not why or how.

They are not devils. Herr von Saale,' he went on, with, for him, considerable earnestness, 'do not believe it. I fancy that you are in danger of falling into the fatal error of supposing that you can play on the violin in the same way that you can whistle an air, by the mere force of the mental faculty. You cannot form a more mistaken notion. The variation of the thirty-secondth of an inch in the sudden movement of the finger on the string will cause the note to be out of tune; and the man who puts his finger on the right spot at the right second of time, though he may have no more mental instinct than a pig, will produce in the utmost perfection the chords of the most angelic composer.'

'I deny it!' cried the master, in a kind of fury, walking up and down the long room, 'I deny it! There is true sympathy and co-operation in the nerves and tissues of this faithful despised servant, the material human frame, even to the finger-tips, with the informing, teaching spirit. There is a tremor, a shading, a trill of meaning, given by the spirit to the nerves and tissues that no instinctive touch of harmony will ever give. The ancient Greeks (as you ought to know, Herr Professor, for you speak of them often enough) had no music worthy of the name, for they had no instruments; but had they had our instruments they would have produced the most ravishing music, for the spirit taught them what music was apart from outward sound, and they talked as beautifully as you talk in your lecture-room of the divine laws of motion and of number, and of the harmonies of sound and of the mind.'

The Professor seemed rather taken aback by this onslaught, and turning to me, said: 'Well, Herr von Saale, you had better come with me: I will show you some of the sights of our kingly city. You shall come to Herr

Veitch to-morrow, when perhaps you will see my daughter.'

He seemed to me strangely willing that I should see his daughter.

He took me into the great cathedral and showed me the gigantic mailed figures that guarded the tombs of the kings, talking very learnedly upon heraldry, about which he seemed to know a great deal. The next morning I went to Herr Veitch at the appointed time and found him alone, playing over a set of old Italian sonatas. He seemed to have been much put out by the Professor's remarks of the day before, and to regard me with kindliness as having been apparently on the opposite side; but when he came to talk to me I did not see much difference between his advice and that of the Professor.

'The Professor is so far right,' he said, 'in that of all instruments the violin needs the most careful study, the most practised fingering, the most instinctive aptitude of ear and touch. It is all very well to talk of expression, but expression with faulty execution is fatal on the violin. It is true that some of the most entrancing players have been self-taught amateurs, but they were such because they had musical genius by birth, and it was therefore possible to them to be amateurs and to be self-taught. In concerted music no amount of expression will enable a performer to take his part or to be tolerated. What pleases me in your playing is that you are able to produce smooth and sweet notes: the scrapy, scratchy period with you has apparently been short. What you want is greater certainty of touch and ear. This can only be obtained by patient labour and study.'

I set to work to play lessons, and while we were thus engaged the door opened and a young lady entered, accompanied by a tall and imposing domestic in the royal livery. I did not need to be told that this was the Professor's daughter, the Fräulein Adelheid, the reader to the Princess. She appeared to me on this, the first time that my eyes rested upon her, a handsome, stately girl, with a steady fixed look, and grave solemn eyes and mouth, which seldom changed their expression or smiled. She was rather above the common height, with fair brown hair and eyes, and was richly dressed in white, with a lace kerchief across her shoulders, and a broad white hat with a crimson feather. She seemed to me a true German girl, with earnest, steadfast truth and feeling; but I did not fall in love with her at first sight.

'This is Otto von Saale, Fräulein,' said the master, 'whom your father introduced to me yesterday, and of whom he may have spoken to you. He is very fond of music and the violin, and your father seemed much taken with him. His *forte* is expression.'

The Fräulein regarded me without embarrassment, with her steady brown eyes. 'Do you play in concert, Herr von Saale?' she said.

'He is not quite equal to that yet,' said Herr Veitch. 'The prospect of playing with you, will, I am confident, inspire him with resolve to practise with the necessary patience.'

'That will be very well timed,' she said serenely, 'as we want to perform a trio before the Princess.'

'He must work some time before he can do that,' observed Herr Veitch decisively.

They set to work to play, and I confess that I felt indescribable mortification in being unable to take a part. All my beautiful fantasias and wind-music seemed at the moment nothing to the power of joining in a concerted piece. The beauty of the playing, however, soon soothed my ruffled vanity and banished every thought save that of delight. The master and pupil were playing in perfect accord both in feeling and sympathetic touch—the old man and the stately beautifully dressed girl—it was a delicious banquet of sight and sound.

After they had played some time, Herr Veitch said, to my great delight: 'Otto will play you a lesson of his which the whispering woodlands of his mountains have taught him. You will like it.'

I took the bow with a tremor of delight and excitement. I played my very best. I endeavoured only to listen to—to think only of the woodland voices that had spoken to the child; and after a few moments I seemed, indeed, once again to be a child beside the lancelike waving rushes with their sunny dance-music, by the pool, or beneath the solemn poplars with the weird and awful notes that sounded amid their distant branches high above me in the sky. When I stopped I fancied that the brown eyes looked at me with a softer and more kindly gaze.

'He will do,' said the master; 'he will play the trio before the Princess anon, if he will be good.'

For several days I was very good: I practised continually scales and passages and shades of accent, both with the master and in my chamber at the 'Three Roses,' where, had I not been in Germany, I should no doubt have been thought a nuisance. I saw the Fräulein Adelheid almost every day, and was allowed once or twice to play in a simple piece. So everything seemed to prosper, when one fatal day I broke waywardly loose from this virtuous and regular course. It was after this manner that it came about.

One morning in the late summer I woke up with a sudden surprising sense of a crisp freshness, of a sudden strain of livelier colour shot through sky and woodland, of a change beginning to work through masses of brown foliage and cloudless summer sky. The touch was that of the angel of decay: but the first signs of his coming were gentle and gracious, with a sense even of life-giving in that new feeling of a change. The first day of autumn had dawned. As I rose, intending to go to the master, the city lay in a wonderful golden mist, through which the old streets and gables and spires seemed strange to the sight, with the romantic vision, almost, of a dream. An intense longing possessed me for the woods and hills. It seemed to me as if a far-off voice from the long past hours of childhood was calling me to the distant rocks and forests: a faint, low voice, like that strange whisper through the short grass, to hear which at all you must lay your ear very close indeed to the ground: a note untuned, uncertain, untrammelled, but with a strange alluring power, making itself felt amid the smooth, cultured, artistic sounds to which I had given myself up, and saying, as in the old harmonic thirds which as a child I had delighted to pick out, 'Come back to me.' I was engaged to Herr Veitch, but it was uncertain whether the Fräulein would be able to come. There was some talk that the Princess would make an excursion with a guest of distinction into the mountains, and her reader might possibly be required to accompany her. The Princess was understood to be very shy, and to surround herself as much as possible with her ladies and women.

The irresistible impulse was too strong for me. I sent a message to Herr Veitch, and hastened out of the confining streets, past the crumbling gates and towers, into the valley and the fields. I wandered down the banks of the stream, by which the road ran, for some hours, until the sun was high in the heavens, and every sound and leaf was hushed in the noontide stillness and heat. Then crossing the river at a ferry, where a little village and some mills stayed its current for a time, I ascended a steep path into the wooded meadows, whence the seductive voice seemed still to come. In a broad upland valley that sloped downwards to the plain and to the river I came upon a wide open meadow skirting the wild pathless wood. Here, at a corner of the outstanding copse, I saw to my surprise a number of horses picketed and apparently deserted by their grooms, and turning the corner of the wood I saw in the centre of the meadow an unexpected and most beautiful sight.

In the midst of the meadow, only, as it

seemed, a few paces from me, was a group of gentlemen in hunting costume, some with long curved horns slung at their backs. Some servants and grooms were collected a few paces behind them, but a little to the side nearest to me, close to two men of distinguished appearance some paces in advance of the rest, stood the most beautiful creature that I had ever seen. She was dressed as a huntress of romance, in green trimmed with white, and a hat fringed with white feathers, and a small silver bugle hung by her side. But it was not her dress, or her figure, that gave her the indescribable charm that made her so lovely: it was the bewitching expression of her face. Her features might possibly have been described as large, but this, as her complexion was of perfect delicacy and freshness, only increased the subduing charm of the shy, fleeting, coy expression about her eyes and mouth. Two ladies stood close behind her, neither of whom was the Fräulein, but I knew at once that this could be none other than the Princess. No family of pure German origin could have produced such a face: she sprang, doubtless, as is becoming to a daughter of kings, from a mixed race.

A perfect stillness and hush, as of expectation, pervaded the scene: even the well-trained horses made no movement as I passed by them. One of the grooms caught a glimpse of me and made a slight sign: then, just as the group had settled itself on my sight, a slight, scarcely perceptible rustle was heard in the wood, and a stag of full age and noble bearing came out into the meadow and stood at gaze, startled but not alarmed. One of the gentlemen in front raised a short hunting-piece, and the Princess, in a soft sweet undertone that penetrated all the listening air and left an imperishable memory upon the heart, exclaimed: 'Oh, do not kill it! How beautiful it is!'

A short, sharp crack, a puff of smoke, and the stag leaped suddenly into the air and fell lifeless, shot between the eyes.

There was a sudden outbreak of exclamation and talk, a rush of the hunters towards the fallen beast. Two or three of the gentlemen drew around the Princess and her ladies, as if to protect her, and in the excitement no one noticed me. I stood for a moment or two, my eyes fixed on this changing, sensitive, inexpressibly beautiful face. Then the beaters and foresters came out of the wood: some remained with the fallen stag, and the rest of the party moved on farther up into the forest followed by the grooms and horses. I returned at once, silent and fancy-struck, to the city, and passed the rest of the day and the entire night in a dream.

The next morning I made my best ex-

cuses to Herr Veitch, and tried to settle to
my work, but I found that this was impossible
until I had made a full confession. He took
it very quietly and as a matter of course:
not so, however, did the Fräulein, a day or
two afterwards, when he revealed the whole
story to her. She looked at me strangely
with her great brown eyes as one who foresaw some great danger awaiting me; and I
wondered, in vain, from what quarter it
would come.

I made great progress under her tuition.
In playing with her in unison I learned more
in a few minutes than in any other way.
The instinct of fingering seemed to come
naturally by her means, by her gentle guidance, by her placid rule. Here again outward harmonies of nature and of art corre-
sponded in its contrast with the life of the
spirit; with the rapt, enthralling passion of
love which had come upon me by the vision

in the forest, and with the calm sympathy which was growing up in my heart with the Fräulein, smooth, broad, tranquil, as the full harmonious chords which she taught me to play. But with all this I confess that the prevailing thought of my mind was that I should some day, and that soon, take my part in this music before the lovely Princess; that I should see again that indescribable, enchanting face.

'We are getting on,' said Herr Veitch: 'we shall be ready soon.'

'Let us have a rehearsal,' said Adelheid, with her grave, gentle smile: 'let us have a rehearsal to-morrow in Das Vergnügen, in the garden-valley of the palace.'

Below the palace, on the side farthest from the city, the wooded valley formed a fairy garden of terraces and of streams flowing down from the hills. In the bottom of the valley were buildings, somewhat on a small scale, after the fashion of the French garden-palaces of Trianon and Marly, and in these little houses some of the court-officials had rooms. The Professor and his daughter occupied one of the most charming suites of apartments opening upon a wide lawn beneath the terraced garden leading up to the palace, broken up by clipped hedges and rows of statues. I had never seen this garden of romance until the afternoon of the rehearsal. In the excitement and nervousness of the hour I was dimly conscious of a solemn blue sky overhead, of the dark foliage of the dying summer rising on the steep hillsides on every hand, of a still afternoon full of sombre tints and sleeping sunlight, of the late-flowering china-roses and the tall asters, of massive wreaths of clematis, of a sense of finished effort and growth, and of a hush and pause before decay set in and brought the end of life and of the year: the little stone palace with its carved pilasters and wreaths of fruit and flowers, the weather-stained, moss-tinted statues and urns,—of all this I was dimly conscious as in a dream.

The Herr Professor was more than usually spruce in his apparel. I had purchased, boylike, a new dress for the occasion. It was the period of frizzled, powdered hair, and lace and embroidery. A man who wore plain clothes and his hair *au naturel* was considered eccentric and of doubtful character. We formed a group on the little in-closed grass-plot outside the windows of the Professor's sitting-room, separated from the great lawns by the low clipped hedges and the wreathed urns. I noticed that the Fräulein seemed anxious and almost expectant, and was continually turning her head in the direction of the palace-gardens. At last she said to her father: 'I fear that I have committed a blunder. I begged to be excused from attending the Princess, and I told her that I was going to practise with the master here, but I said nothing of Otto, or that he would be here. It is quite possible that the Princess may come down through the gardens to hear the master play.'

The Professor shrugged his shoulders. 'It is too late now,' he said; 'the sight of Otto will not kill her.'

'No,' said his daughter doubtfully; but she shook her head as though a catastrophe was very imminent.

A tremor of excitement and of suppressed delight passed through my frame. If the mere thought of the rehearsal had excited me, what must I have felt at such a possibility as this?

We began to practise the trio with the violoncello and two violins. The violin parts were very lively and quick; but the great charm of the piece lay in some perfectly modulated chords of great beauty distributed through the parts in a sustained, broad, searching tone on the fourth string. Herr Veitch played the violoncello with consummate skill. We had played the piece nearly through when Adelheid suddenly ceased, and turned in the direction of the wider lawns to which was access between the urns; and the next moment the same lovely creature I had seen some days before, but now very differently dressed, came through the opening in the low hedge, accompanied by a beautiful young lady, evidently of high rank, whom I also recognised as one of the ladies I had seen in the wood. The Princess looked for a moment serenely at the group, who drew backward a step or two and bowed very low; but the next moment, as her eyes fell upon me, she flushed suddenly, and her face assumed an expression of embarrassment, and even reproof.

'I did not understand that you had strangers here, Fräulein,' she said, and stopped.

'This, Royal Highness,' said Adelheid, bowing very low, 'is a young gentleman, Otto von Saale, who is to play in the trio. It did not occur to me to mention him to the Royal Highness.'

The Princess looked very disconcerted and mortified, but her embarrassment only made the unique expression of her face more exquisitely piquant and enchanting. I would willingly have risked untold penalties to secure such a sight. The young lady who accompanied her regarded me with an expression of loathing animosity and contempt, as much as to say, 'What do you mean by using your miserable existence to get us into this scrape?'

The Professor came to the rescue with great *aplomb*. Herr Veitch evidently regarded the whole matter with lofty contempt.

'If the Royal Highness will deign to take a seat,' said the Professor, 'she may still hear the trio rehearsed. We will regard Otto as second violin merely. One violin is much like another.'

'Oh, sit down, my Princess!' said the young lady coaxingly; 'I should so like to hear the violins.'

The Princess hesitated, and looked still more enchantingly confused and shy, but she sat down at last. It was reported that, as a boy, her brother, the Crown Prince, had been mortally in dread of the Professor. It is possible that his sister may have conceived something of a similar feeling.

We played the trio through. In spite of

my excitement I had the sense to take the greatest pains. I kept my attention perfectly fixed upon my playing, and the clear notes of the great chords came in perfectly true and in time. When we had finished there was a short embarrassed pause. Then Adelheid whispered to me, 'Play that lesson of yours of the woodland breeze.'

Scarcely knowing what I did I began to play; but I had not finished the opening bars before a slight change in the attitude of the Princess attracted my eyes, and suddenly, as if by inspiration, I conceived the fancy that I was playing to a creature of the forest and of the wind. She was sitting slightly forward, her eyes fixed upon the woodland slope before her, her slight, lithe figure and prominent speaking features like no offspring of common clay, but innate in that primeval god-sprung race of the golden hours, before the iron horny-handed sons of men had filled the earth with toil and sorrow and grime: the race from which had sprung the creatures that had filled romance with elf-legends and stories of elf-kings and ladies and beings of gentle and fairy birth; for, as the untrammelled wood-notes that stole across the strings now sunk into a whisper, now swelled into full rich chords and harmonies, I could almost fancy that I saw this glorious creature, while the mystic notes lasted, grow into a more serene and genial life, as though she breathed an air to which she was native, and heard once again the wild notes of the hills and of the winds in the sere antique forest-country that was hers by right of royal ancient birth.

As I played the concluding notes the Princess rose and stood before us once again, as I had seen her stand in the forest-meadow when she had pleaded unavailingly, in those marvellous tones which would never pass from my memory, for the beautiful stag. Then she bowed very courteously to the others, and, taking no notice whatever of me, moved away, attended by her companion.

II

NARRATIVE

There is a gap in Otto von Saale's autobiography which it may be well to fill up from other sources, as we shall by this means obtain a knowledge of some incidents of which he could not possibly have been cognisant.

Two or three days after the rehearsal in the palace-garden the Princess was seated in her own room in the palace, accompanied only by her reader. The relationship between the two was evidently, in private, of the most intimate character.

The room was high in the palace, and a surpassing view lay before the windows.

Immediately in front, over a terrace or glacis planted with sycamore-trees, the roofs and gables and chimneys of the old city lay like a great snake, or rather like several great snakes, climbing the ridges of its steep streets, and crowned with the spires and towers of its cathedral and churches and *rathhaus* and university halls. Over and beyond this stretched a vast extent of wooded valleys and hills, of forest and mountain and glancing river, of distant blue stretches of country indistinguishable and unknown, and in the remote distance along the sky-line a faint range of snow-clad peaks. A vast expanse of cloudland, strange and varied as the earth itself, and almost as tangible and real, filled the upper regions of this landscape with motion and life and varied form. It was evening, and the night-clouds had piled themselves in threatening and lurid forms above the dark wind-tossed forest-land. The white smoke-wreaths from the city curled up before the cathedral towers, and the storks and kites in long trailing flocks wended their way home from the distant fields. The Princess sat, still and silent, looking out over the wide prospect, with searching, questioning eyes, that seemed to penetrate beyond its farthest bound.

'I am still listening,' she said at last, 'to that violin lesson that the young man—Otto von Saale, did you call him?—played the other day. Is he considered to be a great performer? In its echoing repeats I seemed to hear voices that I had never heard before, and yet which seemed as though they were the voices of my kin, that told me whence I came, and who I was, and what I might become.'

'He plays with surpassing feeling,' replied Adelheid, 'and with delicacy of shading and of touch, most surprising as he is only a novice at the violin. You may judge of this when you remember how simple the piece was that he played — a few chords constantly repeated — yet he made them, as you say, speak to the heart, a different utterance for every chord. His *forte* is expression.'

'Is he in love with you?' said the Princess, with the calmest, most unmoved manner and tone.

'No.'

'You are in love with him?'

'Yes, I love him, for he is in every way worthy to be loved. But it is of little importance what I think of him. He is hopelessly, desperately, passionately in love with you.'

'In love with me?' The Princess did not move, and not the faintest shade of deeper colour flushed her cheek; but the faint, shy, kindly smile deepened, and the questioning eyes softened to an expression which was certainly that of supreme, amused beneficence —possibly of something else. 'In love with me! When did he ever see me before?'

'He saw you some days ago in the forest: the day that the Prince von Schöngau shot the stag.'

The Princess sat quite still, looking out upon the southern sky, which was all aglow with a red reflected light. Long dark lines of cloud, like bars of some Titanic prison-house, drew themselves out across the sky; and the masses of cloud, tinged with a sudden glow of crimson, formed a wild contrast with the faint blue of the dying sky, and the green of the waving woodlands below. The deepening glow spread higher over the whole heaven, till the world below became suffused with its sober brilliance, and tower and gable and the climbing ridges of the street and the white smoke-wreaths shone in the mellow light. The distant stretch of country flushed with this mystic light, which certainly was not of earth, seemed instinct with a quivering life—the life of forest and farm-people—the life of hidden townships too distant to be discerned — of rivers bordered with wharves and shipping—the life of a kingdom of earth —and, in her mountain eyrie, with set, wistful eyes, over the regions of her father's rule, the Princess sat at gaze, a creature slight, shy, delicate, yet born of eagle-race.

Her companion waited for some words, but they did not come: then she spoke herself.

'He was born among the forests of the Fichtelgebirge and has listened to the spirits of the wood and mountain from a child; that is why he plays so well.'

'Yes,' said the Princess, 'that is why, in his playing, I heard a talk that I had long wished to hear — a speech which seemed familiar and yet which I had never heard here —the speech of a people from which my race is sprung. And you say that he is in love with me?'

'Yes,' said Adelheid, somewhat sadly; 'at this moment he would give worlds to see you again.'

'Oh, he shall see me again!' said the Princess, with her quaint, shy smile: 'he shall see me again; he shall play before the King. More than that,—he shall marry you!'

.   .   .   .   .

The King was a strikingly handsome, tall, distinguished man, of between fifty and sixty years of age. His father had died when he was a boy, and he had been brought up by his mother as regent of the kingdom. She was a very clever woman, and surrounded her son with the most able men she could attract to her court. She trained him in the most exalted ideas of his position and responsibility, and when she died, after having with much difficulty found a wife whom she considered to be suitable for him, she left him, at the age of five and twenty, profoundly impressed with the conviction that something wonderful was expected of him in every action and word. As he was a man of very moderate capacities, though perfectly good-natured and conscientious, this impression might possibly have placed him in very painful predicaments; but the King very wisely fell back early in life on the obvious alternative of doing absolutely nothing and saying very little. It may surprise some persons to be told how wonderfully the country prospered under this imposing, but silent and inactive monarch. He had been as a boy impressed with the misery of some classes of his people, and he had been known as a young man to absent himself from court for days together, and to wander, attended only by one companion, among the poor and struggling classes; and the only occasions on which he spoke at the privy-council were when he advocated the passing of some measure which his plain common sense told him would be beneficial to his people. He was therefore immensely popular, and was thought, even by many of his familiar courtiers, to be a man of remarkable ability. He had a habit of repeating the last words of any one who spoke to him with an air by which he seemed to appropriate all the wisdom which might be contained in them to himself. 'I have been attending the privy-council, sire.' 'Ah! you have been attending the privy-council, yes.' And it really was difficult not to fancy that you had been listening to a long and exhaustive treatise upon privy-councils generally and their influence on the government of states; so perfect was the manner of the King.

.   .   .   .   .

'Sire,' said the Princess to her father, the same evening on which she had had the talk with Adelheid, 'I wish you to hear a young performer on the violin, Otto von Saale, who is a pupil of Herr Veitch. I heard him once by accident in Das Vergnügen. I wish him,' continued the Princess, with serene candour, after a slight pause, 'I wish him to marry the Fräulein.'

'Yes?' said the King, 'you wish him to marry the Fräulein? I have observed, on more than one occasion, that efforts of this character may be abortive.'

The King paused, as though on the point of saying more, but apparently doubting whether he could safely venture upon further assertion, he remained silent. After a pause he went on: 'You consider this young man to be a promising performer?'

'His *forte*,' replied the Princess, 'as the

Fräulein says, is expression. His playing has a strange fascination for me.'

'Ah!' replied the King, 'his *forte* is expression. Good! When do you wish me to hear this young man?' he continued after a pause.

'I thought we might have a chamber-concert of music after supper, on one of the evenings that the Prince von Schöngau is here. Herr Veitch and the Fräulein will play.'

Except on occasions of great state the King and his family supped in private, a second table being provided for the courtiers. A strict etiquette was observed in the palace, similar to, and founded upon, that of Versailles.

On the evening upon which the Princess had finally decided, a somewhat larger company than usual assembled in the great *salle*. The doors were thrown open shortly after supper, and the chamberlain with his white wand announced, after the manner of the French Court: 'Gentlemen! The King!'

The great *salle* was floored with marble, and surrounded with marble pillars on every side. A thousand lights flickered on the countless jewels that decked the assembly. Great vases of flowers filled the corners, and graced the tables of the room.

The King came forward with long accustomed composure to the seat provided for him, near to a harpsichord in the centre of the *salle:* a step behind him followed the Princess. She was *en pleine toilette*, sparkling with jewels, and if Otto von Saale had had any worlds to give, he might almost have been pardoned had he given them for such a sight; for a creature more delicately beautiful —so absolutely set apart and pure from aught that is frivolous and vain, and yet so winning in the unconscious piquancy of her loveliness —he would scarcely find elsewhere. She was followed by several ladies, and three or four gentlemen, preceded by a prince of a royal house, who had formed part of the King's supper-party, brought up the rear of the procession.

The King sat in his chair a little in advance of the rest: on either side of him were seated the Princess and the Crown Prince, and the ladies and gentlemen who had had the honour of supping with the royal party were seated behind them. Herr Veitch played the violoncello, and the Professor was prepared to accompany on the harpsichord.

The attitude and expression of the King were delightful to watch. He sat back in his chair, his fingers meeting before his chest, a faint smile of serene beneficence on his beautifully-cut features—a gracious, presiding power of another and a loftier sphere.

One or two pieces were played first, then

came a trio of Corelli's, in which the harpsichord took no part.

Did it sound in the Princess's ear alone, or did there run through all the wealth of pure harmonies a strange new quality of tone? Wild, glancing, in tune yet untuned and untunable, like the silver thread of the brooklet through the grass, or the single changeless woodnote of the breeze wailing through the organ-harmonies of the midnight mass in a mountain-chapel. It spoke to the Princess's heart, as she sat some little space backward from her father's chair, her delicate steadfast face fixed upon the scene before her, which, doubtless, she did not see. It seemed to speak of an alluring lawlessness, of that life of unconventional freedom, of that lofty rule and dominion over their own fate and circumstance, of that free gratification of every instinct and faculty, which has such an attraction to the highly-born. It seemed to call her with a resistless power back into a pristine life of freedom which was hers by right of ancient ancestral birth, a world of freedom and love and unquestioned prerogative which belonged to the nobles of the golden age. Almost she was persuaded by the searching power of its magic note to believe that all things belonged to the *élite* 'of earth's children—the favourites of life, those delicately nurtured and born to the purple of the world's prismatic rays. Should she listen to this siren chord it might even happen to her to lose that stainless insight which its wild tone had itself evoked; but, in the perfection of a concerted piece, its wild uniqueness was kept, by grace of finished art, invariably true to the dominant concord of pure harmony, an existence and creation as it were in harmonious sound, of which it formed a part. To the Princess as she listened to the vibrating strings it seemed that, with a vision beyond her years, so potent in suggestion is music, she looked into another world, as one looks down from a lofty precipitous height into the teeming streets of a great city, and the pigmy crowds are instinct with a strange interest—a world of human suffering and doubt and terror, of love unrequited, of righteousness unrecognised, of toil and sorrow and despair unrelieved, until, in the thronged theatres and market-places, where life stands waiting its abiding doom—the times and seasons of the world's harvest being fully ripe—the riddle of righteousness and of wrong is answered, and in the sad gray dawn of the eternal day the dividing sickle is put in.

There was a pause in the wave of sound, and the Princess was dimly conscious that Otto von Saale was playing alone. So magnetic was the searching tone that there seemed nothing in the wide universe save herself and his strange impalpable personality that approached her in mystic sound; but happily beyond and above its sorcery was once more felt the sense of restraining, abiding, cultured harmony—the full, true, settled chords, and the according regular law and sequence of time and pitch.

Then she knew that all were standing up, and she rose in her seat beside the King. A peculiar lustre of gracious courtesy shone in the monarch's attitude and manner.

'Herr Veitch,' he was saying, 'we thank you: the Princess thanks you. Herr von Saale, the Princess thanks you. I perceive——' here his Majesty paused for a moment to give importance to what was to come, 'I perceive, sir, that your *forte* is expression.'

The most wearied cynic must have felt a glow of genuine pleasure as the King said these words, so contagious was the regal, benevolent satisfaction that the exigencies of the occasion had been fitly met.

Otto bowed low before the King, then he turned to salute the Princess; but, as he looked up, his eyes met her marvellous eyes and were fixed by a magic spell, so intense, searching, personal and yet abstracted was the look they met. His entire being was caught up and rapt into hers in an ecstasy of ravishment. Had the gaze lasted another second he must have fainted away.

III

AUTOBIOGRAPHICAL.

I DID not go to Herr Veitch until some days after the concert at the palace. Indeed, I did not care to go. I felt as though I had broken with all continent and decorous life, and was entering upon a delirious course of adventure such as I had read of in some fatal romance of ill-repute, whose course was unnatural and ghastly even in its delights, and whose end was tragic and disastrous. I was appalled even at the splendour of my dream.

But when I did muster courage to go to the master, I was astonished to find that nothing seemed to have happened at all.

Herr Veitch did not even appear to have noticed my absence. He was in a very propitious humour, and complimented me very much on my playing at the palace.

'I never knew you,' he said, 'play with so much certainty and correctness. There is always in your playing a certain originality which might become, as I have often told you, a great snare, indeed fatal in its results. So long, however, as you play as conscientiously as you did the other night, though there will always be a singularity in your style to which some might object, yet you will stand, to my mind, among the great performers on the violin.'

I had never heard the old man utter such praise before.

Nor did I at first notice anything in the manner of the Fräulein towards me which would show that she was conscious of the necessity for any change. But there soon came a change, which was entirely of my own bringing about. I neglected the master and the violin. I hardened my heart against the Fräulein, and especially avoided the hours when I thought she would be with Herr Veitch. Her wistful eyes had no effect upon me, so foolish and delirious had I become.

One day Herr Veitch said to me, 'Yesterday the Fräulein brought us great news. The Princess is betrothed to the Prince von Schöngau, who has been staying so long at the palace. He was present, you remember, on the evening of the concert.'

I was conscious that my face wore a contemptuous, unbelieving sneer. In my madness I thought to myself that I knew much better than to believe such foolish gossip.

At last Herr Veitch took me seriously to task. 'Something has happened to you,' he said. 'You are bewitched, some evil eye has fascinated you. You are no longer the same sensible pleasant lad that you were. The Fräulein notices it also. She says she does not know what is come over you. I tell her that all young men are fools.'

I did not deign to answer the good old man, but left him with my nose in the air. Indeed, I seemed to tread on air. I thought of nothing but palace-gardens and Hyrcanian woods full of terrible delights and secret pleasures. I believed myself to be altogether separate from my fellows, and to be reserved for some supreme exceptional fate. I am not willing to dwell longer than I can help upon this period, the remembrance of which is most distasteful to me. I shall have to describe at some length the supreme and crowning act of folly, and this must suffice the reader.

But in simple honesty, and to relieve my own conscience by public confession, I must relate one incident, so fatuous and unworthy was it, so nobly and graciously forgiven and condoned. I had not been to Herr Veitch for many days; but one morning an unconquerable impulse forced me to visit him. I believe that I was impelled, with all my assumed scepticism, to seek more tidings of the Prince von Schöngau and his reported espousals. I had quite lost count of the Fräulein's mornings, and, indeed, I am ashamed to say, that I had ceased to think of her. I was therefore somewhat chagrined when, on entering the room, I found myself in her presence, as well as in that of Herr Veitch. My manner must have been singularly constrained and boorish, and I could see that the master regarded me with disapproval, not to say contempt. In spite of my affected indifference, I could see that Adleheid was watching me with wistful and pitiful eyes. Some evil demon made my heart harder and

more scornful than ever; and I conceived the
most hateful and injurious thoughts against
one whose sweetness and devotion ought, on
the contrary, to have filled me with affectionate devotion. I played badly, and this only
increased my spiteful and angry mood. So
violent did my passion and an evil conscience
at last make me, that I threw down my violin
in a fit of ungovernable temper and rushed
out of the room. I wandered restlessly about
the streets for some time, in a kind of frenzy
against mankind in general, my mind filled
with the image of the Princess, and with a
sense of intolerable wrong that my exceptional fortune was not recognised by all the
world,—so confident was I in my infatuation.
At last it suddenly occurred to me to go to
the theatre, where the Fräulein had said the
royal family were expected to be present.
Lost in the crowded and enthusiastic audience,
which would doubtless fill the place—the

report of the betrothal being spread throughout the city—I might see the Princess and indulge a secret sense of my exclusive fate.

When I entered the theatre at the bottom of the Peterstrasse, however, I found a rumour already currrent that the King was not well and could not be present, and that the Princess refused to come without him. Whether the strange Crown Prince would visit the theatre alone, no one seemed to pretend to know.

I shall remember that evening as long as I live. The little old-fashioned theatre, as I know now it must have been, so different from the great theatres I have since seen at Dresden and Berlin, seemed to me, then, to be the most gorgeous of pleasure-places, blazing with lights and crowded with what was to me a gay and brilliant throng of superbly dressed and ornamented people. I found a vacant place in the pit near the orchestra. When I entered the curtain had not risen, but the orchestra were playing. The band consisted mostly of violins, and would, no doubt, be considered poor and thin at the present day, but such music has, to my mind, a subtle, delicate tone which is missed now. I did not know what the overture was, and curiously enough I have never heard it again: probably it was some local composition; but there is sounding in my ears, as I write, the simple, thrilling air, the recurring chords. The music ceased and the curtain rose.

Up to this time the royal box opposite the stage had remained empty, and the audience had manifested a restless impatience which paid no attention to anything, either in the orchestra or upon the stage; but the actors had hardly begun their parts when the attention, which was now being attracted towards them, was suddenly diverted in another direction, and a young distinguished-looking man entered the royal box. His breast was a mass of stars and orders, and the rest of his apparel was covered with embroidery and lace; but his tall, slight figure, and the careless self-respect of his manner, enabled him to support so much finery with success. He came down without pause to the front of the box and remained standing, while the actors, dropping their parts, sang a verse of the National Folk-song, accompanied by the audience and supported by the band. The Prince bowed once slightly, then stood quite still, facing the enthusiastic house. From his point of view, doubtless, he saw a waving sea of faces, tumultuous, indistinguishable, indistinct; but in my eyes, and to my thought, as I stood lost in the tossing, excitable crowd about me, there was no one in the whole theatre but myself and him. As I looked at him a wild antagonism, an insane confidence and desire to pit myself against him, took possession of me. My folly even went so far as to picture to my mind a lovely, broken-hearted creature, bound to a betrothal odious to her, stretching out her hand towards another fate. The Prince had sat down in his box, slightly wearied in his daily round of life, not expecting very much entertainment from the play; more pleased, perhaps, at the gay scene the crowded theatre itself presented to his eyes, perfectly unaware, certainly, of the ferocious glances one of the audience in a remote corner was directing towards his unconscious person.

I spent the ensuing night and day in a fever of passionate excitement; but on the next afternoon an event occurred which reduced every other consideration to worthlessness, and exaggerated the delirium from which I suffered to the highest pitch. On my return to the 'Three Roses' from attending a lecture of the university—for I did attend lectures sometimes—I found a royal footman waiting for me with a note from the Princess. The world seemed to swim before my eyes as I took the billet from the man. It had been given him by the Princess herself, he said, who had charged him to deliver it to no one but myself.

I opened the billet and read: 'The Princess Cynthia will be in Das Vergnügen, on the terrace above the cascades, this evening at eleven o'clock. She wishes to see Herr von Saale there without fail.'

Even in the state of exaltation in which I had lived for some days, I could scarcely believe my senses. Yet there could be no possible doubt that the message was a genuine one. The billet was distinguished from ordinary letters by its paper, and was closed with a massive seal bearing the royal arms.

To this moment it is a mystery to me how I passed the intervening hours from the time the man left me till eleven o'clock. I know that at the time the thought of this necessity overwhelmed me with despair. I have some misty recollection of wandering down the valley by the river, of gibbering passing forms which with intolerable intrusion seemed to force themselves between me and the only conceivable event towards which all human history had been tending since the world began.

The garden of Das Vergnügen was defended against intrusion by natural boundaries, very slightly assisted by art. The valley on the palace-side was impregnable, and the steep, rocky, wooded slopes on the farther side of the river were so inclosed at the top as to render intrusion difficult or impossible. The right of *entrée* was given me through my connection with the Professor and the Fräulein, and I had no difficulty in obtaining it on this momentous night.

Mysterious shadows, dark and vast under the pale moonlight, the great trees and banks of leaves, rose in strange distinct outline on every side, as I made my way through the lawns and garden-walks. The nightingales were singing all around me: the festoons of roses, robbed of all colour by the pallid light, hung like the ruined garlands of a dead festival, and sheets of clematis fell like cascades from the tall hedges and forest trees, and filled the air with a stifling perfume that presaged decay. Every now and again a strange whispering music stole through the valley and along the wooded slopes, the echo of wind-harps and harmonica-wires concealed among the terraces and groves. As the night advanced and the moon sank lower in the sky, the starlight grew more intense, with a clear distinct light, in which the sharp dark outlines of the shadows stood out in weird contrast with the beauty which, even in the moment of startled terror, the heart felt to be around. The wayward music that strayed through the leaves, and the fine clear notes of the nightingales, that harmonised with the cold silver light in which valley and river and stone terrace lay in mystic unreality, seemed like a fatal spell to enslave my spirit, a ghost-melody, a pale, beckoning hand to entice me on. And it was not only that these sights and sounds of a pallid and even terrifying beauty lured me on, but my infatuation was so perfect that I traversed the lawns and terraces in the full expectation of finding at the trysting-place the most lovely, the most unique of creatures, a creature born to be the possession and the delight of her own race and kind, and of such only, to whom it would seem presumption and treason for any other even to look. Long years afterwards, writing in the cool blood of middle life, the remembrance of this folly makes me shiver with an intolerable shame; but at the moment, so potent was the wizard spell that untamed, unquestioning youth and the wild, romantic wood-teaching, and the autumnal music of the winds, and the well-spring of fresh hope and love and trust, bursting out like a clear fountain amid the flowering grass and woodland singers, had cast about my path that, as I passed the terraces and the arcades of roses and clematis, I believed confidently that in another moment I should have the Princess, blushing, shy, palpitating, in my arms.

I turned a terraced corner bordered with statues and urns, and shaded with tall yew and holly hedges that grew high up in the woods. I came upon a broad and long terrace, shining in the clear light. On the left hand, far above me, from the mountain summit a single broad cascade fell, like a wall of flashing molten silver, sudden and straight into a deep pool, from which by several outlets, formed by the piers of the terrace-bridge upon which I stepped, it fell again, in four or five cascades of far greater depth, into the valley beneath.

The moon, which was setting a little behind me, cast a full and strong light upon the broad terrace—a light as bright as day. As I turned the corner my heart almost ceased to beat, for I saw, not a dozen yards from me, the Princess herself coming forward to meet me, as it seemed with outstretched hands. The bright light revealed in perfect distinctness the soft, gracious outline of her slight figure and the shy expression of her face. I made a step forward, my heart leaping to my mouth, when suddenly it sank again with a sickening chill, for behind the Princess, only a few steps apart, was the strange Crown Prince, and close to him stood another figure, which I also recognised at once.

The Princess came forward with her faint, bewitching smile.

'You are here, Herr von Saale,' she said: 'I knew you would not fail. We are an awkward number for a moonlight stroll, and I wanted a companion for the Fräulein.'

A sickening sense of self-recognised, self-detected folly—folly too gross and palpable, it might be feared, to escape even the detection of others—crushed me to the earth.

What would have happened, what inconceivably fatal folly I might have committed, I cannot tell—a mad whirl of insane thought rushed through my mind; but the Princess kept her steady eyes fixed full upon mine. 'Herr von Saale,' they said, as plainly as, ay, plainer than, words could speak,—' Otto von Saale, I believe in you. You have taught me something that I never knew before. You have taught me what I am, and you have shown me what I may become. You yourself surely will not fail.'

The steady, speaking eyes, calm in the pale white light—the intense, overmastering power and thought—drew me out of myself, as at the evening concert at the palace; but now, thanks to the purpose and command that spoke in them, with a fortifying help and strength. The boyish nature, fascinated and uplifted even in the depths of its folly and shame, rose—thanks to her—in some sense equal to the pressing need. Surely she must be right. Behind Otto von Saale, the fool, there must be another Otto von Saale who would not fail.

Something of what was passing in my mind rose, I suppose, into my eyes, for the expression of the Princess's face changed, and an inexpressibly beautiful look came into her eyes, amid the quaint reserve which her rank and disposition gave to her habitual look. It seemed to speak, with a start of grateful joy at the sudden gift, of certain abiding faith—faith in herself and in me—faith in the full, pure notes of life's music, which they who are born of the spirit, in the turmoil of the world's passion and desire, alone can hear.

The Princess turned away very quietly towards the Crown Prince. 'You remember Herr von Saale the other evening?' she said; and his Royal Highness bowed.

They moved together towards the other end of the terrace, and I approached Adelheid.

It may be thought that I must have found some difficulty and confusion in speaking to her; but, strange as it may appear, it was not so. It seemed to me as though the demon of vanity and folly had been completely exorcised, as though the courage and faith that shone upon me from the Princess's eyes had blotted out and effaced the miserable, infatuated past as though it had never been. It is given to some natures, at some propitious moments at the turning-points of life, by a happy acquiescence in right doing to obliterate the evil past. The intolerable sense of disgrace and shame had, as it were, stung the lower, vain reptile-self through its vital cord, and it lay dead and withered in the way. The flattering mask was torn from its features, and nothing was left but a shudder at the memory of a creature so contemptible and vile.

I told Adelheid that I did not know how to excuse my conduct of the last few days, that some demon seemed to have possessed me, that Herr Veitch had said truly that this was the case, and that I had been fascinated — by some evil eye, I was about to say; but

I stopped suddenly, remembering that the eyes that had fascinated me had been those of the Princess, those eyes that had restored me to the dominion of the higher self. Escaping from this pitfall as best I could, I promised that I would return to my practising, and this brought us to the end of the terrace, where was a flight of stone steps that led down into the valley. Here the Princess turned to us and said that she wished to show the Prince the cascades from the steps, some little way down: they would return to us immediately on the terrace. They went down the steps and we turned back along the terrace-walk.

The moon by this time had set, and a countless host of stars lit the arched sky above us; and over the leafy walls on every side, darkened and deepened in shade, a delicate, faint, clear light seemed to chasten and subdue the heart—the starlight of the soul. There was no sound but that of the rush of water, for the nightingales and the wind-harps were too far below. There seemed to arise around us, and to enwrap us in its emboldening folds, a protecting mist and garment of solemn, faded light and measured sound. Enshrouded in this mystic veil fear and embarrassment were taken away, and in clear, true vision we saw each other for the first time.

'You have taught me the violin,' I said; 'but there is another instrument, the strings of which vibrate to even higher tones: will you teach these strings also to vibrate in unison to your touch? It has been neglected, and is out of tune: it wants the leading of a master-hand.'

'I fear the instrument is accustomed to another hand,' Adelheid said.

'A violin,' I said, 'is played on by many a one, and they fail; but it is not cast aside.

At last he comes for whom it was predestined long ago, while the wood was growing in the tree, while the mellowing sunshine and the wind were forming it—were teaching it secrets that would fit it to teach mankind in sound. He to whom it was predestined comes. He takes it in his hand, and we know that once, at least, in this life, supreme music has been heard. Will you try this instrument of mine? It may, perchance, be worth the trying, for it is a human heart.'

'I will try it,' she said.

There is not much more to tell. He that is happy has no history; and the life that is in tune with the melodies of heaven, in tune because it is guided by a purer life, inspired by a loftier impulse than its own, cannot fail of being happy. In the sustained and perfect harmonies that result from the concord of full, pure, true notes, there is rest and peace for the wearied and troubled brain; and the harmonies of life, that absorb and hush the discords of the world, are heard only in the private walks and daily seclusions in which love and Christian purity delight. Both harmonies came to me through a teacher of the violin.

And the Princess?

One summer afternoon in the year 1806 a gay city lay smiling in the afternoon sun. It lay in a fair plain watered by shining streams, and surrounded in the blue distance by wooded hills. The newly-built esplanades stretched away into the meadows, and from among the avenues of linden-trees the birds were singing merrily. But a fatal spell seemed to hang over this lovely scene, and the city might have been a city of the dead. Not a chance figure could be seen in its streets and boulevards: the windows of its houses were all fastened, and the blinds and jalousies drawn down and closed.

And more than this: every few moments a deathly terror tore the serene, calm air, and, alighting like a shrieking fiend, crashed into house and grove. The Prussian army was in full retreat across the fords of the river lower down, and the city was being bombarded by a battery of the French.

The blinds in the long streets were all drawn and the shutters closed; but there was one house in which not a blind was down nor a window closed. This was the palace, which stood in the centre of the city, looking upon the Grand Platz, and surrounded by chestnut and sycamore trees. The King was with the army on the distant Thuringian slopes; but it was known through all the city that the Queen was still in the palace and had refused to leave; and in the hearts of the citizens, wherever a few met together, or in the homes where they spoke of this, despair and anguish were soothed into gratitude and trust.

But gradually as the evening drew on matters became worse. The terrible cannonade, it is true, ceased; but a party of French chasseurs, followed by infantry, occupied the market-place, and the work of plunder was systematically begun. The crash of doors burst in and the shrieks of the inhabitants were heard on every side. At seven o'clock in the summer evening houses were in flames in front of the palace, and the light was so intense that people could read handwriting, both in the palace-court and in the market-place.

Then, suddenly, a most wonderful thing occurred. The great iron gates of the court-yard, which had remained closed, were thrown open, and a state carriage, gorgeously caparisoned and drawn by six white horses, accompanied by servants in full liveries, issued forth in the evening light, amid the added glare of the flaming houses. It passed on its stately way through the crowded, agitated Platz, the lawless soldiers standing back astonished and abashed, till it reached the great hotel of the 'Three Kings,' where a marshal of France, a brother-in-law of the Emperor, had taken up his quarters for the night an hour before. It did not remain long; but in a few moments it was known throughout the city that the Queen's intercession had prevailed, that orders had been given to extinguish the conflagration, and that the pillage would immediately cease.

The people, young and old, swarmed into the streets. From by-lane and causeway and boulevard, rich and poor, without distinction, child and old man and grandam, crowded around the stately carriage with the white horses, wherein sat a beautiful woman of middle age, serene and stately, but very pale with long watching and with grief. Sobs, and words of blessing, and cries of love and joy, resounded on every side; but amid that countless throng there was no heart so full of a strange pride and gratitude to God as was that of an unknown stranger, by chance in the city, standing unnoticed in the dark shadows of the palace groves. I knew her—had known her longer than they all; for it was the Princess Cynthia of the old, unforgotten, boyish days.

II

THE MARQUIS JEANNE HYACINTHE DE ST. PALAYE

THE MARQUIS JEANNE HYACINTHE DE ST. PALAYE

I

In one of the mountainous districts of the south of France, which in the last century were covered with forests, the highway ran up through the rocky valley by the side of a roaring torrent. On the right hand and on the left the massive foliage descended to the banks, and filled up the small and intervening ravines with a bosky shade. Here and there a lofty crag broke out from the sea of green leaves, and now and then the pointed roofs of a château or the spire of a village church witnessed to the existence of man, and gave an interest and a charm to the beautiful scene.

It was a day in the late autumn of the year 1760. The departing smile of nature, which in another hour would be lost in death, was upon every tree and leaf. The loveliest tints and shades, so delicate that at the moment of their perfection they trembled into nothingness, rested upon the woodlands on every side. A soft wind whispered through the rustling leaves laden with mellow odours and with the pleasing sadness that comes with the falling leaf. The latest flowers of the year with unconscious resignation wasted, as it might seem, tints which would not have disgraced the warmest hues of summer upon heaps of withered leaves, and dry moss, and rotting wood. The loveliest hour of the year was the last.

The highway crossed an ancient bridge

of great height with a cunningly pointed arch. Just beyond the bridge a smaller path turned up on the left hand as you ascended the valley. It wound its way up the wooded valleys as though with no definite end, yet it was smooth and well kept, more so, indeed, than the highway itself, and doubtless led to some château, by the orders of whose lord the peasantry kept the road in good repair. Let us follow this road on an evening at the end of October in the year we have already mentioned, for we shall meet with a pretty sight.

Some distance up the road on the left was a small cottage, built to mark and protect the path to a natural terrace formed, as far as art had had a hand in the proceeding, by some former lord of the domain to command a view of the neighbouring mountains and country. Several of these terraces existed in the wood. At the point where the path entered the private road to the château the wood receded on every side, and left a wide glade or savannah across which the sunshine lay in broad and flickering rays. Down this path there came a boy and girl, for they were little more, though their dress and the rank of life they held gave an appearance of maturity greater than their years. The lady was of supreme beauty even for a heroine of romance, and was dressed with a magnificence which at any other period of the world would have been fantastic in a wood. She was clinging to the arm of a handsome boy of some two and twenty years of age, whose dress, by its scarf and some other slight peculiarities, marked the officer of those days. His face was very handsome, and the expression on the whole was good, but there was something about the eyes and the curve of the lips which spoke of violent passions as yet unsubdued.

The girl came down the path clinging to his arm, her lovely face upraised to him, and the dark and reckless expression of his face was soothed and chastened into a look of intense fondness as he looked down upon it. Rarely could a lovely autumn afternoon receive its finishing touch from the passing of so lovely a pair.

The valley was perfectly solitary; not a single sound was heard, nor living creature seemed astir. It was as if Nature understood, and held her breath to further the purposes of their lonely walk. Only for a moment however. At the instant they left the path and entered upon the grassy verge that bordered the way to the château, they both started, and the girl gazed before her with an expression of wild alarm, while the young man's face grew darker, and a fierce and cruel look came into his eyes. But what they saw would seem at first sight to give little cause for such emotion. A few yards before them, walking leisurely across the grass from the direction of the road, appeared a gentleman of some twenty-eight or thirty years of age, of whom at first sight there could be no question that he was one of the most distinguished and handsomest men of his day. He was carefully dressed in a style which only men of exceptional figure can wear without extravagance, but which in their case seems only fitting and right. He wore a small walking sword, so hung as not to interfere in the least with the contour of his form, with which his dress also evidently harmonised. His features were faultlessly cut, and the expression, though weary and perhaps almost insolent, bore slight marks of dissipation, and the glance of his eyes was serene and even kindly. He saw the pair before him and instantly stopped. It is probable that the incident was equally embarrassing on both sides, but the visible effect was very different. The two young people stood utterly silent and aghast. The lady was evidently frightened and distressed, while her companion seemed prepared to strike the intruder to the earth. On the other hand the Marquis, for such was his rank, showed no signs of embarrassment.

'Pardon, Mademoiselle,' he said; 'I perceive that I have committed a *gaucherie*. Growing tired of the hunt, I returned to the château, and hearing from the servants that Mademoiselle had gone down into the forest to visit her old nurse at the cottage by the terrace, I thought how pleasant it would be to go to meet her and accompany her home. I had even presumed to think,' he continued, smiling, and as he spoke he turned to the young man with a gesture of perfect courtesy —'I even presumed to think that my presence might be some small protection to Mademoiselle in the wilds of the forest. I was unaware, of course, that she was guarded with such loyal and efficient care.' He paused for a moment, and then continued with greater dignity and kindliness of expression, 'I need not add, Mademoiselle, as a gentleman whose name hitherto, I believe, has been free from taint—I need not add that Mademoiselle need fear no embarrassment in the future from this chance encounter.'

It was perhaps strange, but it seemed that the politeness and even friendliness of the Marquis, so far from soothing, irritated the young man. He remained silent, but kept his black and angry glance fixed upon the other.

But the girl seemed differently affected. She hesitated for a moment, and then took a step forward, speaking with her clasped hands before her, with a winning and beseeching gesture.

'You see before you, Monsieur le Marquis,' she said, 'two as miserable young creatures as, I hope, exist upon the earth. Let me present to you Monsieur le Chevalier de Grissolles, of the regiment of Flanders—'

The gentlemen bowed.

'—Who has known me all my life,' continued the girl, speaking rapidly; 'who has loved me—whom I love. We meet to-day for the last time. We should not have told you—I should not have mentioned this to you—because I know—we know—that it is useless to contend against what is fixed for us—what is decreed. We meet to-day for the last time; the fleeting moments are running past—ah! how quickly—in another moment they will be gone.' . . .

Here the emotion that overpowered her choked her utterance. She stopped, and to prevent herself from falling, she clung to the Chevalier's arm.

The Marquis looked at her in silence, and his face became perfectly beautiful with its expression of pity. A marble statue, indeed, might almost have been expected to show emotion at the sight of such beauty in such distress. There was a pause. Then the Marquis spoke.

'I am most honoured,' he said, 'to be permitted to make the acquaintance of Monsieur le Chevalier, whose name, if I mistake not, is already, though that of so young an officer, mentioned with distinction in the despatches of Monsieur de Broglie. For what you have said to me, Mademoiselle—and what you have condescended to confide to me has torn my spirit—I fear I can offer you but little consolation. Your good sense has already assured you that these things are settled for us. They are inevitable.

And in the present case there are circumstances which make it absolutely essential to the interests of Monsieur le Comte, your father, that these espousals, at any rate, should take place at once. Even were I'—here he turned to the Chevalier with a smile—'even were I to pick a quarrel with your friend, and, a few seconds sooner than in the natural course of events it probably would, allow his sword to pass through my heart, I fear the result would be simply to substitute another in my place—another who, I, with perhaps a natural vanity, may fancy, would not place matters in a happier light. But let us not look at things too gloomily. You say that this is your last hour of happiness; that is not necessary. It is true that the espousals must take place at once. The interests of your father require this. But there is no need that Mademoiselle's feelings should not be consulted with regard to the

K

final consummation of the nuptials. These need not be hurried. Monsieur le Chevalier may have other opportunities of making his adieux. And I hope that my influence, which, in after years, may be greater than it is at present, will enable me to further any views he may have with regard to higher commands in the service of his majesty.'

The words were those of ordinary compliment, yet the manner of the Marquis was so winning that, had it been possible, it would have affected even the Chevalier himself; but if a highwayman is threatening your life it is not much consolation that he offers to return you a franc piece.

The Chevalier remained cold and gloomy.

The Marquis looked at him for a moment; then he continued, addressing himself to the girl—

'But I am intruding myself on Mademoiselle. I will continue my walk to the terrace;

the afternoon is delightfully fine. As you are aware, Monsieur le Comte is hunting in the valleys to the west. All the *piqueurs* are withdrawn to that side of the forest. I should hope that Mademoiselle will not again be interrupted in her walk.'

Then without another word he courteously saluted the young people, and continued his walk up the path. He never turned his head, indeed he would have allowed himself to be broken on the wheel rather than have done anything of the kind, but the others were not so reticent; several times they stopped and looked back at the Marquis as he paused every now and then as if to admire the beauties of the scene. At last he reached the corner of the cottage and disappeared from their view.

The beauties of the scene, however, did not entirely occupy the mind of the Marquis. At the most enchanting point, where opening valley and stream and mountain and distant tower burst upon his view, he paused and murmured to himself, 'Some men, now, might have made mischief out of this. Let us wait and see.'

II

THE Château de Frontênac was built upon a natural terrace half way up the slope of the forest, with the craggy ravines clothed with foliage surrounding it on every side. It consisted of two courts, the oldest of which had been built in the earliest days of French domestic architecture, when the detached buildings of the mediæval castle were first brought together into a compact block. In accordance with the singular notion of those days that the south and west were unhealthy aspects, the principal rooms of this portion of the château faced the north and east. They consisted of vast halls and saloons succeeding each other with apparently purposeless extension, and above them a suite of bed-chambers of solemn and funereal aspect. These saloons and bed-chambers had been left unaltered for centuries, and the furniture must have been antique in the reign of Henri Quatre. The other court had been built much more recently, and, in accordance with more modern notions, the chief apartments faced the south and west. From its windows terraced gardens descended into the ravine, and spread themselves along the side of the hill. The architecture had probably, when first the court had been added to the château, contrasted unpleasantly with the sombre pile beyond; but the lapse of centuries with their softening hand had blended the whole into a unity of form and colour, and adventurous plants creeping silently over the carved stone-work of the straggling fronts wrought a soft veil of nature's handiwork over the artificial efforts of man.

The saloons in this part of the château were furnished more or less in the modern taste with cabinets of ebony and ivory of the days of Louis Quatorze, and buhl-work of the eighteenth century; but as the modern articles were added sparingly, the effect on the whole was quiet and pleasing. The De Frontênacs, while enjoying the more convenient portion of their abode, prided themselves upon the antique apartments, and kept them in scrupulous repair. In these vast and mysterious halls all the solemn meetings and ceremonies of the family had place. Here when death had touched his own, the De Frontênacs lay in state; here the infant heir was baptized; here the important compacts of marriage were signed; here the feast of *Noël* was held. It is true that for the last century or so these ideas had been growing weaker, and the usages of modern life and the fascinations of the capital had broken in upon these ancient habits, and weakened the attachments and associations from which they sprang; but the De Fronténacs were a fierce and haughty race, and never entirely lost the characteristics of their forefathers. Now and again, at some distaste of court life, or some fancied slight on the part of the monarch, they would retire to their forest home, and resume for a time at least the life and habits of a nobler and a prouder day.

In the largest of these old saloons, the day after the meeting in the forest, the whole household of the château was assembled. At a long table were seated several gentlemen well known in Paris as among the highest of the *noblesse de robe*, and rolls of parchment and masses of writing, with great seals hanging from their corners, covered the table. The walls of the saloon were hung with portraits of several epochs of art, including the works of artists then alive; for it was a peculiarity of the De Frontênacs that, venerating as they did the antique portion of their château, they invariably hung the portraits of the family as they were painted in these old and faded rooms, reserving for the modern apartments the landscapes and fancy pictures which from time to time they purchased.

When the moment had arrived at which the contracts were to be signed, there was a movement in the room, and Mademoiselle de Frontênac, accompanied by her mother, entered and advanced towards the table. She was perfectly collected, and bowed to the Marquis with an unembarrassed grace. No one ignorant of the circumstances of the case would have supposed that anything approaching to a tragedy was being enacted in that room.

The Marquis signed more than one document, and as he stepped back from the table he ran his eyes carelessly over the room, with which he was unacquainted. Fronting him, above a massive sideboard with the full light of the opposite window upon it, was the portrait of a young man in the cuirass of an officer of cavalry of a previous century, whose eyes were fixed upon the Marquis with a stern and threatening glance. It seemed that, stepping from the canvas, there confronted him, as a few hours before he had met him in the forest, the Chevalier de Grissolles, whom he had found with Mademoiselle de Frontênac.

Nothing probably could have made the Marquis start, but he gazed upon the portrait with interest not unmixed with surprise, and as soon as Mademoiselle had retired, which she did when her signatures had been obtained, he turned to the Count with a courteous gesture.

'These apartments, Count,' he said, 'are

certainly as fine as anything of the kind in Europe. I have seldom, indeed, seen anything that can be compared to them. And doubtless the portraits upon the walls are of exceptional interest. By your leave, I will glance round them;' and, accompanied by the Count, he passed through several of the rooms, listening attentively to the descriptions and anecdotes which the different portraits required and suggested. There was somewhat of sameness perhaps in the story, for the French nobility had little scope of action other than the battle-field, and the collection lacked the pleasing variety of an English portrait-gallery, where the variety of costumes, here a soldier, there a divine, now a lawyer or judge, and then a courtier, charms the eye and excites the fancy. The Marquis came back perhaps all the sooner to the great saloon.

The saloon was empty, and the lawyers

and rolls of parchment were gone. The Marquis went straight to the portrait which had attracted his attention, and stood facing it without saying a word; the Count, after glancing carelessly round the room, followed his guest's example.

The vast hall was perfectly empty. The tables had been pushed aside into the windows, and the superb figure of the Marquis, standing upon the polished floor, would have been of itself sufficient to furnish the scene, but in proportion as the interest which the portrait had excited was manifested in the attitude of the Marquis, so much the more the figure on the wall seemed to gather life and intensity, and to answer look for look with its living opposite.

'That painting,' said the Count, after a moment's pause, 'is the portrait of a cadet of my family, or rather, I should say, of a female branch of it, a Chevalier de Grissolles.

He was a youth of great promise, a favourite and aide-de-camp of the Prince de Condé; and he fell at Jarnac by his master's side. Enough of him,' and the Count's manner changed as he glanced round the chamber, and advanced confidentially to the Marquis. 'Enough of him; but I am not sorry your attention has been directed towards his portrait, because it enables me to introduce, with somewhat less embarrassment, a subject to which I have hitherto shrunk from alluding. I am sorry to say,' continued the Count, with an uneasy smile, 'that the chevalier whose portrait you see before you was not the last of his race. There have been others who have borne the name, and there is one now. He is a lad in the regiment of Flanders, and was brought up in my family. Unfortunately he was allowed to attend Mademoiselle de Frontênac in her recreations, and a boy and girl attachment was formed between them, from which harmless child's play no one foreboded any evil. The young fool is constantly breaking away from his regiment, in which he is a great favourite, and is hanging about my daughter; and from what Madame la Comtesse tells me—I—I hardly like to say it, it is so absurd!—she is positively attached to him, seriously and devotedly attached. Positively I cannot sleep sometimes; this stupid affair has given me so much annoyance.'

It did not increase the good humour of the Count, who was already in a sufficiently bad temper, to notice, as he could not help doing, that the Marquis did not seem in the least surprised at the information he had received, and what was still more irritating, that he seemed to regard it with perfect indifference. He appeared, in fact, to be much more interested in studying the portrait before him, probably admiring it as a work of art.

'My dear Count,' he said at length, 'I am really sorry that you should allow yourself to be so much annoyed over what seems to me to be a mere trifle. This marriage-contract, so honourable to me, is now signed ; at the present moment *les messieurs de robe* are engaged, I doubt not, in arranging those pecuniary matters which you explained to me were of so much importance : why, then, should we trouble ourselves ? As to this little *pastorale* which it seems is being enacted as a sort of interlude to the more serious business of the stage, it is what I imagine invariably takes place. What would become of the poets and romancists otherwise ? We must think of our own youth, Count, and not be too hard upon the young people. Positively I feel quite old when I think of those delightful days — that spring-time of existence, those first loves,' and the Marquis closed his eyes and sighed deeply, apparently from his heart.

The Count took a turn or two in the saloon, but it did not seem to soothe his temper.

'This is all very well,' he said sharply, 'and very witty; in delicate badinage we all know no one can equal Monsieur de St. Palaye, but I assure you this is no laughing matter. This affair has grown beyond a joke. When my daughter has the honour—an honour, I am well aware, far higher than any she had a right to expect—of signing herself Madeleine, Marquise de St. Palaye, it will not be my place, of course, to say a word. Then her honour will be in her husband's keeping—her honour and his. But while she remains in my house she is my daughter, and in my care, and I tell you plainly that this matter is past a joke.'

A fleeting expression of extreme *ennui* passed over the Marquis's face, and he evidently suppressed an inclination to yawn. Then with more *bonhomie* than he had previously shown he put his hand on his companion's arm.

'Well, my dear Count,' he said smilingly, 'I will do anything you wish—anything, that is, short of unpleasantly hurrying the nuptials —that I cannot do. It would be—in fact, it would be such wretched taste—tears!—a scene!—a—an *esclandre* in general, my *dear* Count!'

Then linking his arm in that of the Count, he led him, still sulky and grumbling, out of the saloon, and into the modern court of the château; and the long lines of ancestors on the walls followed them as they passed with angry and vindictive looks, as though enraged that they could not descend from their places and join again in the turmoil of life.

III

The second morning after the contract had been signed, the Marquis was seated in his dressing-room, about an hour before *déjeuner*, reading, apparently with great entertainment, though not for the first time, *Le Taureau Blanc* of Monsieur de Voltaire. While he was thus agreeably occupied the door was violently thrown open, and the Count, heated and excited, burst into the room.

'Marquis,' he said, utterly regardless of any who might hear, 'let me beg of you to get to horse at once and come with me. I have positive information that my daughter is at this moment giving an interview to that young scoundrel on one of the terraces in the wood. While we speak they may be planning an elopement—nay, even carrying it into effect. Let me beg of you to come at once!"

The Marquis laid down his book, crossed one knee over the other, and leaning back on his chair looked the Count in the face steadily for a second or two, as who should say, 'This man will be too much for me; I shall have to press forward the nuptials, I see, in self-defence.' Then he sighed deeply and rose from his seat.

'Very well, my dear Count,' he said, 'I will be as quick as possible. Pierre, see that they bring some horses round; come into my closet yourself, and send Charles and Alphonse and all the men here at once. I will make haste, my dear Count, indeed I will.'

Whether the Marquis did make haste as he said, or whether the number of valets impeded each other, it is certain that it was a long time before he descended to the court of the château, where he found the Count pacing up and down, fuming and cursing his delay. They got to horse as soon as possible, and rode down the forest road, but the Marquis reined his horse in so often, and made such inappropriate remarks upon the beauty of the morning and of the view, that the Count could bear it no longer.

'Monsieur le Marquis,' he said, 'I am sorry I have disturbed you so much; I am very anxious to press forward, but I will not hurry you, I will ride forward at once.'

'Pray do not delay a moment on my account,' said the other; 'I shall rejoin you anon.'

The Count put spurs to his horse, and, followed by his servants, was lost to sight behind the windings of the path.

The moment he disappeared the Marquis

drew his rein, and turning to his valet, said in a tone perfectly different from that which he had hitherto used—

'On the north terrace, do you say?'

'Yes, Monsieur le Marquis,' replied the man, with a smile; 'on the north terrace to the left: not on the old terrace, as the Count is wrongly advised. They have been there a long time; I should think they must be about parting.'

The Marquis turned his horse, and, followed by his men, retraced his steps until they reached a scarcely perceptible path which, now on their right hand, found its way down into the road. Here he dismounted, and taking his riding-whip with him in place of a cane, began leisurely to ascend the path. When he had gone a yard or two, however, he turned to the valet and said—

'Wait here with the horses, and should

Monsieur le Comte return, say to him that I have taken the opportunity of the fine morning to enjoy one of the numerous views on his delightful estate. Say that to him, neither more nor less.'

When the Marquis reached the head of the path he found himself at the end of a long and grassy terrace, from which the path was screened by thick bushes. Standing for a moment so concealed, he became conscious of the presence of the two young lovers whom he had met some few days ago in the forest. Again he could see the face of the young girl, and again he was moved by the sight. He waited till they had reached the other end of the terrace, and then came forward, so as not to startle them by his sudden appearance. They met half way.

'I am sorry once again,' said the Marquis, speaking simply and without affectation, 'to intercept Mademoiselle, especially as this time I have no excuse, but have acted with prepense. Monsieur le Comte, your father, is ridden out in hot haste and temper upon some mischievous information he has received concerning Mademoiselle and Monsieur le Chevalier. I did what I could to delay him, and finally left him, having better information, it appears, than he had. But he will be here anon. I was compelled to leave my horses in the road below, and when he returns from his fruitless quest he will doubtless follow me here. Monsieur le Chevalier will doubtless see the propriety of avoiding an unpleasant meeting.'

'I have to thank you, Monsieur le Marquis,' said the young man, whose manner seemed compounded of an intense dislike and a sense that politeness was due to one who, under singular circumstances, had behaved in a more friendly manner than could have been looked for; 'I have to thank you for previous courtesy, and for, I have no doubt, much consideration to-day. I will not linger any more.'

He took the girl in his arms and imprinted a kiss upon her lips, which, under the circumstances, was perhaps scarcely courteous; then, gloomily bowing to the Marquis, he plunged into the thickest of the wood and disappeared.

The Marquis took no notice of the warmth of his leave-taking, but having his riding-whip and hat in one hand, he offered the other arm to the girl, saying—

'If Mademoiselle will honour me by taking a turn upon the terrace before her father's arrival I shall esteem it a favour, as it will give me the opportunity of saying a single word.'

The girl took his arm willingly, and as she did so she said, with a winning and confiding gesture—

'Monsieur le Marquis, I think you are the best and kindest of men.'

'I wish to put before Mademoiselle,' said the Marquis, speaking gently, but very gravely, 'one or two considerations; and I could wish that it were possible for her to regard it as the advice of an absolutely impartial friend. The first is one of which I hesitate to speak, because it seems to cast a slur, in some manner, upon the character of Monsieur le Chevalier. But man is very weak, especially when exposed to such temptation as, fortunately for him, rarely in this world crosses his path. These shady groves and grassy banks are the places where the deceitful god delights to work his mischief—a mischief which is never repaired. I know, of course, that there are many who speak of these things lightly, and who even view these flowery but dangerous paths with approbation; but I cannot think that

Mademoiselle would tread them without violating the *bienséance* which alone makes life tolerable, or tainting the purity of those lustrous ranks of which she will be the brightest star. I pass at once to another thought which it is not impossible Monsieur le Chevalier has already suggested.' He paused, as the tremor of the girl's hand upon his arm showed that he was not speaking in vain. 'I mean,' he continued, 'the project of seeking in another land that happiness which I fear appears to Mademoiselle to be denied her in this. Could I see any permanent prospect of happiness in such a course I would not shrink, Quixotic as it might seem, from advising you to adopt it. But there appear to me insuperable objections to such a course. I do not see how it is possible for Mademoiselle so to elude the affectionate solicitude of her family as to obtain more than a couple of hours' start.

Couriers on swift horses would be sent to the *Intendants* of the provinces, to the postmasters on the great roads, and to the officers on the frontiers. After experiencing toil and hardships, which it is pitiful to think of, Mademoiselle would probably be overtaken before she reached the frontier. But supposing that such was not the case; supposing that she succeeded, by the skill of Monsieur le Chevalier and the swiftness of his horses, in reaching a foreign land, the Chevalier is a sworn servant of the King of France. He would be arrested in any court and city of Europe; he would be brought back to France, and the Bastile, or some inferior prison, would be his home for life. When I add to this the hardships of life in a foreign land, of the rupture of family ties, of hatred and animosity where there should be nothing but serenity, of the failure of family schemes and hopes, and of the tie which binds persons of our rank all over the world to discountenance actions which are regarded as subversive of family order, and even life—I cannot, I say, when I think of such certain hardship, of such possible disgrace and misery—I cannot advise Mademoiselle to adopt such a course. The certainty that she would soon be separated from her friend seems to me to decide the matter.'

The Marquis paused; but as the girl made no reply, he continued—

'For myself, I say nothing; it is my misfortune that I have been introduced to Mademoiselle under circumstances which render it impossible that I should make that impression which it would have been the ambition of my life to achieve; but this, perhaps, I may say, that should Mademoiselle decide to let matters take their course, and as far as circumstances will permit, to repose in me her confidence, it would indeed seem a fatality no less strange than sad should she prove the first who, in the long course of centuries, had reason to regret that they placed confidence in the word of a St. Palaye.'

It seemed that something in the words of the Marquis, strange as they may appear to some people, or something in his manner as he spoke them, did not affect the girl unpleasantly, for she was in the act of saying, what indeed she had said before, but now with one slight but important modification—

'Marquis, you are the best and kindest of men,'—when her father, heated with riding and with anger, burst through the trees at the end of the terrace, and overlooking in his fury what was before his eyes, exclaimed—

'Well, Marquis, I told you how it would be: I cannot find them! This wretched girl——' he stopped suddenly, open-mouthed, as straight before him, apparently on the most friendly terms, the girl hanging confidingly upon her companion's arm, stood the Marquis, and she of whom he was in such desperate chase. It was impossible for either to conceal a smile.

'My dear Count,' said the Marquis, 'I am sorry you have had so much unnecessary trouble. The truth is that after you left me it occurred to me that, in the little domestic scene you were anticipating, I should play an insignificant, not to say a somewhat ridiculous figure. Warm as is the interest which I must naturally feel in everything that concerns Mademoiselle, I think that these family matters are always best managed by the family itself. I therefore turned aside to enjoy perhaps the most beautiful of the many beautiful views to be found on this estate, and to my delight I found Mademoiselle engaged in a precisely similar occupation. It augurs well.

I am sure, for our future happiness, that at this early period our tastes are found to be so similar.'

The Count saw that he was being laughed at, and indeed it may as well be confessed at once that the Marquis erred in the manner in which he treated the Count. This, however, should be remembered in extenuation, that nothing could be more intolerable to him than the part of jealous husband and lover which the Count appeared determined to force him to play. It was not in human nature but that he should take a little quiet revenge.

'But did you see nothing of the Chevalier?' blundered out the Count.

'Really, my dear Count, I have not had time, had I possessed the power, to challenge my adversary to mortal combat, to run him through the heart, to cut him up into small bits, and to bury him beneath the sod.

Besides, you will observe that the grass all around is perfectly undisturbed. I assure you solemnly,' continued the Marquis, apparently with the greatest earnestness, 'that the Chevalier does not lie murdered beneath my feet.'

The words were spoken in jest, but they were recalled to memory afterwards by more than one.

The Count turned sulkily away, and his daughter and the Marquis followed him back to the château.

IV

A FEW days after these events the Count removed his family to Paris, travelling in several large carriages, and accompanied by numerous servants on horseback. The Marquis accompanied them, and, by what might appear a curious coincidence, on the very morning upon which they set out on their journey the Chevalier received, at the little *auberge* on the farther side of the forest, where he lodged, an imperative order to join his regiment without delay. Furious at the success of what he conceived to be the interference of the Marquis and the Count, he obeyed the order, resolved to return to Paris at the earliest opportunity.

The winter passed in Paris as winters in great cities usually do. The Chevalier stole up from the frontier more than once, and at court balls, at the theatre, and at the private assemblies he succeeded in seeing Mademoiselle de Frontênac more often than he perhaps had expected, but though his opportunities exceeded his hopes, the result was not proportionally favourable. Whether Mademoiselle had succumbed to the paternal influence, or whether the Marquis had succeeded in substituting his own attractions for those of the Chevalier, it was evident that her manner became colder and more reserved at each interview.

The winter at last was over, and one evening in summer, after a royal concert at Versailles, when the king's violins had performed such delicate and yet pathetic music of Monsieur Rousseau's that the court was ravished by it, the Chevalier met his mistress by appointment in one of the pavilions of the orangery. He had secret means of obtaining admission to the precincts of the palaces which were well understood by the courtiers of those days.

Mademoiselle de Frontênac was perfectly pale as she came into the pavilion, and she seemed to walk with difficulty; she stopped immediately when within the door, and spoke at once, as though she were repeating a lesson.

'Do not come any nearer, Monsieur le Chevalier,' she said; 'I am the wife of another.'

He stopped, therefore, where he was, on the other side of the small pavilion, and across the summer evening light that mingled with the shimmer of the candelabras, he saw her for the last time.

Neither spoke for a moment or two, and then she said, still as though conning a part—

'I have promised, Monsieur le Chevalier de Grissolles, to be the wife of the Marquis de St. Palaye, and I will keep my word.'

'You are not speaking your own words, Madeleine,' he said eagerly; 'let your own heart speak!' and coming forward across the pavilion, he was on the point of taking her hand.

Then the door by which she had entered opened again, and the Count de Frontênac, with a quiet and firm step, glided in, and stood by his daughter's side.

At this sight, which revealed to him, as it seemed, the faithlessness of his mistress, and the plot which was woven around him on every side, the Chevalier lost his self-control.

'I was aware, Monsieur le Comte,' he burst forth, 'that in this *pays du diable* the privileges of parents were numerous and inalienable, but till this moment I did not know that eavesdropping was one of them.'

The Count made no reply, except by raising his hat; and his daughter, bowing with a mechanical grace that was pitiful to see, said—

'I wish you farewell, Monsieur le Chevalier.'

'Madeleine,' said the young man, 'I wish you farewell for ever; and I pray God, with what sincerity will be known when we stand, each of us, before His judgment bar, that you may not bitterly regret your words this night.'

Then, perfectly pale, but more composed than before he had spoken, he too raised his hat courteously, and left the room.

That evening there were enacted within a stone's throw of each other two very different scenes.

When the Marquis de St. Palaye returned to his hotel he was told that the family lawyer, Monsieur Cacotte, was waiting to see him, having at the first possible moment brought him some deeds which Monsieur le Marquis was very anxious should be completed.

The Marquis would see him at once, and after a few minutes' delay, he entered the room, in which the lawyer was seated at a table which was covered with parchments. The room was one in which the Marquis usually sat when the festivities of the day, whether at home or abroad, were over; it was richly furnished as a library, and upon the wide hearth there burned a fire of wood, though it was summer. Greeting the lawyer with great friendliness of manner, St. Palaye threw himself somewhat wearily into a chair, and gazed at the blazing wood-ashes.

A servant entered the room with wine.

'I am sorry, Monsieur le Marquis,' said the lawyer, 'to come to you at so unseasonable an hour; but your instructions were so precise that the moment this first will was ready it should be brought to you to sign, that I did not dare to wait till the morrow.'

'You did quite right, Monsieur Cacotte,' said the Marquis. 'No one can tell what may happen before the morrow.'

'I have indeed,' continued the lawyer, 'prepared both wills, so that Monsieur can satisfy himself that they are both exactly alike. The one will be signed immediately after the marriage; the other at once. They both contain the same clauses, and especially the one upon which Monsieur le Marquis so much insisted: "That the sum of fifty thousand louis d'or, charged upon the unsettled estates in Poitou and Auvergne, should be paid within three months of the death of the testator to Monsieur le Chevalier de Grissolles, for a purpose which he will appreciate and understand." Those, I think, were the words Monsieur wished to have used.'

'They seem quite correct,' said the Marquis.

'I am sorry,' continued the lawyer, 'that this extra expense, which seems to me unnecessary, should be entailed.'

'In that,' said the Marquis politely, 'you only show, Monsieur Cacotte, that care and interest in the good of the family which you have always manifested both in the time of my father and of myself. My father, the late Marquis de St. Palaye, always expressed to me the obligation under which he conceived himself to be in this respect, and this obligation is, of course, much increased in my case.'

'The obligation, Monsieur le Marquis,' said the lawyer, 'if such there be, has been too liberally repaid both by your father and yourself.'

'To tell the truth, Monsieur Cacotte,' said the Marquis, leaning back in his chair, with his feet stretched out towards the fire, and speaking with an appearance of being perfectly at home with his companion, and desirous of confiding in him—'to tell the truth, I am, even in this age of science and encyclopædias, somewhat superstitious, and I have a presentiment—the St. Palayes often had it—that I have not long to live. Do not suppose that I shrink from this prospect, though it is a singular statement for a man to make who is about to marry, and to marry such a bride as mine! Yet I do not mind confiding to you, Monsieur Cacotte, that I am somewhat wearied of life. The world grows very old, and it does not seem to mend.'

'Monsieur le Marquis has been too long unmarried,' said the lawyer. 'I am not surprised that he should be wearied of the enjoyments which he has had the opportunity of tasting to such repletion. He will speak differently when he has a lovely woman by his side, and knows the felicity of wife and child.'

'Ah, Monsieur Cacotte!' said the Marquis, smiling, 'you speak, as they all do, of felicity. There is such a thing, believe me, as the intolerable weariness of a too constant felicity. When I hear even of the joy of the future, and of the bliss of heaven, it seems to me sometimes that the most blissful heaven is to cease to exist.—Let me sign the deed.'

A servant was called in as a witness, and the Marquis signed the first will. Then he said to Monsieur Cacotte—

'The marriage will take place in six weeks in Auvergne; I hope that Monsieur Cacotte will honour the ceremony with his presence. I can assure you from my own experience that you will have nothing to complain of in the hospitality of Monsieur le Comte.'

. . . . .

The Chevalier returned to his lodging about the same time that the Marquis entered his hotel. His valet awaited him that he might change his dress as usual before going into the town to spend the remainder of the evening. The man perceived at once that his master was excited and unhappy. He was an Italian by birth, and had accompanied the Chevalier in his campaigns, and in his secret visits to the Château de Frontenac. He saw that the crisis had arrived.

'Does Monsieur go down into Auvergne this autumn?' he said.

'We go down once more,' said the Chevalier gloomily. He had divested himself of his court dress, and was taking from his valet a suit of dark clothes somewhat resembling a hunting suit. 'Yes, we go down once more: this cursed marriage will take place a month hence.'

'Monsieur takes this marriage too much to heart,' said the Italian,—and as he spoke he handed the coat, which his master put on, —'it may never take place. A month hence in the country they will begin to hunt—to hunt the boar. No doubt the party at the château will divert themselves in this way while the nuptial ceremonies are arranged. It is a dangerous sport. Many accidents take place, many unfortunate shots—quite unintentional. Monsieur le Chevalier is a finished sportsman. He has a steady hand and a sure eye. *C'est un fait accompli.*'

The Chevalier started: in the large glass before him he saw a terrible figure dressed as for the chase, but pale as a corpse, and trembling in every limb as with the palsy. He shuddered and turned away.

V

THE *piqueurs* sent up word to the château that a magnificent boar had been lodged in a copse at the foot of the forest road. An answer was sent down accordingly that the Marquis would drive him early in the morning, and that he should be turned if possible towards the château.

In the morning, therefore, very early, the whole household was astir. The ladies were mounted, and, divided into parties, cantered down the road and along the forest paths to those points where, according to the advice of their several attendant cavaliers, the hunt would most likely be seen to advantage. The Marquis, it was said, had been down at a still earlier hour to rouse the boar. Every now and then a distant horn sounding over the waving autumn forest told that the sport had commenced.

The ladies were gay and delighted, and those of the gentlemen who, like Monsieur Cacotte, were not much accustomed to country life and scenes, shared their enjoyment to the full. And indeed it seemed a morning out of fairyland. From every branch and spray upon which the leaves, tinted with a thousand colours, were trembling already to their fall, hung sparkling festoons of fairy lace, the mysterious gossamer web which in a single night wreathes a whole forest with a magic covering which the first hour of sunlight as soon destroys. Yellows, browns, and purples formed the background of this dazzling network of fairy silver which crossed in all directions the forest rides.

But though the morning was so lovely the ladies grew tired of riding up and down waiting for the hunt. The horns became fainter and more distant, and it became evident that the chase had drifted to the eastward.

'Why do you stay here, Monsieur de Circassonne?' said Mademoiselle de Frontênac, smiling, to a young man, almost a boy, who had with the utmost devotion remained by the side of herself and a very pretty girl, her companion. 'Why do you stay here? You are not wont to desert the chase. What can have happened to the Marquis and the rest?'

The boy looked somewhat sheepish, and replied to the latter part of the question only.

'I fancy that the boar has broken out, in spite of the *piqueurs*, and that the Marquis has failed to turn him. They have probably lost him in the forest.'

'But is not that very dangerous?' said the pretty girl. 'If they do not know where the boar is, he may burst out upon us at any moment.'

The boy looked at her as though much pleased.

'That is quite true,' he said. 'It was one reason why I stayed.'

Monsieur de Circassonne was not far wrong in his opinion. This is what had happened.

When the Marquis arrived at the cover, very soon after sunrise, he found that the boar, ungraciously refusing to wait his opponent's convenience, had broken cover, and wounding one of the *piqueurs*, who attempted to turn him, had gone down the valley. He was described as an unusually fine animal, and the dogs were upon his track.

The course which the boar had taken lay

through the thick of the forest. It was rugged and uneven, and he could only be pursued on foot. After some distance had been traversed, the scent was suddenly crossed by a large sow, who, as frequently happened, apparently with the express purpose of diverting the pursuit from her companion, crossed immediately in front of the dogs and went crashing down through the coppice to the right. Most of the hounds followed her, and the *piqueurs*, with few exceptions, followed the dogs. The Marquis, however, succeeded in calling off some of the oldest hounds, and, accompanied by two or three *piqueurs*, followed the original chase. Some distance farther on, however, the boar had taken to the water, and the scent was lost. At the same time the horns sounding in the valley to the right showed that the deserters had come up with their quarry, and distracted the attention of both *piqueurs* and dogs. The former were of opinion that the boar had simply crossed the river, and taking the dogs across they made a cast on the opposite bank, where the dogs ran backwards and forwards baying disconsolately. The Marquis, however, believing that the boar had followed the course of the stream for at least some distance, kept on the left bank, and forcing his way round one or two craggy points, found at last the spot where the boar, apparently but a few moments before, had scrambled up the bank. He sounded his horn, but either from the baying of the dogs, or the noise and excitement in the valley below, he was disregarded, and pushing aside the branches before him, the Marquis found himself at the foot of a ravine down which a mountain torrent was rushing to join the river below. The bed of the ravine was composed of turf overstrewn with craggy rock, and on either side rugged cliffs, out of the fissures of which lofty oaks and chestnuts had grown for centuries, towered up towards the sky.

The Marquis waited for a moment, but hearing no reply to his horn, he entered the ravine alone.

As he did so, the strange shapes which the hanging roots and branches of the trees assumed might seem to beckon and warn him back; but, on the other hand, a thousand happy and pleasing objects spoke of life and joy. The sun shone brilliantly through the trembling leaves, birds of many colours flitted from spray to spray, butterflies and bright insects crossed the fretted work of light and shade. The chase was evidently before him—why should he turn back?

Some fifty yards up the valley the rocks retreated on either side, leaving a wide and open grassy space, down which the torrent was rushing, and over which fragments of basaltic rock, split from the wooded cliffs above, were strewn. At the summit of this grassy slope, standing beneath a bare escarpment of basalt, the Marquis saw the boar.

Its sides and legs were stained with mud and soil, but the chase had been very short, and the animal seemed to have turned to bay more out of curiosity and interest than from terror or exhaustion. It stood sniffing the air and panting with excitement, its hair bristling with anger, its white and polished tusks shining in the sun.

When the Marquis saw this superb creature standing above him on the turf, a glow of healthy and genuine pleasure passed over his face. He swung his horn round far out of reach behind his back, and drew his long and jewelled knife. The boar and he would try this issue alone.

For some seconds they stood facing each other. Then the posture of the Marquis changed inexplicably. He rose to his full height, his gaze was fixed as if by fascination upon a long range of low rocks above him to the left, and an expression of surprise, which did not amount to anxiety even, came into his face. Then he dropped his knife, threw his arms up suddenly over his head, and falling backwards, rolled once òver and lay motionless upon the uneven turf in an uneasy posture, his head lower than the limbs. A puff of white smoke rose from the rocks above, and the reverberating echo of a hunting piece struck the rocks and went on sounding alternately from side to side down the valley.

The boar, startled at the shot, and still more, probably, by the sudden fall of his adversary, crept into the thicket, and, while a man might count sixty, an awful silence fell upon hill, and rock, and wood. The myriad happy creatures that filled the air with murmur and with life became invisible and silent, and even the rushing torrent ceased to sound. Then a terrible figure, habited in the costume of the chase, but trembling in every limb as with a palsy, rose from behind the rocks upon the left. With tottering and uneven steps, it staggered down the grassy slope, and stood beside the fallen man. The Marquis opened his eyes, and when he saw this figure he tried to raise himself from the uneasy posture in which he had fallen. When he found it was impossible, a smile of indescribably serene courtesy formed itself gradually upon his face.

'Ah, Chevalier,' he said, speaking slowly and at intervals, 'that was scarcely fair! Make my regrets to the Marquise. Monsieur Cacotte—will speak to you—about—my—will.'

Then, the smile fading from the lips, his head fell back into the uneasy posture in which it had lain, and the Marquis Jeanne Hyacinthe de St. Palaye rested in peace upon the blood-stained grass.

III

THE BARONESS HELENA VON SAARFELD

THE BARONESS HELENA VON SAARFELD

TRAVELLING in Germany on one occasion, I passed the evening at a small inn among some mountains with a middle-aged man whom I soon discovered to have been an actor. In the course of the evening he told me the outlines of the following story, together with much interesting detail relating to an actor's life. I have endeavoured to work into the story what I could recollect of his observations, but not being able to take notes at the time, and having little intimate knowledge of German life, I have lost much of the local colouring and graphic detail which interested me so much at the time. This short introduction will suffice.

In a considerable town in Germany (said the actor) there have been for several generations a succession of dukes who have patronised the German theatre and devoted the principal part of their revenue to its support. In this city I was born. My grandfather had been an actor of some repute, whose acting in some of his principal characters Schiller is said greatly to have admired. His son, however, did not follow in his father's art, but degenerated, as most would call it, into a stage-carpenter and inferior scenepainter. He was, however, a man of considerable reading, and of a certain humour, which mostly took the form of bitter sarcasm and dislike of the theatrical profession. From my birth he formed a determination to bring me up as a printer, for besides that his fondness for reading naturally caused him to admire the art by which books are produced, he believed that education would make gigantic steps within a few years, and that in consequence printers would never want for occupation. In this expectation, at any rate in one respect, he was mistaken.

Upon the production of a new piece which the reigning Duke had himself written, the juvenile actor who was to have taken a boy's part sickened and died, and the company did not at the moment possess any child who was fitted to take his place. My father was requested, or rather commanded, to allow me to learn the few words attached to the part. He was extremely averse to the proposal, but was compelled to consent, the matter appearing so trifling. The play was very successful. The applause was unanimous, and indeed was so enthusiastic that, not satisfied with lauding the talent of the noble author and with praising the intelligence of the chief actors who had so readily grasped the intentions of genius, it had some encomiums left for the child actor, and discovered a profound meaning in the few words the Duke had put into my mouth, which it asserted I had clearly and intelligently rendered. The Duke, pleased at finding himself so much cleverer than even he had ever suspected, joined in the applause. He never failed to testify his approbation at the way in which I piped out the very ordinary words of my single line, and finally, when the play was withdrawn for a time, he sent an order to my father to repair one summer afternoon to the ducal Schloss which overlooked the town. I have since sometimes thought that it was curious that this play, so full of genius and of humour, was not re-acted even on this partial stage oftener than it was, and that, in all the theatres of Germany where I have played my part, I never once saw it performed, nor even so much as heard it mentioned; so difficult of recognition is merit in my profession.

The ducal Schloss rose directly above the tall houses of the superior quarter of the town, the backs of which looked out upon forest trees which had been planted, and had grown to great size, upon the steep mountain slope upon which the Schloss was built. My father, taking me by the hand, led me up the winding road, defended at the angles by neglected towers, which led to the castle gardens. On the way he never ceased to impress upon me the misery of an actor's life.

'The poorest handicraft,' he said, 'by which a man can earn his crust of bread in quiet is preferable to this gaudy imposture which fools think so attractive. In other trades a man is very often his own master, in this he has so many that he does not even know which to obey. In other trades a man has some inducement to do his best, in this to excel is in most cases to starve. The moment an actor ceases to assist the self-love of his fellow-actor, or to minister to the worst passions of his auditors, he is hated or despised. He works harder than the simplest journeyman for poorer pay, he is exposed to greater risk of accident, and the necessities of his part require such a delicacy of organisation that the least accident ruins it.' The great trunks of the trees were throwing a fitful shadow over the steep walks as my father, still holding me by the hand, poured these dolorous opinions into my ears, and we reached the long terraces of the ducal gardens.

We were passed on from one gorgeous domestic to another until at last we found ourselves before the chasseur, a magnificent man of gigantic height, but with an expression of face perfectly gentle and beautiful. I had often noticed this man in the theatre, and had always thought that he would be admirably fitted to represent St. Christopher, a picture of whom hung in my mother's room. He surveyed us courteously and kindly, and informed us that the Duke was taking his wine with a friend on one of the terraces on the farther side of the hill. Thither he led us, and we found the Duke seated at a small table in front of a stone alcove ornamented with theatrical carvings in bas-relief. The view on this side avoided the smoke of the town and commanded a magnificent prospect of wood and plain crossed by water, and intersected by low ranges of hills. The afternoon sun was gilding the tree-tops and the roofs and turrets of the Schloss behind us.

 The gigantic chasseur introduced us to the Duke, who sat at his wine, together with a gentleman of lofty and kindly expression, whom I never saw before or since. On the table were wine and dried fruits. I remember the scene as though it had occurred only yesterday.

'Ah, my good Hans,' said the Duke—he prided himself on his accurate acquaintance with every one attached to the theatre, and my father's name was Karl—'ah, my good Hans, I have sent for you because I have taken an interest in this little fellow, and I wish to make his fortune. I will take his future into my hands and overlook his education in his noble profession of player.'

My father looked very uncomfortable.

'Pardon, your highness!' he said, 'I do not design him for a player. I wish him to be a printer.'

The Duke raised his hand with a magnificent gesture as of a man who waives all discussion.

'My good fellow,' he said, 'that is all past. This boy has developed a talent for the highest of all possible professions. He has shown himself unconsciously appreciative of genius, and able to express it. His future is mine.'

My father looked very downcast, and the gentleman who sat by the Duke, with a kindliness of demeanour which has endeared him to me for ever, said—

'But this good man seems to have decided views about his own son.'

'My dear Ernest,' said the Duke, 'on every other subject I am most willing to listen to, and to follow, your excellent advice, but on this one topic I think you will admit that I have some right to be heard. We have here,' he continued, leaning back in his chair, and waving his two hands before him, so that the fingers crossed and interlaced each other, as his discourse went on, with a continuous movement which fascinated my eyes, 'we have here the commencement of an actor's life. We look forward into the future and we see the possibility of an existence than which nothing more attractive presents itself to the cultured mind. What to other men is luxury is the actor's every-day life. His ordinary business is to make himself familiar with the highest efforts of the intellect of his day, but this even is not all; every movement of his life is given to the same fascinating pursuit; whenever he walks the street he is adding to his store; the most trifling incident—a passing beggar, a city crowd—presents to him invaluable hints; his very dreams assist him; he lives in a constant drama of enthralling interest; the greater stage without is reflected on the lesser stage of the theatre; his own petty individuality is the glass in which the universal intellect and consciousness mirrors itself. It is given to him of all men to collect in his puny grasp all the fine threads of human existence, and to present them evening after evening for the delight, the instruction, and the elevation of his fellow-men. We have before us an individual, small, it is true, and at present undeveloped, before whom this future lies assured. Shall we hesitate for a moment? This worthy man, looking at things in a miserable detail, sees nothing but some few inconveniences which beset this, as every other, walk in life. It is fortunate that his child's future is not at his control.'

My father said nothing more; but as he was shown off the final terrace by the least gorgeous of the domestics, he muttered to himself so low that I could only just hear him, 'We shall see what the mother will say.'

But—when we reached our house, which was a lofty gabled dwelling in the poorer part of the town, but which had belonged to my grandfather and to his father before him, and had once been a residence of importance; when we climbed to the upper story and found ourselves in the large kitchen and dwelling-room which commanded views both ways, into the street and to the ramparts at the back—he got no help from his wife.

My mother did not like reading, and even thought in her secret mind, though she did not say it aloud, that her husband would be much better occupied in working for his family than in puzzling his brains over the pages of Kant. She had, therefore, no great admiration for the great printers of the day, nor was Johann Gutenberg likely to replace St. Christopher over her bedside. She knew nothing of the vast stride that education was about to make, nor of the consequent wealth that awaited the printer's craft, but she did know the theatre and she knew the Duke. That the Duke had promised to make her son's fortune was not denied; surely there was little left to desire. It was decided that night that I should be an actor.

'My son,' said my father, some time afterwards, as he took me to the lodgings of an actor who had promised to teach me to repeat some famous parts, 'my son, I have not been able to train thee to the occupation which I should have desired. I pray God to assist thee in that which fate has selected. I have one piece of advice which I will give thee now, though I hope I shall be able to repeat it often. Never aspire to excellence; select the secondary parts, and any fine strokes of acting which you may acquire throw into these parts. In this way you will escape the vindictive jealousy of your fellows; but if unavoidably you should attract such ill-feeling, leave the theatre at once, travel as much as possible, act on as many boards as you can. You will achieve in this way the character of a useful player who is never in the way. In this way, and in this only, you probably will never want bread ; more than this I cannot hope for.'

．　　．　　．　　．

I shall not weary you by relating the story of my education as an actor ; it will suffice to say that I found neither my father's estimate of the profession, nor that of the Duke, to be precisely correct. If on the one hand I have found littleness and jealousy to exist among players, on the other I have seen numberless acts of unpretending and self-denying kindness. It must be remembered that the actor's life is a most exciting and wearing one, and most certain to affect the nerves and make a man irritable and suspicious. His reputation and his means of existence are dependent upon the voice of popular applause — an applause which may be affected by the slightest misunderstanding or error. It is no wonder, therefore, that he is apt to take alarm at trifles, or to resent with too much quickness what seems to be a slight or an unfairness. With regard to the Duke's ideal view of the profession, I did not find this even altogether without foundation in fact. I found, amidst all its trivialities and vexations, the player's training to give an insight into human life in all its forms, and to encourage the study and observation of the varieties of city existence more than perhaps any other training does. I studied the works of the great dramatists and novelists with attention, not only for my own parts, but that I might understand the parts of others. I followed my father's advice throughout my life. I confined myself systematically to secondary parts, but I watched carefully the acting of the great players, and endeavoured to lead up to their best effects, and to respond to the emotions they sought to awaken. By this means I became a great favourite among the best players, for it is surprising what an assistance the responsive action of a fellow-actor is in obtaining an effect, while on the other hand it is very unlikely that the attention of the audience should be diverted from the principal actor by what tends indeed to increase the impression he makes. Several of the greatest actors then in Germany often refused parts unless I played the secondary character. I was not particular. I would take any part, however unimportant, provided my salary was not reduced in consequence, and I endeavoured to throw all my knowledge and training into any part I undertook. By this means I became a great favourite with authors, who, if they are worth anything, endeavour to distribute their genius equally among their characters, and whom nothing irritates so much as to see everything sacrificed to promote the applause and vainglory of a single performer. I grew up, much to the surprise of all who knew me, a very handsome young man; and I generally took the parts of lovers, when these were not of the first importance, such, for instance, as the part of Romeo, which, true to the rule I had adopted, I never attempted. In this way I had visited most of the cities of Germany, and was well known in all of them, when, at the request of one of the chief actors of the day, who studied the parts of the great tragedies which he undertook with the most conscientious care, I accepted an engagement at the theatre of one of the great cities of the empire, to which he had also engaged himself for a considerable time.

The theatre was a large one, and the company numerous and varied. I might occupy you for a long time with divers descriptions of character and with the relation of many curious and moving incidents, but I do not wish to make this a long story, and I will therefore confine myself to the chief events.

The German stage, as you are aware, is different from your own in England, in that it does not present such marked contrasts. There is a great gulf, as I understand, between your highest actors and your pantomime players; but this is not the case in Germany. As far as I can understand, we have nothing resembling your pure pantomime, and what we have which resembles it is introduced in interludes and after-pieces, and is taken part in, to a considerable extent, by the same actors who perform in the more serious pieces. There was, for instance, in the theatre to which I was attached, an old actor named Apel, who would take the part of grave-digger in *Hamlet*, and the same evening, in the after-piece, act the part of what you call the clown. This part on any stage is the one most liable to accidents, and this man, in the course of a long professional career, had met with several, in falling through trap-doors open through the carelessness of carpenters, or stumbling over unforeseen obstacles. These accidents had seriously affected his physical system, and he was rapidly becoming a helpless cripple. He had one child, a daughter, who danced, for a German, with remarkable grace and agility, and sang with a rich and touching voice. Of all the avocations which necessity has forced the unhappy daughters of man to adopt—

> 'The narrow avenue of daily toil,
> For daily bread,'

that of a pantomime dancer, who has a song, is the hardest. I have stood upon the stage by such a girl as this, and marked the panting exhaustion with which she completed her dance, and the stupendous effort with which she commenced her song. Even without the exertion of the dance, I know of few things more touching than to see a girl labouring conscientiously through a long, and possibly an unattractive song, before a wearied and unsympathising audience who reck nothing of the labour, the pains, and the care which the performance involves. The girl of whom I speak, whose name was Liese, had her share, and perhaps more than her share, in this hard lot. She was a fine German girl of no particular talent, but perfectly trained; she came of a family of actors, and displayed a kindliness of disposition and a devotion which were truly German. As her father's incapacity increased, her exertions redoubled. While they both were able to take their full part, the income of the pair was comparatively ample; but as he was obliged to relinquish part after part of his accustomed performance, she redoubled her exertions, and took every trifling part which was in kindliness offered her by the management. I acted with her in innumerable parts of light comedy as lover and sweetheart, as brother and sister, as betrayer and victim, and, in turn, as jilted and deceived. I have never been able to this day to decide whether I was really in love with her or not, but I rather think my feelings were those of a devoted and affectionate brother, and I am certain of this, that no man ever reverenced a woman more than I did this girl. At last the old man's paralysis became so confirmed that he could scarcely stand; he had to be carried to the side scenes, and went through hours of agony when his short part was over.

One afternoon, about this time, after rehearsal, at which neither father nor daughter had been present, and whose fines for non-attendance I paid, a proceeding which, as I was known to be so intimate, passed as a mere matter of arrangement between ourselves, I went, at the request of the manager, to inquire whether either would be present at the evening performance.

Herr Apel had been obliged to leave his former lodgings owing to the reduction of his earnings, and I had not far to go to the dreary, shabby street near the theatre, where he occupied two rooms on the first floor. Liese received me in one of the lower rooms, and I noticed a strange expression in her face which I had never seen before.

'We could not come to the rehearsal,' she said; 'we have been rubbing him all day, and he has been in such pain! I do not think that even he can possibly play to-night. We have our fines ready.'

'There is no question of fines,' I said, 'with you. You do not think so badly of Herr Wilhelmj as that, I hope.'

She looked at me curiously, but made no remark. After a pause she said—

'I sometimes think that nursing him and seeing him suffer affects me too. I feel at times a strange numbness and pain stealing over me. What would become of us if I became like him!'

'You must not think of such things,' I said; 'you have plenty of friends who will help you in every way. Let us go up to him.'

We went together upstairs into a little room where the old clown lay. He had the expression of an idiot, and seemed absolutely crippled and helpless; but I was not surprised at this, for I had seen him even worse before, and known him act the same evening with much of his old genius and fire. It was a most extraordinary fact that this man, helpless and idiotic to the last inch of the side scenes, regained, the moment the footlights flashed in his face and he saw the crowded theatre before him, all his strength, recollection, and humour, and went through his part apparently without an effort, only to collapse the moment he tottered behind the scenes.

He was whining and moaning as I sat down beside him on the sofa.

'No one pays any attention, no one takes any care of me,' he said; 'I am a poor old man. I have entertained people in my day—thousands and thousands; no one does anything for me. My daughter, even, does nothing; she might do much, but she does nothing; she is only thinking of herself and her own gains.'

She stood leaning on the end of the couch,

looking me full in the face with a sad, but not unhappy, look in her eyes. I could return her glance freely. The old man's state was so evident, it did not embarrass any one whatever he said. She leaned over her father.

'Shall you play to-night, papa?' she said: we used many French words in the theatre.

A contortion of pain passed over the old man.

It was a curious thing, but as I half rose, involuntarily, to help, I saw the same spasm of pain pass over the daughter's form, and she seemed bent down for a moment by it; then she stood upright, and looked at me with a wistful, earnest, inquiring gaze.

It is just possible—at this hour I do not think that I should—but still it is just possible that I might have asked what she had in her thoughts, when the door opened, and a female servant announced—

'The Count von Roseneau.'

I rose in my seat as a very handsome young man, of some two and twenty years of age, came into the room. He was well known to us all as a constant frequenter of the green-room, as you call it in England. He spoke kindly to the old man, who seemed to brighten at his presence, nodded to me, but took little notice of Liese. I know not what prompted me, but I stood for a moment silent, comparing myself with him. He was handsome, though of a more boyish style of beauty than mine; he was noble, though said not to be rich. He was far from clever, and of very moderate education. I was handsomer than he, trained in every art that makes the possessor attractive—elocution, gesture, demeanour; my mind stored by the intelligent familiarity with the highest efforts of human genius; yet it never occurred to me to put myself for a moment into competition with him. After a few ordinary phrases, I took my leave.

From this day it seemed to me that Liese was more distant and reserved with me; she seemed, too, to act with indifference and even carelessly, and to be often *distraite* and forgetful. Her father grew worse and worse. He crept through his part, the mere shadow of his former self. At last the manager informed his daughter that it was impossible to allow him to appear any longer upon the stage.

'We will give him a benefit,' he said, 'in a week or two, at which all the strength of the theatre will assist. He shall be brought on in a chair, and shall sing his popular song. That must be the *finale*.'

In about a month's time the benefit took place. The theatre was crowded, everything being done to make the entertainment attractive. Several actors came from distant cities to take part in the performance, for the old clown was one of the best-known men in the profession, and was associated with pleasant recollections in the memory of most players. Two favourite pieces were given with great applause, and in the interval Herr Apel was brought in in a chair, which was placed in front of the footlights, and sang his song.

To the last moment, and even as he was carried across the stage, he seemed almost insensible of what was passing, but once in front of the lights, and of the great theatre rising tier over tier before him, every one upon his feet, with waving of handkerchiefs and fans, and a tumult of applause and of encouraging cries, he raised himself in the chair, his face assumed the old inimitable comic expression, and amid the delighted excitement of the vast crowd, he gave his song with as much power and wit as he had

ever done in the course of his long career.
Nor was this all, for the song being over,
and the last two verses given twice, in
response to the repeated encore, the long
applause having a little subsided, the old man
rose, and, without help, tottered forwards
towards the lights, and amid the breathless
silence of the house, and with a simple dignity
which contrasted touchingly with his feeble-
ness and his grotesque dress, spoke a few
words of natural regret, of farewell, and of gratitude for the favours of a lifetime. He even,
in the concluding sentence, turned slightly
to the stage, which was crowded, and included
his fellow-actors in the expression of kindly
reminiscence and thanks. The excitement
was intense. Men wept like children, not
only in the theatre but on the stage ; many
women fainted, and it was some time before
the curtain could rise again for the second
piece. Herr Apel was taken home in a

comatose state, and scarcely moved or spoke again during the remainder of his life.

Two days after this performance, as I was leaving the theatre after the morning rehearsal, I was accosted by a tall chasseur, who reminded me instantly of my old friend, St. Christopher, in the ducal court.

'Sir,' he said, with great deference, 'the Baroness Helena von Saarfeld wishes to speak with you in her carriage, which is close by.'

I followed the man to a handsome carriage which was standing a few doors from the stage entrance, a little way down the street. There, as I stood bareheaded at the open door, I saw for the first time the most beautiful woman, without exception, that I have ever seen.

Helena von Saarfeld was the only child of the late Baron, who was enormously wealthy and possessed of vast ancestral

estates. He was a man of great intellect
and of superior attainments, and he undertook
the entire education of his only child and
heiress. Helena was taught everything that
a man would know, and her father discussed
all social and religious questions with her.
He held very singular opinions upon social
problems, and in religion he was much attached to the mystical doctrines of the Count
Von Zinzendorff. At a very early period
he had contracted his daughter in marriage
to the young Count von Roseneau, to whose
father he had been much attached; but as
the boy grew up, having been deprived early,
by death, of his father's care, the Baron
became dissatisfied with the young man, and
it was well known that at his death, which
had taken place about two years before I saw
his daughter, he had left a codicil to his will
entirely exonerating her from any obligation
to the young Count, and leaving her future

destiny in her own hands, expressing every confidence in her judgment and discretion. All these facts were known to me as I approached the carriage.

The Baroness was at this time between two and three and twenty, in the full possession of her youth. She was of a perfect height, with brown hair, lighter than her eyes, and beautifully cut features; her mouth was perhaps rather large, but this only increased the wonderful effect of her smile, which was the most bewitching ever seen. She spoke with animation, and her smile was so constant that the most wonderful thing about it was that its charm never flagged. This was the woman who was presented to my gaze as I stood in the sunshine bareheaded by the carriage-door.

'I have wished to speak to you, Herr Richter,' she said, throwing a world of fascination into her face and manner as she spoke; 'will you oblige me by driving a short distance with me in the carriage? I will not take you far out of town.'

I entered the carriage, and the coachman having orders to drive slowly, we passed through the crowded streets.

'I was at the theatre the other night,' the Baroness said, 'and I was extremely touched, as, indeed, we all were, at the sight of that poor old man; though I do not know that I should call him poor who all through his life has contributed to the gaiety and innocent enjoyment of the world, and could at his last breath speak words so touching and so noble as he did. May I ask of you, Herr Richter, what will become of him—I am so ignorant of these things—and whether it were possible for one like I am to help him in any way?'

'I shall be very glad, Madame la Baronne,' I said, 'to undertake to apply any help you may be most kindly disposed to afford. I am very intimate with Herr Apel, and can easily find ways of doing so; and I fear, from what I know of his circumstances, that any aid will be most welcome.'

'That was what I feared,' she said; 'and it seems to me so sad that such should be the end of a life of toil like his!'

I saw at once that the Baroness was saying these last words by way of introduction to something else, and I did not reply. Probably she noticed this, for she said without the slightest hesitation—

'He has a daughter, I believe.'

'He has,' I replied.

'She is a very clever actress, I am told.'

'She is a very conscientious, hard-working *artiste*,' I replied, 'and has, for a German, remarkable grace, and she sings charmingly.'

'And she is a very good girl.'

'She is one of the best girls I ever knew.

She is devoted to her father, and, I fear, is injuring herself by her exertions to make up the deficiency which is involved in his failing health. She is a thoroughly true and excellent girl.'

The Baroness looked at me for a moment before she replied; then she said—

'You speak, Herr Richter, as I was given to expect. Fräulein Apel is fortunate in having so true a friend.'

There was a pause. I knew something was coming, but I did not know what. Then she said, still without the slightest hesitation—

'The life of an actress is a difficult and exposed one, Herr Richter?'

'It is, Madame la Baronne; but like all other ideas, this one has been exaggerated. A girl in this, as in other walks, has ample means of protection, and I have never heard that Fräulein Apel has even needed such.'

She looked at me again for a moment. I began to think that she was the most lovely creature that ever walked the earth.

'But gentlemen and nobles court their acquaintance a good deal, do they not? This must be a great temptation in their sphere of life.'

'Some gentlemen frequent the greenroom,' I replied, 'and are fond of talking to the actresses. In some theatres it is forbidden.'

'Has Fräulein Apel any friends of this kind?' said the Baroness; and now for the first time I detected a slight hesitation in her manner; but it was so trifling that no one but an actor would, I think, have perceived it. 'The Count von Roseneau, for instance.'

'The Count is a frequenter of the theatre,' I said, 'and I have seen him speaking to Liese—to Fräulein Apel—in fact, I have met him at her house.'

The Baroness was looking straight before her now. She said without hesitation, but still seriously—

'I fear that any acquaintance between them will not be for good.'

There was a pause. I scarcely knew what to say. It was the Baroness who broke it.

'I will not take you farther out of your way,' she said. 'I do not ask you to understand me, or not to misinterpret anything that I have said, for it is notorious that Herr Richter can do nothing but what the noblest gentleman might think. I hope I may see you again.'

It is impossible to describe the superb courtesy with which she said this. The carriage was stopped, and I alighted, and made my adieux.

As I walked back into the city, pondering over this strange interview, I made up my mind decisively that, in spite of any obstacle and misunderstanding, the Baroness was deeply attached to the Count von Roseneau. You will have an opportunity of judging for yourself whether this was the fact or not, but I ask you to remember that this was the impression upon my mind, because it probably influenced my after conduct in an important crisis.

After this, matters went on for some time much as usual. The Baroness sent me several sums of money, which I tried to appropriate to the wants of Herr Apel and his daughter, but I found more difficulty in doing this than I expected. Liese showed a shyness and reserve towards me which I had never seen before. Once or twice I thought I noticed the same wistful glance that I had noticed before, but there was no reason why I should inquire into her thoughts, and I did not do so. I adopted the simple plan of placing the money in comparatively small sums in the old man's hand, and I have reason to know that he immediately gave them to his daughter. Matters went on in this way for some time.

At last one evening there was a second piece at the theatre which somewhat resembled the first part of your pantomimes. There was a kind of love-story running through it, but broken in upon by every kind of absurdity. We had played *Hamlet* for the first piece, considerably cut down, in which I took the part of Horatio. The actor who played Hamlet said courteously to me amid the applause that closed the play—

'Half of this, Richter, belongs to you,' and insisted on taking me by the arm as he went before the curtain.

I played the lover in the second piece. I had noticed during the evening that the manner of Liese was unusually excited; she spoke much, and to every one; she was unusually friendly with me, and when the piece came on she took every opportunity of clinging to me, and playing her part in the most lively and charming way. I never saw her look more attractive. Towards the end of the piece, when the climax of absurdity was nearly reached, there was a scene in which the King, the Lord Chancellor in his robes, and the two lovers meet in conclave to consult partly over state affairs, and partly over the fate of the two latter. Towards the end of the consultation, apparently as a relief to more serious business, it occurs to the Chancellor to sing a song and dance a hornpipe. After performing his part to admiration, and careering round the stage several times, he disappeared through the side scenes, and the King, inspired apparently by his example, waved his ball and sceptre, advanced to the footlights, and, singing his song, also danced round the stage, his robes greatly encumbering him, and, finishing up with a pirouette, which under the circumstances was highly creditable, also vanished from the scene. It then came to my turn, and leaving the side of Liese, by whom I had stood hitherto, I also sang two verses of a popular melody, and finished by a dance; as I came back, amid applause, Liese regarded me with a glance full of kindliness and congratulation, and glided forward to the footlights with the most graceful motion, to sing her song. I did not leave the stage, but stood watching her. She wore the dress of a Swiss country girl, and I some picturesque lover's costume. I noticed an unusual stillness in the crowded theatre, and fancied something uncommon in the rich tones of her voice. She was encored, and repeated the last verse; then she commenced her dance, coming round the stage three times. Each time that she passed me she made a graceful motion of her hand, to which I replied by kissing the tips of my fingers in an attitude of extreme devotion, which indeed was little exaggeration of what I really felt. After the third time she came forward to the footlights, and made her pirouette higher than usual, amid a thunder of applause. Then she fell, flat and motionless, upon the boards.

I had her in my arms in a moment. There was a rush of actors upon the stage, and the curtain fell with a crashing sound. We could hear the excitement and confusion amid the audience without. The manager went before the curtain in response to repeated calls, and said that an unfortunate accident had happened to Mademoiselle Liese. Except as far as she was concerned the piece would go on. He begged the forbearance of the audience for a few minutes.

Meanwhile I had carried Liese to a couch. She was quite conscious and spoke, but she could not move a limb. She never moved again.

Amid the crowd around her, some one at last forced his way. I turned and recognised Von Roseneau.

'Richter,' he said, 'my carriage is close at hand; we will take her home.'

His manner was so wild and excited that I turned and looked at him. He was not in his evening dress, but appeared dressed for a journey.

'You do not generally have your carriage here, Count,' I said.

'No,' he replied distractedly; 'but for this accursed accident she would have been mine to-night.'

I looked at him for a moment.

'The paralysis is, then, only half to blame, Count von Roseneau,' I said.

. . . . .

We saw no more of the Count, and learnt that he had left the city. It appeared that he was deeply in debt, and, though he evidently had considerable sums of money at his control, that his person was not safe from arrest. The family estates had been heavily encumbered even in his father's time, though had he lived he would probably have succeeded in freeing them from debt. The Count had deposited a sum of money with an agent to be applied to the support of Herr Apel. Some days afterwards the agent called upon me and informed me that this sum was still at our disposal. I declined to receive it.

It seemed that, uncertain of my feelings towards her, haunted by a terrible dread of approaching paralysis, and overwhelmed with the charge and burden of her father's state, Liese had yielded to the proposals of the

Count, which promised ease and luxury to them all. If I could have made up my mind sooner, had I spoken to her more openly and freely, and endeavoured to win her confidence, it might have been different. Poor Liese!

'I will tell you what we must do, Liese,' I said as cheerfully as I could two days after the accident, as I was sitting by her bed. She had recovered so far as to be able to move one arm a little. 'I will tell you what we must do. You must marry me. We will then live all together and take care of the old man as long as he lives. Then when you have rested a long time and got quite well, we shall be as happy as the day is long.'

And so—I am telling a long story—we settled it. The Baroness came to see Liese several times. We were married in her room by a priest—most of us actors profess to be Catholics—and the Baroness was present at the ceremony. We moved to an old house in a better part of the town, where we had a large room with a long low window at either end commanding cheerful views, the one into a market-place, the other over the distant country with mills and a stream. Here Liese lay in a clean, white bed, with the old man seated beside her; he became much quieter and gentler after he had given up acting; and in the same room we had our meals, and lived. We were rather straitened for money, for now that I was bound to the city and theatre by my wife's state, some little advantage was taken, and I was told the theatre could not afford so high a salary. It is the way of the world. Indeed we should have been very poorly off, more than once, but for the Baroness, who sent me money openly from time to time. I took it without hesitation. One day she came to see us when I was at home, and remarked how comfortable we were in our large room, and the cheerful picturesque view at the back, like a landscape by an old master, and how happy the old man seemed. When she went down to her carriage, and I was handing her in, she said, looking straight before her, and with a kind of strange scorn in her voice—

'There is some difference, Herr Richter, between a noble of the empire and you!'

We went on in this way for more than a year. I was content enough; indeed, I should have been a wretch to have been impatient, for I knew it could not last very long. The doctors went on giving us hopes and expectations, but I knew better. I could see that the malady was gradually stealing over Liese's faculties and consuming her life. She had lost the use of both arms, and would lie for hours without the least sign of life, and she took nothing but a little broth. The old man died first: he went away very peacefully in his chair in the evening sunlight, saying that it was time to dress. Some two months after his death, I was sitting by Liese in the afternoon, learning my part. It was autumn, and the room was full of a soft light; opposite to the bed was an old clock, upon the dial of which was an accidental mark. I had noticed that if I left when the minute hand reached this mark, I could reach the theatre easily without hurry. I sat watching the hand slowly approaching the spot. The room was perfectly still, nothing but the loud ticking of the clock being heard. The hand was within three minutes of the mark when Liese, who had lain motionless and unconscious for hours, suddenly stirred. I turned towards her in surprise; she looked up full in my face and smiled, and at the same moment she raised her right arm, which had never moved since the fatal night, and held out her hand to me. I grasped it in mine, and the next moment she was gone.

. . . . .

I acted that night as usual, for the public must not be disappointed. But I took a holiday soon after, and went a tour through the mountains. Not that I wish you to suppose that I was overwhelmed with grief; on the contrary, now that I have no temptation that way, I am ashamed to remember that I felt a sense of relief. Were the temptation to occur again, no doubt I should feel the same.

When I returned from my little tour I found myself courted. Now that I was free to go where I liked, the management suddenly found that I was very useful, and offered me a considerable increase of salary to remain. Indeed, I was so flattered and courted that I became somewhat vain and light-headed. I dressed finely, and went much into society, for I was invited to some of the best houses in the city as an agreeable and entertaining guest. I saw the Baroness frequently, and was always invited to her garden-parties, which she received at a small but beautiful château, a mile or two from the city, by the stream which flowed before poor Liese's room. Indeed, I was quite at home at the château, and the servants treated me almost as an inmate.

At the conclusion of one of these parties, about two years after Liese's death, the Baroness took an opportunity, as she passed, to say to me—

'I am going to-morrow to spend a few days at Saarfeld, which I think you have never seen. It is a strange, old, romantic place among the Bavarian Alps, and I think would please you. I wish you would arrange to come over and stay a night or two. I shall be quite alone, as I go on business of the estate.'

I promised to go.

As the travelling chaise wound up from the valleys by long and gradual ascents, and the beauties of the mountain forests revealed themselves one by one, I seemed to be entering an enchanted land of romance and witchery. Light mists hovered below the lofty summits, and over the thick foliage of the oaks and beech-trees. They were illumined with prismatic colours by the slanting sunbeams which shot in strange and mystic rays through mountain crag and forest glade, throwing up portions in wild relief and depressing others into distant shade. The huts of hunters and woodmen, and the wreaths of smoke from the charcoal burners, were the only signs of life in this wild land of forest and hill. The lofty woods of black pine climbing the higher summits shut in the view on every side.

At last I reached the château, which stood

high up in the forest, commanding an extensive and surprising view.

It was indeed a strange, wild old place of immense size, with long rows of turrets and windows, and massive towers of vast antiquity. We entered a court-yard, surrounded by lofty walls, so completely covered with ivy that the windows could scarcely be seen. It seemed as though the real and living world were entirely shut out and lost sight of. The whole place, however, was in perfect repair, and was richly furnished. The staff of servants was ample. The majordomo, who always accompanied his mistress, welcomed me with great kindness. The Baroness, he said, was at that moment engaged with the steward; if I would take some slight refreshment after my journey, she would receive me presently in the grand *salon*. I was shown into a dining-room, where a slight repast was awaiting me.

The rooms were hung with portraits of the old barons of Saarfeld, with tapestry of strange device, and with still stranger pictures of the old German and Italian masters, and were furnished with cabinets and sideboards, evidently of extreme antiquity. The sense of glamour and of mystery increased upon me at every step; I seemed to be acting in a wild and improbable piece.

When I had taken what refreshment I wanted, I asked to be shown my room that I might arrange my dress before seeking the Baroness. I had scarcely finished before the major-domo again appeared, and informed me that his mistress was waiting for me in the grand *salon*. I found this to be a magnificent apartment, with a long row of lofty windows in deep recesses overlooking the wild forest. Tall portraits of more than life-size hung upon the walls, and a massive stone chimney-piece, the height of the room, and carved with innumerable devices, fronted the windows. The polished oak floor would have been dangerous to walk on, but an actor is always equal to such feats.

The Baroness was standing in the centre of the vast room, which was clear of furniture. I seemed to see her at last in her full perfection, as though such a lovely creature required such a setting as this before she could be fully and perfectly seen. She was easy and composed, and began to speak at once.

'I wish to tell you, my dear friend,' she said, 'why I have asked you to come here, because it is only fair to you that you should know it at once.'

She paused for a moment, and I could only look at her in silent admiration. I had not the remotest idea what she was going to say, but it seemed to me more and more that I was acting a strange and unnatural part.

'You are aware, my dear friend,' she repeated, 'that my father had some thought of marrying me, had he lived, to the Count von Roseneau, but long before his death he saw in that unhappy young man what made him change his intention. He spoke to me often with great freedom on this as on every other subject; it was the wonderful privilege which I enjoyed with such a father. He spoke to me much of the relationship between man and wife, of the peculiar duties and trials of each, and of the necessity of long and careful thought and of seeking for the best guidance in such a matter. He impressed upon me the value of eternal principles rather than of accidental forms; and though he insisted continually on the necessary observance of outward forms and decencies, yet he pointed out to me that circumstances might arise where all the necessary principles and qualities which alone give forms any value could exist, though some of the form itself might appear wanting. Finally, in the most solemn manner he assured me, and confirmed it in his will, that he was perfectly satisfied to leave the matter in my hands, convinced that I should follow out the great principles upon which his life had been based, and show myself worthy of the confidence and education he had bestowed upon me. I believe that I am about to act in a manner that would meet his full approval. I believe that those circumstances have actually arrived which he foresaw, and that I have found the man whom he would welcome as a son. I offer you my hand.'

She pronounced these words, even to the last, without any hurry of manner or the slightest sign of excitement beyond the charming animation with which she always spoke. You will naturally suppose that their effect upon me was overwhelming, but if so you are mistaken. It has been a matter of profound astonishment to me, in every succeeding moment of my life, that I acted as I did. Afterwards, of course, reasons appeared which justified, and even approved in the highest degree, my conduct; but that, at the instant, when in another moment I might have had this glorious creature in my arms, I should have remained unmoved, has never ceased to fill me with astonishment. I can only account for it by one wild and seemingly improbable supposition. You will not believe it, but I am firmly convinced that during the whole interview I thought that I was on the stage, I thought that I had a part given me, and that I spoke words which I had already carefully conned. I am the more convinced that this was the case because I made no longer pause than would have been proper could you conceive such a scene to be enacted upon the stage.

'Baroness,' I said, and I see the words now before me as plainly as if I read them from a play-book, 'Baroness, it cannot be necessary to say that the offer you have made overwhelms me to the earth. I do not use such phrases as gratitude, and favour, and condescension; words at any time are unequal to the task of expression, and to use them now would only be an insult to your heart and mine. But I should be utterly unworthy of the amazing regard which you have shown to me, and of the undeserved approbation with which your own goodness has led you to regard me, were I to hesitate for a moment to urge you to reflect before you commit yourself to such a step. You have yourself allowed that your father insisted on the necessity of submission to the forms and decencies of outward life. Think for a moment of the consequences to yourself of such a step as you now, with the sublime unconsciousness of the highest natures, propose to me. You have created out of your own nobleness an image which you call by my name, but you will find the reality an idol and a delusion, and you will find the world's verdict, on the whole, to be right. I entreat you to pause.'

'Herr Richter,' she said, looking me full in the face, and no language can express the beauty of her confiding glance, 'every word you say only confirms my choice. I offer you my hand.'

This second trial was very hard.

'My conscience is not at rest,' I said. 'I entreat you to reflect.'

A very slight shade passed over the beautiful face, and a look of something like incredulity came into the wonderful eyes.

'You refuse my offer?' she said.

'I entreat you to weigh well what I have said.'

'I might well say, Herr Richter,' she said, 'that there is some difference between you and other men.'

There was a pause. The interview became embarrassing. I turned slightly towards the window, and it occurred to me to walk into the embrasure and look out. When I turned round, after a minute or two, I found that the Baroness had taken advantage of my action and had left the room.

I went out into the park. The moment I was alone a host of reasons rushed into my mind, all of them insisting with one voice on the propriety of the course I had, as it were involuntarily, taken. I was firmly convinced that whether she knew it or not the Baroness was attached with all the tenacity of her girlhood's recollections to the Count von Roseneau. Supposing this to be the case, I could well see that the position, when novelty had played its part, of the player-husband would not be a dignified or enviable one. I knew, none better, the effect of the overpowering sympathies of rank and class, and of the revulsion which inevitably follows action, which is the result of excited feeling. I knew the ultimate irresistible power of the world's verdict. Of course some demon might have suggested that I should take the temporary wealth of delight which was offered to me, and, when the inevitable catastrophe came, go my quiet way unharmed, but I should hope that there are few men who would desire a temporary pleasure at so stupendous a cost.

I wandered in the park and forest for a couple of hours. Then I came back to the château. I was uncertain what to do, but I did not like to leave without seeing the Baroness again. I went to my room. Here I found one of the valets arranging my toilette for the evening. I had not been in the room many minutes before the major-domo entered. His manner was even more urbane and polite than in the morning.

The Baroness, he said, earnestly hoped that I would favour her with my company at dinner; the meal would be served in less than an hour.

The man's manner was so marked that I could not help looking at him. Was it possible that the household could have any idea of what had taken place?

I found the Baroness in an ante-chamber which opened upon one of the lesser dining-rooms. There were several servants standing about between the two rooms, but she seemed utterly indifferent to their presence. Her manner was perfectly unembarrassed, and she came forward to greet me, holding out her beautiful hand.

'My dear friend,' see said, 'I feared you had left Saarfeld in displeasure. I hope you will not deprive me of what I value so highly. I have quite recovered from the little natural vexation I felt at your refusal of my offer. I will not offend again. Let us go to dinner.'

'On one condition, Baroness,' I said, as I gave her my arm, 'that you are not too fascinating. I might take you at your word.'

'Your chance is gone by, sir,' she said, with a delightful *moue*. 'The ivory gates are closed.'

I still felt as though I were performing in a play. I never exerted myself to please as I did that night. When the evening was over, I said, 'I fear I shall not see you in the morning. I must be at the theatre to-morrow night.'

'I shall not stay here many days,' said the Baroness. 'You must call on me the moment I return, my friend.'

I raised the hand she gave me, and kissed

the tips of her fingers, but I did not press her hand. When a man is walking in slippery places he is wary of his steps.

.   .   .   .   .

I visited the Baroness immediately on her return, and found her as friendly and unembarrassed as ever. The months glided by with great quietude. The theatre was under good management; it was prosperous, and the best actors frequently visited it. It was one of those halcyon periods which visit all theatres at times. My popularity increased, and I could have demanded almost any salary. I was invited to other cities, but these visits I made very sparingly. What, however, might perhaps have been expected occurred, and caused me great annoyance. A report spread through the city that I was about to be married to the Baroness. It was universally believed.

'Have you heard the news?' men said

one to another. 'The beautiful Helena von Saarfeld, for whom princes were not high enough, or cultured, or religious enough, who was almost too good to walk the earth, is going to marry Richter the player! What do you think of that?'

'Have you heard the news, Herr Richter?' said the Baroness one afternoon as I entered her drawing-room.

'Yes,' I said. 'It has annoyed me beyond expression. Who could have originated such a report?'

'Oh,' she said, with a bewitching underglance of her eyes, 'such things cannot be hidden. It is not my fault that it is not true.'

'That is all very well, my pretty friend,' I thought to myself, 'while the Count is away and out of mind, but what will happen should he return?'

I was congratulated on all hands, and

could only deny that there was a word of truth in the report.

'It is most annoying to me,' I said. 'I shall have to give up visiting the Baroness.' My friend would not hear of this, however, and seemed to take every opportunity of appearing with me in public. This had very much the desired effect, for when people saw we had nothing to conceal, they grew wearied of talking about us, and the matter pretty much dropped.

One evening as I was dressing in the theatre I received a note from the Baroness, asking me to come to her château the next day at one o'clock, without fail. I was true to the time, and found her in a little morning-room where she transacted business. She seemed excited beyond her wont.

'My dear friend,' she said, 'I have sent for you because I want your advice and protection. I have good reason to know that

I am safer in your care than I am in my own. There was a man here yesterday, a kind of Jew lawyer, who made an excuse to see me, though his business might well have been settled with the agent. When he had said what he had to say, however, he became very mysterious, and said that he had lately seen the Count von Roseneau, and that he had something to communicate which it very much concerned me to hear. His face wore a low, cunning expression as he said this, which disgusted me, and I told him that I had nothing to say on such subjects to him, and that if he had anything to communicate it must come through my agent. He told me he could tell it to no one but myself. I thought immediately of you; and told him that if he liked to call here to-morrow at this time I would ask a gentleman, a very intimate friend, to be present, and then he could say what he wished. He hesitated at this, but I turned my back upon him, and left the room.'

'Do you know any evil of the man?' I asked.

'I know nothing of such people,' she said scornfully. 'I know no more evil of him than I do of a toad, but I shudder at both.'

The man was speedily announced. He was evidently of the lowest type of his profession, and had a mean and hang-dog look. I do not know whether he knew me or not, but he took little notice of any but the Baroness.

He began his tale at once.

He had lived in Berlin, where the Count von Roseneau was, and had been engaged in some inferior business connected with the mortgage on the Count's estates.

'The Count's affairs,' he said, 'were getting more and more involved; he was deeply in debt, was very short of money, and indeed had been more than once under arrest. The mortgages were foreclosed on all his estates, and the estates themselves offered for sale, when one day, going over some deeds in the office of the lawyer who was engaged in managing what little remained to do on his behalf, I discovered a most important memorandum, signed by the Count himself. It is not necessary to explain before the Baroness,' he continued, turning to me, 'the exact nature of the complicated business, but you will understand that the paper had been given in lieu of deeds which never seem afterwards to have been executed, and was the sole evidence which decided the possession of the estates, or, at least, of the most considerable one. It had been inclosed by mistake in a parcel of copies that had been returned to the Count. I found him alone, and placed the paper in his hands. It was some time before he understood its character, but when at last he was convinced that its possession restored him to wealth and honour, a singular expression came into his face.

'"This is a nice homily, my good fellow," he said, "on you men of business, with all your chicanery of deeds, and evidences, and papers, and signing, and counter-signing, and all the rest of the devil's game. What do you want for this paper? You did not bring it for nothing, I presume."

'"Well, I said, "a thousand marks would not seem too much for such a service."

'"A thousand marks," said the Count, rising, "is all I have in the world; nevertheless I will give it for this paper."

'"I should think so," I said. "A thousand marks are not much for estates and wealth."

'The Count went to his *secrétaire*, took out a rouleau of gold, and handed it to me.

Then he sat down again, and looked at the paper steadily for some time.

'"Neat," he said to himself more than to me: "pretty, very pretty, but not my style; never was the Von Roseneau style, that I ever heard."

'Then he bowed me politely out of the room. What happened I heard from his valet. As soon as I had left the Count sat down at the *secrétaire*, wrote some lines in an envelope, fastened up the paper in it, directed it, and called the servant.

'"You will take this to the address," he said, "and give it to the principal. If he is out, wait for him, though it be all day. You will give it into no hands but his. Tell me when it is done."

'The Count is now,' continued the Jew, 'in absolute penury. He has applied for a commission in the Bavarian Infantry, which he is certain to receive. The miserable pay will be all he will have to live on. He has business in this city which requires his presence. I expect him here, for a few hours, in a day or two.'

The Baroness rose from her chair, and I could see that she was pale.

'You will settle with this—this gentleman,' she said to me, and left the room.

'Well,' I said to the man. 'You want something for the communication, I suppose?'

I saw that he did not know who I was, for his manner was deferential, as to a gentleman of rank.

He said he left it to the Baroness.

I gave him a heap of notes, as I knew it would be the Baroness's wish, and he left well satisfied.

I went into the drawing-room to the Baroness.

She was standing in the window, looking

at the gorgeous flowers that were heaped together in profusion—a soft and pensive light in her eyes. She was evidently thinking of the Count, and of their early days.

Her attitude and expression were so lovely that I stopped involuntarily to gaze. She looked up, and saw, I suppose, something in my look which she had not seen before, for she flushed all over, and said, with a softened, pleased expression, which was bewitching to see—

'You are a strange man, Richter; I know you love me.'

'Yes, I love you, Baroness,' I said, 'better than I love myself.'

'That is nothing,' she said, flushing again. 'Do you think I did not know that? Do you think I should have acted as I have done had I not doubted whether in all Germany, nay, in Europe itself, there could be found a man so good as you!'

'Let us hope, Baroness, for the sake of Europe, there may be a few.'

'Well,' she said, sitting down, 'I want you to do something for me. A very little thing this time. I want you to find out when the Count comes, to go to him, and to get him to come over to Saarfeld to me.'

'What are you going to say to him?' I said.

She looked up suddenly, as in anger, but the next instant a touching look of humility came over her face, and she said—

'I am going to make him the same offer that I did to you, sir!'

I shook my head. 'Do you know so little of your own people—of your own order—as that,' I said. 'He will refuse.'

'I am not only a noble,' she said, almost pitifully, 'I am a woman too.'

There was a pause. Then she said, 'Why do you say that he will refuse?'

'He has the distinguishing vice of his order,' I said, 'insolent, selfish pride. It is notorious that he took great umbrage at what he considered interference in his affairs by your father and yourself, and at the blame which the breaking off of the match implied. He will think that you make him the offer now out of pity. His pride of race will rebel, and he will refuse a future, however splendid, marked by favours received and restrained by gratitude, and, he may even think, by compulsion. I have a better plan. I will seek him out; and if I find that he does not refuse to talk with me, and I do not see why he should, I will let him understand that you are kindly disposed towards him. I will recall his early days, and I will endeavour to make him believe that he is performing a chivalrous action, and forgiving injuries, and is conferring rather than receiving a favour. I hope to succeed. You said to me this morning that you were safer in my keeping than in your own. Trust to me now, though God knows I only do it to please you; I am not responsible for the result.'

'No,' said the Baroness, getting up from her seat. 'I am a woman, and I will go my own way. I will have him at Saarfeld, where we were so happy as children. I will tell him all myself.'

'She trusts to her charms,' I said as I left the house. 'It cannot be wondered at. Come what may, I will not marry her. The world shall *never* say that this divine creature married Richter the player.'

. .

Some few days afterwards I learnt that the Count had arrived. In the interval I had urged the Baroness to dispense with my advocacy altogether, and simply to send a message; but this she refused to do. I had nothing left but to do my best.

I called at the hotel at which the Count was staying, and sent in my name. I was immediately shown up to a private room.

'I see you are surprised to see me, Count von Roseneau,' I said, 'but I am not come to revive any reminiscences of the past. I simply bring you a message from the Baroness Helena, who asked me to tell you that she wished to see you at Saarfeld.'

'If I showed any wonder, Herr Richter,' said the Count, 'it was simply that I was surprised that you should condescend to call upon me. As you have mentioned the Baroness, I am glad of the opportunity of saying that I am convinced that she can have no truer friend than yourself.'

'The Baroness,' I said, 'is of the opinion that I might become the best means of telling you that she still cherishes the recollections of her early childhood. If I might venture to say anything, I would say that we do not war against women, and that though doubtless many things may have happened founded upon exaggerated reports, yet the Count von Roseneau will not cherish such paltry recollections in such a moment as this.'

'The Baroness,' said the Count, 'has chosen well, though I fancy I can see that she has acted against the advice of her best friend. I will go to Saarfeld at any moment she may appoint, and anything that is within my power, and which is consistent with the honour of my family, I will do; the more willingly because by doing so I know I shall oblige you.'

This was all very well, and I did not see what else I could say. There was a polished coldness about the Count's manner which seemed to imply that the Baroness and he moved in a charmed circle within which it was intrusion for any one to venture. I had delivered my message, to the words of which the Baroness had almost limited me, and I rose to take my leave; but I was not prepared for what ensued.

The Count followed me to the door. 'Herr Richter,' he said, speaking in a very different tone from that which he had hitherto used, 'I wish to say something else. I wish, if I can possibly say it, to say something which will cause you to think less hardly of me with regard to one who is dead; which will offer you some thanks, though thanks from such a source must be utterly worthless —for—but there are no words which can express what I mean—if you do not see it, there is no help.' ..

I stood looking at him across the threshold for a moment.

'In the matter of which you speak, Count von Rosencau, if I understand you, and I think I do, I also was to blame. It is not for me to judge another. If you owe me thanks for anything that is past, let me entreat you to weigh well every word you say at Saarfeld.'

'I promise you,' said the Count.

. . . . .

With regard to the interview at Saarfeld, I only know what the Baroness told me. I believe that she told me every word that fell from the Count, but her own words and manner I had to collect as best I could. It was evident that she adopted a very different method from that which she had done toward myself. She received the Count indifferently, and put off the important moment as long as possible. No doubt she brought to play the whole fascination of her manner and person, but she selected the great *salon* as the scene of her final effort. In what way she introduced the subject I do not know, but she told me that she was standing in one of the embrasures of the windows when the Count replied—

'Helena, I am unworthy of you, but I am grateful all the same. I cannot allow you to sacrifice yourself simply out of pity to me. I am a ruined man—ruined in purse and reputation. The auguries which influenced your opinion of me when we were younger are fulfilled — more than fulfilled. What would the world say if, when the fear alone of possible consequences rendered your union with me unsuitable, I were to avail myself of such a union when all these dreary predictions have been verified? Let the world say what it will, the Von Roseneaus are proud; that which was denied me because I was unworthy I cannot accept because I am poor. Besides, I cannot forget one who is dead.'

The Baroness was standing against the embrasure of the window which was lined with tapestry. She was evidently anxious to retain her perfect composure, but as the Count continued speaking with a manly openness of purpose, her calmness was sorely tried. The last words came to her help. She grew composed instantly, and her face darkened with displeasure.

'You should take lessons from the stage, Count,' she said, somewhat bitterly. 'The actor declines a supreme favour with better grace than you.'

The Count said nothing; he was probably not displeased at the loss of temper which would bring the interview to a close.

'Then you refuse my offer?' she said at last.

'I cannot accept.'

'Mine is a strange fate, Count von Roseneau,' she said. 'In this hall, beneath the portraits of my ancestors, I have, in violation of all the customs of my sex, offered my hand to two men, one an actor and one a noble, and have been rejected by both.'

'The actor, madam,' said the Count, stepping back, 'you may well regret; the noble is not worth a thought.'

.   .   .   .   .

The Baroness did not bear her second disappointment so well as the first. She looked sad, though the smile lost nothing of its sweetness, nor her manner of its vivacity. She had a wistful look in her eyes sometimes when they met mine, which, it might be thought, must have made my resolution hard to keep. If you like you may call my determination a selfish fancy which my vanity alone enabled me to maintain. The Baroness spoke a great deal of the Count, and talked to me much of her early days, and of the confusions and ill-feeling when the young Count's conduct first began to arouse the fears of her father.

'I get very old and prosy, my friend,' she said—she grew lovelier every day—'and I fatigue you with this talk; but I have no friend but you to whom I can speak of these things.' She devoted herself to charity and good works; she visited the hospitals, and her carriage was to be seen in the worst purlieus of the city.

One day she told me she had received an invitation to travel in Italy with some cousins of her mother's, the head of the party being a superb old gentleman whom I had often met, and who reminded me of Don Quixote. This old gentleman had at first been very cold and haughty, but after some time his manner changed suddenly, the cause of which alteration the Baroness explained to me.

'The old gentleman,' she said, 'took me to task very severely upon the danger of my intercourse with you, and gave himself much trouble in repeating at great length the most wise maxims. I let him run on till he was quite out of breath, and then I said: "My dear cousin, all that you have said is quite true, and shows your deep knowledge of the world. There has been the greatest danger of what you dread taking place. I offered my hand to Herr Richter years ago, and any time within the last five years, excepting one short week, I would have married him if he would have had me." I saw that the old Baron was very polite the next time you met.'

The Baroness wanted me to accompany her to Italy, and offered to settle a large sum of money on me absolutely, so that I might give up my profession.

'No, Baroness,' I said, 'let us go on as we have begun. We have had a fair friendship, for which I do not say how much I thank you, and which no breath of calumny has ever stained; do not let us spoil it at last.'

So we parted, but only for a time.

When the party had left for Italy I felt less tied to the city, and accepted engagements elsewhere. I acted in Berlin, and so far departed from my rule as to take one or two principal parts with more success than I had expected. This was chiefly owing to the fact that in Germany the new reading of any part is welcomed with enthusiasm, and a host of critics immediately discover numberless excellences in it, chiefly to show off their own cleverness. Many of these gentlemen were kind enough to point out many beauties in my acting of which I was entirely unconscious. This led to my receiving invitations to other cities, which I accepted. In the course of my wanderings I arrived at a city on the French frontier, where I accepted an engagement for several nights to play Max

Piccolomini. In the midst of this engagement the war between Germany and France suddenly broke out, and before we were aware we found ourselves involved in the marches and counter-marches of armies. The theatre was closed and the company dispersed. I attempted to return into Saxony, but the advancing armies so blocked the roads that I was compelled to turn back. The French were advancing with equal rapidity, and I found myself shut in between the opposing troops. The campaign was so complicated that what was the rear one day became the advanced guard the next. The utmost confusion seemed to prevail.

At last I found myself in a little suburb of some large town devoted to *Lusthauses* and gardens of pleasure; pretty little cottages appeared on every side surrounded by gardens and grass-plots dotted with alcoves

T

and sheltered by lofty trees. The French made a sudden advance, and held the adjoining slope, but did not come into the suburb. A small detachment of German Uhlans had halted in the village, and were watching the French.

I was standing in the door of one of the cottages with the officer of the little troop, when the chasseur of the Baroness, whom I knew so well, rode up. I sprang forward to meet him, and learnt that a skirmish had taken place outside the town, and that the wounded men were being brought from the front in charge of an ambulance corps to which the Baroness had attached herself.

A few minutes afterwards the corps arrived, bringing with them several wounded men. I shall never forget the look of glad surprise in the face of the Baroness when she saw me. It is the most cherished recollection of my life.

'You come, as always, in the right time, my friend,' she said. 'In a few minutes we shall be in the thick of the battle. Whenever I want help and protection, you appear. How did you learn that I was here?'

'I did not know you were in Germany, Baroness,' I said. 'It is the will of God that we should meet; something is going to happen which concerns us both.'

She wore the ambulance dress, with the white cross upon her arm, and looked more lovely than ever.

We had not stood above five minutes before we heard firing to the right and left; and the Uhlans mounted and rode off, advising us to retire into the cottages with the wounded. It was too late, they said, for the ambulance corps to retire further into the rear.

Having deposited the wounded as best we could, the Baroness and I went into an upper room which looked out to the side over a small grass-plot flanked by a low wall and a plantation of willows. The firing came nearer and nearer, and all along the slope on our left we could see the French lines and the artillery officers riding up and down. We did not know what was going on.

Suddenly a roar like hell itself shook the earth from end to end; the cannon balls came crashing through the branches of the trees, and a hail of lead swept off the leaves, tore up the grass in faint lines, and shook the wall of the cottage with their dull thud. We could see a strange commotion among the plantations on our right, and the next moment a form which we both knew too well vaulted over the low wall and came across the grass. A second after him other officers leaped the wall, and without waiting to see if their men followed, hurried across the lawn, and up the slope. They had no need to pause. The next moment the Bavarian infantry, the men falling at every step, cleared the fence, and in spite of the torrent of fire which seemed to burn the earth before it, crossed the garden, and ascended in almost unbroken line the hill beyond, half concealed by the shattered trees. Other regiments followed, equally steady, and equally exposed to the never-ceasing storm, and in about eight minutes the firing lulled ; the French had fallen back.

We went out of the cottage. Never in the wildest stage effect could such a transformation be beheld as this village scene presented. Eight minutes ago, smiling in the sunshine, peaceful, bright with flowers, and green grass and trees — now shattered, mangled, trodden down, the houses in ruins and in flames, the trees broken and leafless, the ground strewn with the dying and the dead. The ambulance was already at work, but the Baroness did not stop.

'Let us go to the front, my dear friend,' she said.

I knew what she meant. The chasseur, who kept close to his mistress, followed us, and we went forward up the slope, picking our way among the fallen men, and now and then stopping while the Baroness gave some poor fellow a drink of water, and assured him that the ambulance corps would be up immediately. As we ascended the slope and looked back for a moment, we could see that the village and the whole line of country was occupied by the main body of the German troops—a magnificent sight.

At last, near the top of the slope, we met two Bavarians who were carrying an officer between them. The Baroness knelt down, and, without hesitation, the men laid their burden before her, in her arms.

'We do not think he is dead, lady,' said one of them, the tears streaming down his face. 'He moved once as we came along.'

He lay perfectly still, to all appearance lifeless, his eyes closed.

'Speak to him,' I said; 'perchance he may hear *you*.'

'Von Roseneau,' cried the Baroness, in a tone I never wish to hear again, 'Von Roseneau, will you marry me now?'

The despairing tremor of her voice seemed to recall the departed spirit already wandering in other lands. The dying man opened his eyes, a brilliant smile lighted his face, his gaze met that of the Baroness, and he held out his hand, but he could not speak The next moment he fell back dead within her arms.

'And what became of the Baroness?' I asked, for the actor paused.

'She became a canoness, and devoted herself entirely to the mystical religion of the Count von Zinzendorff.'

IV

ELLIE

A STORY OF A BOY AND GIRL

ELLIE

A STORY OF A BOY AND GIRL

WHEN I came home from Eton one vacation, I found a new inmate at Abbot's Calvert: one whom at first I was very much surprised at, and afterwards very much delighted with. This was a little girl, of about fifteen, the daughter of a very distant cousin of my father's, who, having lived a life of privation, partly, I believe, caused by errors of his own, had died prematurely, without either choosing or being able, I do not know which, to interest his noble relatives in his behalf. When he died, and his little daughter was left alone and helpless in the world, my mother had caused inquiries to be made about her, which resulted in her being sent for into the country. The moment she arrived at Abbot's Calvert it was plain that she was permanently established there. It was impossible for any creature to be with her for five minutes without loving her. My mother, who had no daughters of her own, adopted her altogether as one; and the Marquis himself, who rarely spoke to any one except my mother and his eldest son, condescended to pet her. She was even then a remarkably graceful girl, tall, and giving great promise of that extraordinary loveliness which two years afterwards she possessed. It was not astonishing, then, that I, a boy of seventeen, used to ladies' society and fond of it, fell desperately in love (with the desperation of seventeen) with this charming little creature; or, on the other hand, that she, transferred from the narrow poverty of her father's life to a stately old mansion with 'parks and ordered gardens great,' with ponies to ride, and boats upon the river, with carriage drives, and picnics, was very happy, and thought a good deal of her young companion, who, whenever he arrived, took the greatest trouble and felt the greatest pleasure in pleasing her. In spite of all these pleasures, it was rather dull most of the year at Abbot's Calvert, for my mother did not take Ellie to London, but left her nominally in the schoolroom, under the care of her governess, a lady recommended by the single but invaluable characteristic of never being in the way. It was not astonishing, then, that in this new life of hers the girl was very happy, or that she was very fond of 'Fred.'

'Fred' is very different now, so it is not conceited to say that I was then a good specimen of an English lad, such as you may see scores of in the public schools, with well-cut features, and auburn hair, tall, but not too tall, well-built, active, holding my place in all games, used to society, just bashful enough to be well-mannered, and no more. If I am to tell my story at all, I must be allowed to say thus much, so that it may be understood.

I do not want it to be a long story, so it will be enough to say things went on in this way for two years, till I left Eton finally in June, and came down home for the vacation, looking forward to going up to Cambridge to Trinity at the beginning of the term. I had not seen Ellie for nearly six months, for I had not been in the country at Easter, having spent the holidays in London. It was my brother Lord Canham's first session in Parliament, and the family had been in London longer than usual. When I got into the hall, then, and found her there waiting for me, I scarcely knew her, such a perfectly lovely creature had she grown. She was standing beneath the picture of the last Abbot, with the sunlight falling on her coloured by the old armorial bearings of the Abbey which still remain in the windows (for the Calverts had been tenants of the old monks for centuries, and have always preserved a kindly feeling towards their memory, as indeed was not unreasonable, seeing that they had come in for by far the largest part of their lands). She was tall, and very slightly formed, her features and complexion perfectly faultless, her eyes large and dreamy, what some people thought heavy and expressionless (though they lighted up enough many times that I knew of), her hair of the palest auburn, wavy all over and very abundant. I felt shy and bashful for a moment, but, fortunately for myself, I crushed down this feeling and kissed her, as I should have done a year ago.

That year's summer was a glorious one, day after day of lovely skies, soft showers, warm quivering air, sultry 'all-golden' afternoons, short wonderful nights, like dreams of day, full of perfume, of cool zephyrs, of rustling voices in the trees. Parliament sat late, and the house was almost deserted the most part of the time; we were not without neighbours, and formed parties of pleasure every few days, but these only served to point and intensify the zest with which Ellie and I spent the intervening days alone. In the gardens, on the croquet-lawn, on the river, riding or wandering in the lanes, galloping over the grassy slopes of the Chase (I had taught Ellie to ride myself, and she did my instruction the greatest credit), driving a miniature basket phaeton into the neighbouring town to the Cathedral service and to the shops, day after day of this delightful summer flew by unheeded. I imagine, from the novels I have read, that it will be thought by some people very wrong that we should have been left together in this way, and that they will say that it is highly improbable and absurd to suppose that my mother should have permitted this intimacy to go on in so unchecked a way. All I can say is, that these ideas never entered into any phase of society with which I was acquainted; a perfect absence of any feeling of the kind, of any approach to what I have seen described as a restless meddling propensity to match-making, or to an equally restless fear of it, characterised, or would have characterised, if any one had ever thought of it, the people among whom I lived, and no one more so than my mother. The Marquis and Marchioness were down for a few days in the middle of summer, and Canham also for a week. I know that my father spoke to Canham about us, but that he pooh-poohed the whole affair, called Ellie a charming little thing, whom he had a great mind to fall in love with himself, and that my father thought no more, or little more about us. I do Canham the justice to say he never did interfere with us, being wholly occupied with preparing a speech on the tenant-right of Ireland, a subject about which he knew nothing and cared less, only, as the family had large estates in that island, it was thought well for him to make a speech, which, while not embarrassing the Government, might rouse great enthusiasm in his favour among the Irish: and this he found was quite sufficient to occupy him while at Abbot's Calvert.

When I first came home in June Ellie had told me something which had not affected us much at the time, when we had all the holidays before us, but which, as time passed by, assumed a more formidable appearance.

This was that my mother had decided that she should spend a year at least at a ladies' school, of which great things had been told her, in a little village in the northern counties, called Southam, which boasted of a fine old minster or collegiate church, and aped in all its arrangements a small cathedral city. Ellie did not object to this arrangement. My father and mother were going to Italy at the end of October, and the house would be very dull all the autumn. She looked forward to this school-life with expectation of amusement.

September arrived, and the day when Ellie was to leave was very near, when my mother, one morning at breakfast, expressed great annoyance at the illness of Allen, her favourite maid, who, she informed us, had been selected as Ellie's escort.

'Who was to take Ellie now,' she said, 'she did not know?'

I struck in with the happy audacity of my age and class.

'It was absurd to talk in that way; who should take Ellie except myself? I had never thought of anything else.'

My mother immediately acquiesced, with that outward indifference with which she received most things, and with that unconscious and undemonstrative but profound conviction, that everything that her family did, or proposed to do, was right.

'Oh very well,' she said; 'if you think of doing so that will be very nice; that will settle everything pleasantly. Ellie will be very willing, no doubt.'

I looked across at Ellie; no one could have found fault with her eyes for dulness at that moment.

'Yes, she was very willing.'

At this moment my father, who rarely took any notice of our conversation, raised his eyes from his newspapers and letters, and asked what we were talking of.

'Oh nothing,' my mother said, 'only Allen is so unwell that she cannot take Ellie to school, and Fred very kindly says he will go with her.'

'Hum,' said my father.

As he went out of the breakfast-room he told me to follow him into the library, and seating himself in his favourite chair, in the great oriel window, he turned to me with the air of a man who is saying a good thing—

'I have not the least objection, of course, sir, to your making a fool of yourself; you will do so with great success, doubtless, many times during the next few years, but you will please to remember that a man of your name ought not to make a fool of any one else.'

I had not the faintest idea what to say, so I said—

'Certainly not, my Lord.'

I very seldom called my father 'My Lord,' perhaps because he very seldom spoke to me; but this seemed to be one of those rare occasions when it was dramatically consistent, at least, to do so.

I went back into the morning-room, which was also the music-room, where Ellie was practising at the grand piano. I half lay on a couch watching her, a ray of sunlight piercing the drawn blinds and lighting up her hair, and beyond a Choir of Angels by Sabbatini that hung over the piano.

Both my brother and myself had, when quite little boys, been trained by my mother, who was a very clever woman, to watch our own motives and feelings, and to look events as they occurred in the face, and to trace, as far as we could, the succession of cause and effect in them, relatively to ourselves; not very much, however, with a view to arranging our own future, but as a matter of pure philosophy. It was, therefore, impossible for me to act in any circumstances perfectly thoughtlessly or without reflection; but, as I lay watching Ellie, I was conscious that I was acting, and should go on acting, under the influence of a sort of instinct, which told me I was safe and right. Looking back on those days now, with no possible motive for self-deception, I believe I was right; I believe that, even had things happened very differently to what, alas! they did, both Ellie and I were safe.

When the morning came for us to set out, we were driven down to the cathedral town, and travelled to Southam by express.

'Look here,' I said to the guard, as we got into the carriage, 'I will give you a sovereign at Southam if no one gets in here beside ourselves.'

No one attempted to get into that compartment between Bishopstone and Southam. We had a delightful and comfortable ride, wrapped up in a corner of the carriage like the babes in the wood, and the only fault we found with the journey was that it was too short.

At Southam we were expected, and found a fly waiting to take us up to the school. We passed the grand old minster, with its Norman towers, sleeping in the evening sunshine, and reached the school, a pleasant country house surrounded with gardens, and fields planted with rows of beeches, in which the rooks were cawing.

Ellie was taken away upstairs, and the servant, telling me that some ladies were at tea with her mistress, suggested that I should join them. I had sent in my card 'Lord Frederick Staines Calvert,' on which I had added, rather patronisingly, ' Miss Elinor Calvert, for Ellie had no cards. I entered a large pleasant room, where several ladies and one or two clergymen were at tea at a long table. I fancy they had expected an older and more imposing person from my card, for they seemed uncertain as to who I was, as I came in, and no one rose to welcome me.

A pretty and clever looking young lady, whom I took to be the chief manager in the school, held out her hand to me without rising as I came up the room, and, as I bowed over it, showed me a chair which had been placed next to her. At the top of the table was a severe looking old lady, to whom I was introduced, evidently the mistress of the school; and just opposite me was a little pleasant looking bright old lady, who took the greatest interest in everything, and began to talk to me at once.

'We expected a much older gentleman from your card, Lord Frederick,' she said, looking very sharply at me; 'Miss Calvert cannot be your sister?'

'It is all the same,' I said; 'we have been brought up together.' Which was a fib.

'You are a very good brother,' she said, still looking at me very hard; 'I know many who would think it a great "bore," as they call it, to bring their sisters to school.'

Her eyes were so sharp and full of meaning that I could not help wincing, and am not even sure that I did not blush, especially as the clever looking young lady by me seemed amused.

At this moment the door opened, and Ellie was shown in. She had changed her dress, and was looking fresh and beautiful. I had never before been so conscious of her really extraordinary loveliness, nor so proud of it, as when I saw the effect it produced on these people as she came up the room.

Room was made for her by the austere old lady herself, whose face softened and quite beamed with kindness as she turned to her.

'We were just saying, my dear,' she said, 'how good it was of your brother—cousin, I believe he is, but he says it is all the same—to bring you here. That was before we saw you; we do not wonder at all now that he was glad to do so.'

'No,' said the little old lady; 'I was going to ask you, Lord Frederick, what you travelled down together for; I have no need to ask anything of the kind now.'

We sat some time at tea, and talked pleasantly. The pretty young lady was very intelligent and amusing. Canham's tenant-right speech had after all turned out a very good one, and one of the clergymen spoke to me about it. They were all quiet intelligent people, and I enjoyed myself. After tea we went into a drawing-room, which opened into the room where we were, and stood about, still talking. Ellie sat rather apart upon an ottoman. I went to her, and, sitting down by her side, said mischievously, alluding to the cosy way in which we had travelled—

'What did we travel down together for, Ellie?'

She was shy and sad now, and could scarcely smile. I sat some time by her, talking of what we should do at Christmas, and how pleasant it would be, and she cheered up a little to remind me of a sort of interlude I had promised to write, and to insist on my not forgetting some little playful hit, which we had concocted against one of the family. I was conscious that we were the object of great interest to the people in the room. The clever young lady told me afterwards in that very room (ah me, on what a different day!) that they had all taken it as a settled thing—a match desired by the family.

At last I rose to go away. Ellie came out with me to the door. She hung about my neck for a moment—one, two kisses—and then a third, and she was taken upstairs, and I drove away, under the beech-trees, where the rooks were gone to rest, and by the great old towers of the minster, upon which the moon was just risen, as I looked back.

I went down to Ryde, to Canham, who had his yacht there. We cruised about the Channel for a few days, and took part in a regatta, and then he took me round the east coast to Cromer, and I came up to Cambridge, and entered at Trinity at the beginning of the term.

The excitement of yachting, and of the new life at Trinity (and especially the boating, into which I entered with great zest, having been in the first boat at Eton), put Ellie almost entirely out of my head, so that for many days I scarcely thought of her at all.

The splendid summer of that year was prolonged into a superb, but moist and unhealthy, autumn, with a luxuriant vegetation, caused by the sultry and showery summer, and causing, in its turn, fever, and in some places cholera. Cambridge was lovely during day after day of golden misty sunlight on the gorgeous foliage of the 'Backs.' Of course I had many friends already among the Eton men, and had plenty of company, but I did not altogether forget Ellie, and had even begun to work upon the interlude for Christmas, having found a man who had a taste for such things. But for two or three days our boating coach had been working us very hard, and I think that I had scarcely thought of Ellie once, when one evening I came down from my rooms (which were on the staircase which turns up opposite the Hall, looking into the Neville Court), and stood on the steps, looking down into the great quadrangle, a little before Hall. A cloudless blue sky was overhead, the sun was just setting on the quaint buildings, the grass-plots, the fountain—on that beautiful court, in short, on which, that he might look once more from his death-bed, a late master made them draw up the blinds of his sick-room. The evening was close and sultry, and the court was very quiet, though the men were all standing about, waiting for Hall. As I stood upon the steps, some one came across from the porter's lodge with a paper in his hand. It was handed about among the men, 'Lord Frederick Calvert,' and with a joke or two, was passed on to me. I see as plainly as I shall ever see anything in life the scene before me, as I stood with it, a moment, unopened in my hand, the old buildings, the chapel, the blue sky, the grass, the fountain, the men in their blue gowns standing about, the next moment it was rolled away like a scroll altogether out of sight. 'Ellie is dying,' the message from my mother said; 'come down to Southam at once. She says nothing but "Fred."'

I got to the station a few minutes before the train started; I caught the express at Huntingdon, and came on all night; I heard nothing but Ellie's voice calling me by name. My father was well known on the Great Northern, and they stopped the express for me at the nearest station on that line to Southam, and I got a carriage and two horses, and came on as fast as I could bribe the man to go. As we got near our journey's end the dawn broke, and the sun, true to the character of that year, rose upon a splendid autumn morning. The few birds that were left sang gaily, the moist trees and grass and brambles were covered with a thousand glittering drops, the blue sky was streaked with varied colour, everything sang of new life, new hope, new beauty, the resurrection from the night. Only in my heart I felt a chill hatred of this beautiful nature, of this lovely, unsympathising companion which mocks our grief; in my heart I felt, as I have felt since at calmer and more solemn times, that this beauty of nature has little in common with our deepest sorrows and our highest hopes.

The grand old minster towers, with their Norman tracery, were shining in the slanting glory of the rising sun; the rooks were wheeling above the beeches. We had come rather slowly the last few miles, but we swept through the village and up the drive at a gallop. The house was ghastly with the white blinds. The maid who opened the door was the same who had waited upon us at tea that evening, and knew me at once before I spoke. Ellie was gone. From the first moment the plague had struck her down she had said but one word, at first continually, then at longer and longer intervals, but always the same—' Fred.'

'Why did we travel down together, Ellie?' Such a little way through life.

In the far-off spaces of Eternity—in the Light which no man can approach unto—we shall know.

V

AN APOLOGUE

AN APOLOGUE

There was a pause in the game. Spades were trumps, and the two Besique Knaves were lying on the table side by side. The Professor held sequence cards almost entirely, and it required careful play on the part of his adversary to prevent his getting both the sequence and the double besique. Therefore there was a pause in the game.

The King of Diamonds and the King of Clubs were lying side by side, and began to talk. The King of Clubs was a stupid king. He always said the same thing over again. No matter what excellent reasons you gave him, nor how clearly you showed him what foolish remarks he made, he always repeated the last words he had said. This was, no doubt, very stupid; but it gave him a great advantage in argument.

The King of Diamonds, on the contrary, was very clever. His intellect was of so rare a quality, and of so hard and fine a temper, and had been so carefully and sharply cut and elaborated into crystals, that it was enabled to pierce further into a millstone than that of any other card—yes, even that of the cleverest of the Knaves, for the intellect of these latter is always spoilt by a sort of worldly cunning, and a too great reference to the gains and advantages of present good.

'I tell you,' said the King of Clubs, in a loud and positive voice, 'that it is all chance. In an affair in which I was lately engaged, and in which my suite were trumps, there were with me the two Aces, my brother, the King of Clubs, my own consort, the two Tens, and one of the Knaves. Now, I ask you, what could any skill effect against such a force as this ?'

As this was the ninth time the king had related this anecdote in precisely the same words, the King of Diamonds began to feel the conversation a bore, and if his perfect culture would have permitted such a thing, he would have felt irritated, which, of course, he never did. He therefore replied with extreme politeness, in a soft and melodious voice—

'The force of your reasoning, my dear Clubs, and the interesting anecdote you have just related, admit of no reply. I see clearly that everything is the result of chance, and I also see, I think clearly, that chance forms itself under certain contingencies into a sort of system by which unexpected results are obtained. Thus, I have often noticed that when everything seemed clear before us, and the game our own, in the most unexpected way everything is changed; instead of lying peaceably on our own side of the table, we are transferred to the enemy's camp. The play of one particular card appears to have subverted the most formidable combinations, and conclusions which I fancied certain dissolve into air.'

The King of Clubs did not understand a word of all this, but, as his companion appeared to be agreeing with what he himself had stated, he did not think it worth while to relate his anecdote over again, and remained silent.

'I think it must be plain to every one,' continued the King of Diamonds, still with extreme politeness, 'even to the most stupid, that we are governed by a higher intellect than our own; that as the cards fall from the pack, in what you so forcibly describe as chance-medley merely, they are immediately subjected to analysis and arrangement, by which the utmost possible value is extracted from these chance contingencies, and that not unfrequently the results which chance itself seemed to predict are reversed. This analysis and arrangement, and these results, we cards have learnt to call intellect (or mind), and to attribute it to an order of beings superior to ourselves, by whom our destinies are controlled. These truths are taught in our Sunday schools, and will, I think, scarcely be denied. But what I wish to call your attention to, is a more abstruse conception which I myself have obtained with difficulty, but which your more robust— that is the term, I think, you Liberals use —intellect will, I doubt not, readily grasp. It has occurred to me that even the fall of the cards is the result merely of more remote contingencies, and is resolvable into laws and systems similar to those to which they are afterwards subjected. I was led at first to form this conception by an oracular voice which I once heard, whether in trance or vision I cannot say. The words I heard were somewhat like these :—

'" If we could sufficiently extend our insight we should see that every apparently chance contingency is but the result of previous combinations : that all existence is but the result of previous existence, and that chance is lost in law. But side by side with this truth exists another of more stupendous import, that, just as far as this truth is recognised and perceived, just so far, step by step, springs into existence a power by which law is abrogated, and the apparent course of its iron necessity is changed. To these senseless cards" (whom the voice here alluded to I fail to see)—"to these senseless cards, doubtless, the game appears nothing but an undeviating law of fate. We know that we possess a power by which the fall of the cards is systematised and controlled. To a higher intelligence than ours, doubtless, combinations which seem to us inscrutable are as easily analysed and controlled. In proportion as intellect advances we know this to be the case, and these two would seem to run back side by side into the Infinite Law, and Intellect which perceives Law, until we arrive at the final problem, whether Law is the result of intellect, or intellect of Law." These were the remarkable words I heard.'

'I do not understand a word you have said,' replied the King of Clubs. 'I remember in an affair in which I was engaged——'

Here the King of Spades suddenly came down upon the table at his brother monarch's side, and the game was played out.

When the game was over, and the other player was gone, the Professor's little daughter came to the table, and began to play with the cards.

'Why does the Herr Councillor, who is so rich, come and play with you, papa?' she said.

'We were boys together, and he likes to come and hear me talk; for while he has been growing rich and great, I have been thinking, which he has no time to do.'

The Professor would not have said this to any one else, but it was only his little daughter, and there was no reason why he should not say what was in his mind.

'Why did you not ask God to make you rich and great?' said the little girl.

'I asked the All-father,' said the Professor, looking very kindly at the child, 'to give me all that was good, and He has given me everything, even a little girl.'

The child was taking all the royal cards in her hands and placing them side by side upon the table, so that she made a pretty picture, bright with colours and gay forms;

but one card was wanting, so that the royal dance-figure was not perfect, and one place was vacant.

A card was lying on the floor with its back uppermost.

'Pick me up that card, papa,' said the Professor's little daughter. 'It is a king.'

The Professor stooped down and picked up the card. It was a paltry seven of hearts.

Now the father could not complete the picture for his child, for the wise King of Diamonds had fallen by misadventure into the large pocket of the rich councillor's embroidered coat, and was gone.

THE END

MESSRS. MACMILLAN AND CO.'S PUBLICATIONS.

BY THE SAME AUTHOR.

A CHEAPER EDITION OF

MR. SHORTHOUSE'S NOVELS.

Just published.   Crown 8vo.   3s. 6d. each.

JOHN INGLESANT: A ROMANCE. [*Ready.*

ACADEMY—"That which gives surpassing interest to the book is its picture of a human soul, strong and acute beyond that of ordinary mortals, performing its task for good or for evil with unflinching resolution."

PALL MALL GAZETTE—"It is one of the most remarkable books, not only of the season, but of a good many seasons."

SPECTATOR—"History, romance, and philosophy, Mr. Shorthouse has managed to blend them in one harmonious whole, without making his readers feel that he is dealing unfairly with history, or unduly weighting romance with the deeper interests of philosophy."

STANDARD—"As a picture of the Civil War and of the Commonwealth, it is almost excellent. . . . 'John Inglesant' is a book which one can hardly read without being the wiser for it. If one reads aright its lessons of charity, one must be the better for it too."

DAILY NEWS—"'John Inglesant' is probably the best written novel which has issued from the press for some years. There is no doubt whatever that Mr. Shorthouse has made a careful study of the seventeenth century, and has brought many of the celebrated characters of the day into his story."

ST. JAMES'S GAZETTE—"The romance takes up a wide space of historic ground, and the author peoples it with men and women singularly lifelike. Not many other men of our time that we are aware of could have written so many passages of spiritual wisdom and insight as we find in 'John Inglesant.' We commend it for the knowledge it displays, the charm of its descriptions—clear and calm as the reflections in a mirror—its philosophic insight, and the force and purity of its style."

SATURDAY REVIEW—"An interesting and remarkable book. . . . In the creation of this character, at once weak and dignified, Mr. Shorthouse has shown great knowledge of many of the deeper and less commonly analysed forces of human thought."

SIR PERCIVAL. [*Ready.*

LITERARY WORLD—"It is the work of a man who to great literary power unites a deep insight into the hidden mysteries of spiritual life."

A TEACHER OF THE VIOLIN: AND OTHER TALES.
[*Ready.*

THE LITTLE SCHOOLMASTER MARK: A SPIRITUAL ROMANCE. Complete.

ACADEMY—"Such a story as 'The Little Schoolmaster Mark' is worth a dozen first-rate novels."

THE COUNTESS EVE.

MACMILLAN AND CO., LONDON.

MESSRS. MACMILLAN AND CO.'S PUBLICATIONS.

POPULAR NOVELS BY MR. MARION CRAWFORD.

Crown 8vo.   Cloth.   3s. 6d. each.

MR. ISAACS: A Tale of Modern India.

DAILY NEWS—"The best novel that has ever laid its scene in our Indian dominions."

ATHENÆUM—"A work of unusual ability."

DR. CLAUDIUS.   A True Story.

ATHENÆUM—"Mr. Crawford has achieved another success."

A ROMAN SINGER.

TIMES—"A masterpiece of narrative. . . . In Mr. Crawford's skilful hands it is unlike any other romance in English literature."

ZOROASTER.

GUARDIAN—"An instance of the highest and noblest form of novel. . . . Alike in the originality of its conception and the power with which it is wrought out, it stands on a level that is almost entirely its own."

MARZIO'S CRUCIFIX.

A TALE OF A LONELY PARISH.

GUARDIAN—"The tale is written with all Mr. Crawford's skill."

SATURDAY REVIEW—"Unlike most novels, goes on improving up to the end."

PAUL PATOFF.

ATHENÆUM—"The originality of the story, the charm of the description, and the brilliancy of the narrative are undeniable."

WITH THE IMMORTALS.

SPECTATOR—"To do justice to Mr. Crawford's remarkable book by extracts would be impossible. . . . It cannot fail to please a reader who enjoys crisp, clear, vigorous writing, and thoughts that are alike original and suggestive."

GREIFENSTEIN.

SATURDAY REVIEW—"With the exception of 'Saracinesca,' his most consistent work, Mr. Crawford has not written anything so good as his last novel, 'Greifenstein.'"

ACADEMY—"During the whole of his literary career Mr. Marion Crawford has produced nothing quite so powerful as one or two of the situations in 'Greifenstein.'"

SANT' ILARIO.

ATHENÆUM—"The plot is skilfully concocted, and the interest is sustained to the end. The various events, romantic, and even sensational, follow naturally and neatly, and the whole is a very clever piece of work."

SCOTSMAN—"The book is full of passages of remarkable power. A reader will find it hard to decide whether this is not the best of Mr. Crawford's novels."

MACMILLAN AND CO., LONDON.

MESSRS. MACMILLAN AND CO.'S PUBLICATIONS.

In Crown 8vo, Cloth extra, price 3s. 6d. each.

UNIFORM EDITION OF THE COLLECTED WORKS OF

CHARLES KINGSLEY.

WESTWARD HO!
HYPATIA.
YEAST.
ALTON LOCKE.
TWO YEARS AGO.
HEREWARD THE WAKE.
POEMS.
THE HEROES.
THE WATER BABIES.
MADAM HOW AND LADY WHY.
AT LAST.
PROSE IDYLLS.
PLAYS AND PURITANS, &c.
THE ROMAN AND THE TEUTON.
SANITARY AND SOCIAL LECTURES AND ESSAYS.
HISTORICAL LECTURES AND ESSAYS.
SCIENTIFIC LECTURES AND ESSAYS.
LITERARY AND GENERAL LECTURES.
THE HERMITS.
GLAUCUS, OR THE WONDERS OF THE SEASHORE. With Coloured Illustrations.
VILLAGE AND TOWN AND COUNTRY SERMONS.
THE WATER OF LIFE, AND OTHER SERMONS.
SERMONS ON NATIONAL SUBJECTS, AND THE KING OF THE EARTH.
SERMONS FOR THE TIMES.
GOOD NEWS OF GOD.
THE GOSPEL OF THE PENTATEUCH, AND DAVID.
DISCIPLINE, AND OTHER SERMONS.
WESTMINSTER SERMONS.
ALL SAINTS' DAY AND OTHER SERMONS.

Now Ready, on fine paper, complete in XIII Vols. Globe 8vo. 5s. each.

EVERSLEY EDITION.

CHARLES KINGSLEY'S NOVELS AND POEMS.

PALL MALL GAZETTE—"No English author has ever appeared in a more charming form. This is not an *edition de luxe*, but it is that much better thing for work-a-day readers—an edition of admirable taste and most pleasant use."

WESTWARD HO! Two Vols.   YEAST. One Vol.
TWO YEARS AGO. Two Vols.   ALTON LOCKE. Two Vols.
HYPATIA. Two Vols.   HEREWARD. Two Vols.
POEMS. Two Vols.

MACMILLAN AND CO., LONDON.

MESSRS. MACMILLAN AND CO.'S PUBLICATIONS.

RE-ISSUE OF THE SIXPENNY EDITION OF

CHARLES KINGSLEY'S NOVELS.

Medium 8vo, sewed, 6d. each.

WESTWARD HO!	*ALTON LOCKE.*
HYPATIA.	*HEREWARD THE WAKE.*
YEAST.	*TWO YEARS AGO.*

UNIFORM EDITION OF THE NOVELS OF

THOMAS HUGHES.

Crown 8vo, Cloth extra, 3s. 6d. each.

TOM BROWN'S SCHOOLDAYS. With Illustrations by A. HUGHES and S. P. HALL.
TOM BROWN AT OXFORD. With Illustrations by S. P. HALL.
THE SCOURING OF THE WHITE HORSE, and The Ashen Faggot. With Illustrations by RICHARD DOYLE.

SIXPENNY EDITION.

TOM BROWN'S SCHOOLDAYS. A Sixpenny Edition. Uniform with the Sixpenny edition of CHARLES KINGSLEY'S Novels. Illustrated. 8vo. 6d.

UNIFORM EDITION OF NOVELS AND TALES

BY MRS. CRAIK.

(The Author of "John Halifax Gentleman.")

Crown 8vo, Cloth extra, 3s. 6d. each.

OLIVE. With Illustrations by G. BOWERS.
THE OGILVIES. With Illustrations by J. McL. RALSTON.
AGATHA'S HUSBAND. With Illustrations by WALTER CRANE.
HEAD OF THE FAMILY. With Illustrations by WALTER CRANE.
TWO MARRIAGES.
THE LAUREL BUSH.
MY MOTHER AND I. With Illustrations by J. McL RALSTON.
MISS TOMMY: A Mediæval Romance. With Illustrations by FREDERICK NOEL PATON.
KING ARTHUR: Not a Love Story.

MACMILLAN AND CO., LONDON.

MACMILLAN'S TWO-SHILLING NOVELS.

Globe 8vo, 2s. each.

BY MRS. OLIPHANT.
  THE CURATE IN CHARGE.
  A SON OF THE SOIL.
  YOUNG MUSGRAVE.
  HE THAT WILL NOT WHEN HE MAY
  A COUNTRY GENTLEMAN.
  HESTER.
  SIR TOM.
  THE SECOND SON.
  THE WIZARD'S SON.

BY THE AUTHOR OF "HOGAN, M.P."
  HOGAN, M.P.
  THE HONOURABLE MISS FERRARD.
  FLITTERS, TATTERS, and the COUNSELLOR, WEEDS, and other Sketches.
  CHRISTY CAREW.
  ISMAY'S CHILDREN.

BY GEORGE FLEMING.
  A NILE NOVEL. | *THE HEAD OF MEDUSA.*
  MIRAGE. | *VESTIGIA.*

BY MRS. MACQUOID.
  PATTY.

BY W. E. NORRIS.
  MY FRIEND JIM. | *CHRIS.*

BY HENRY JAMES.
  DAISY MILLER; AN INTERNATIONAL EPISODE; FOUR MEETINGS.
  RODERICK HUDSON.
  THE MADONNA OF THE FUTURE; and other Tales.
  WASHINGTON SQUARE.
  PRINCESS CASAMASSIMA.

BY FRANCES HODGSON BURNETT.
  LOUISANA, and THAT LASS O' LOWRIE'S. Two Stories.
  HAWORTH'S.

BY HUGH CONWAY.
  A FAMILY AFFAIR. | *LIVING OR DEAD.*

BY D. CHRISTIE MURRAY.
  AUNT RACHEL.

BY HELEN JACKSON.
  RAMONA: A Story.

MACMILLAN AND CO., LONDON.

MESSRS. MACMILLAN AND CO.'S THREE-AND-SIXPENNY SERIES.

In Crown 8vo. Cloth extra. 3s. 6d. each.

By Rolf Boldrewood.
ROBBERY UNDER ARMS. | *THE MINER'S RIGHT.*
THE SQUATTER'S DREAM.

By Frances Hodgson Burnett.
LOUISIANA; and *THAT LASS O' LOWRIE'S.*

By Sir H. Cunningham.
THE CŒRULEANS. | *THE HERIOTS.*
WHEAT AND TARES.

By D. Christie Murray and Henry Herman.
HE FELL AMONG THIEVES.

By Thomas Hardy.
THE WOODLANDERS. | *WESSEX TALES.*

By Bret Harte.
CRESSY.

By Henry James.
A LONDON LIFE. | *ASPERN PAPERS.* | *TRAGIC MUSE.*

By Annie Keary.
CASTLE DALY. | *JANET'S HOME.*
YORK and a *LANCASTER ROSE.* | *OLDBURY.*

By Margaret Lee.
FAITHFUL AND UNFAITHFUL.

By Amy Levy. | By Lord Lytton.
REUBEN SACHS. | *THE RING OF AMASIS.*

By D. Christie Murray.
AUNT RACHEL. | *SCHWARTZ.*
JOHN VALE'S GUARDIAN. | *THE WEAKER VESSEL.*

By Mrs. Oliphant.
A BELEAGUERED CITY. | *NEIGHBOURS ON THE GREEN.*
JOYCE. | *KIRSTEEN.*

By W. Clark Russell. | By Mrs. Humphry Ward.
MAROONED. | *MISS BRETHERTON.*

Uniform with the above.

STORM WARRIORS. By the Rev. John Gilmore.
TALES OF OLD JAPAN. By A. B. Mitford.
A YEAR WITH THE BIRDS. By W. Warde Fowler. Illustrated by Bryan Hook.
TALES OF THE BIRDS. By the Same. Illustrated by Bryan Hook.
LEAVES OF A LIFE. By Montagu Williams, Q.C.
LATER LEAVES. By Montagu Williams, Q.C.
TRUE TALES FOR MY GRANDSONS. By Sir S. W. Baker.
TALES OF OLD TRAVEL. By Henry Kingsley.

Other Volumes to follow.

MACMILLAN AND CO., LONDON.

Catalogue of Books

PUBLISHED BY

MACMILLAN AND CO.

BEDFORD STREET, COVENT GARDEN, LONDON

May, 1891.

NOTE.—In the following Catalogue the titles of books belonging to any Series will only be found under the Series heading.

	PAGE		
Art at Home Series	3	ÆSCHYLUS.	See pp. 2, 31, 32.
Classical Writers	8	BLACK (William).	See p. 28.
English Citizen Series	12	BOLDREWOOD (Rolf).	See pp. 5, 29.
English Classics	12	CÆSAR	See pp. 31, 32.
English Men of Action	13	CICERO	See pp. 8, 31, 32.
English Men of Letters	13	CRAIK (Mrs.)	See pp. 9, 29.
Twelve English Statesmen	13	CRAWFORD (F. M.)	See pp. 9, 29.
Globe Editions	16	DEMOSTHENES	See p. 32.
Globe Readings from Standard Authors	17	EURIPIDES.	See pp. 13, 31, 32.
Golden Treasury Series	17	HARDY (Thomas)	See p. 29.
Historical Course for Schools	21	HARTE (Bret)	See p. 29.
Indian Text-Books	22	HERODOTUS	See pp. 20, 32.
Six-Shilling Novels	28	HOMER	See pp. 21, 31, 32.
Three-and-Sixpenny Series	29	HORACE	See pp. 21, 31, 32.
Two-Shilling Novels	29	JAMES (Henry)	See pp. 23, 28, 29.
Half-Crown Books for the Young	30	JUVENAL	See pp. 24, 32.
Elementary Classics	30	KEARY (A.)	See pp. 24, 28, 29.
Classical Series for Schools and Colleges	32	LIVY	See pp. 26, 31, 32.
Geographical Series	33	OLIPHANT (Mrs.)	See pp. 29, 39.
Science Class-Books	33	OVID	See pp. 31, 32.
Progressive French and German Courses and Readers	34	PHÆDRUS.	See p. 31.
		PLATO	See pp. 32, 33, 41.
		PLAUTUS	See pp. 33, 41.
		PLINY	See pp. 33, 41.
		PLUTARCH	See pp. 33, 41.
Foreign School Classics	35	POLYBIUS	See pp. 33, 41.
Primary Series of French and German Reading Books	35	SALLUST	See pp. 33, 44.
		SCHILLER	See p. 35.
		SHAKESPEARE	See pp. 12, 45.
Nature Series	39	TACITUS	See pp. 33, 47.
Science, History, and Literature Primers	42	THUCYDIDES	See pp. 32, 38, 49.
		XENOPHON	See pp. 31—33, 54.

ABBOTT (Rev. E. A.).—A SHAKESPEARIAN GRAMMAR. Extra fcp. 8vo. 6s.
—— CAMBRIDGE SERMONS. 8vo. 6s.
—— OXFORD SERMONS. 8vo. 7s. 6d.
—— FRANCIS BACON: AN ACCOUNT OF HIS LIFE AND WORKS. 8vo. 14s.
—— BIBLE LESSONS. Crown 8vo. 4s. 6d.
—— PHILOMYTHUS. Crown 8vo. 3s. 6d.

ABBOTT (Rev. E. A.) and RUSHBROOKE (W. G.).—THE COMMON TRADITION OF THE SYNOPTIC GOSPELS, IN THE TEXT OF THE REVISED VERSION. Crown 8vo. 3s. 6d.

ABBOT (Francis).—SCIENTIFIC THEISM. Crown 8vo. 7s. 6d.
—— THE WAY OUT OF AGNOSTICISM; or, The Philosophy of Free Religion. Cr. 8vo. 4s. 6d.

ADAMS (Sir F. O.) and CUNNINGHAM (C.)—THE SWISS CONFEDERATION. 8vo. 14s.

ÆSCHYLUS.—THE "SEVEN AGAINST THEBES." With Introduction, Commentary, and Translation by A. W. VERRALL, Litt. D. 8vo. 7s. 6d.
—— AGAMEMNON. With Introduction, Commentary, and Translation, by A. W. VERRALL, Litt. D. 8vo. 12s.
—— THE SUPPLICES. Text, Introduction, Notes, Commentary, and Translation, by Prof. T. G. TUCKER. 8vo. 10s. 6d.
See also pp. 31, 32.

ÆSOP—CALDECOTT.—SOME OF ÆSOP'S FABLES, with Modern Instances, shown in Designs by RANDOLPH CALDECOTT. 4to. 5s.

AGASSIZ (LOUIS): HIS LIFE AND CORRESPONDENCE. Edited by ELIZABETH CARY AGASSIZ. 2 vols. Crown 8vo. 18s.

AINGER Rev. Alfred).—SERMONS PREACHED IN THE TEMPLE CHURCH. Extra fcp. 8vo. 6s.

AIRY (Sir G. B.).—TREATISE ON THE ALGEBRAICAL AND NUMERICAL THEORY OF ERRORS OF OBSERVATION AND THE COMBINATION OF OBSERVATIONS. Crown 8vo. 6s. 6d.
—— POPULAR ASTRONOMY. With Illustrations. Fcp. 8vo. 4s. 6d.
—— AN ELEMENTARY TREATISE ON PARTIAL DIFFERENTIAL EQUATIONS. Cr. 8vo. 5s. 6d.
—— ON SOUND AND ATMOSPHERIC VIBRATIONS. With the Mathematical Elements of Music. 2nd Edition. Crown 8vo. 9s.
—— GRAVITATION. An Elementary Explanation of the Principal Perturbations in the Solar System. 2nd Edit. Crn. 8vo. 7s. 6d.

AITKEN (Sir W.)—THE GROWTH OF THE RECRUIT AND YOUNG SOLDIER. With a view to the selection of "Growing Lads" for the Army, and a Regulated System of Training for Recruits. Crown 8vo. 8s. 6d.

ALBEMARLE (Earl of).—FIFTY YEARS OF MY LIFE. 3rd Edit., revised. Cr. 8vo. 7s. 6d.

ALDIS (Mary Steadman).—THE GREAT GIANT ARITHMOS. A MOST ELEMENTARY ARITHMETIC. Illustrated. Globe 8vo. 2s. 6d.

ALDRICH (T. Bailey). — THE SISTERS' TRAGEDY, WITH OTHER POEMS, LYRICAL AND DRAMATIC. Fcp. 8vo. 3s. 6d. net.

ALEXANDER (T.) and THOMSON (A.).—ELEMENTARY APPLIED MECHANICS. Part II. Transverse Stress; upwards of 150 Diagrams, and 200 Examples carefully worked out. Crown 8vo. 10s. 6d.

ALLBUTT (Dr. T. Clifford) —ON THE USE OF THE OPHTHALMOSCOPE. 8vo. 15s.

AMIEL (Henri Frederic).—THE JOURNAL INTIME. Translated by Mrs. HUMPHRY WARD. 2nd Edition. Crown 8vo. 6s.

AN AUTHOR'S LOVE. Being the Unpublished Letters of PROSPER MÉRIMÉE'S "Inconnue." 2 vols. Ex. cr. 8vo. 12s.

ANDERSON (A.).—BALLADS AND SONNETS. Crown 8vo. 5s.

ANDERSON (L.).—LINEAR PERSPECTIVE AND MODEL DRAWING. Royal 8vo. 2s.

ANDERSON (Dr. McCall).—LECTURES ON CLINICAL MEDICINE. Illustrated. 8vo. 10s. 6d.

ANDREWS (Dr. Thomas): THE SCIENTIFIC PAPERS OF THE LATE. With a Memoir by Profs. TAIT and CRUM BROWN. 8vo. 18s.

ANGLO-SAXON LAW: ESSAYS ON. Med. 8vo. 18s.

APPLETON (T. G.).—A NILE JOURNAL. Illustrated by EUGENE BENSON. Crown 8vo. 6s.

ARATUS.—THE SKIES AND WEATHER FORECASTS OF ARATUS. Translated by E. POSTE, M.A. Crown 8vo. 3s. 6d.

ARIOSTO.—PALADIN AND SARACEN. Stories from Ariosto. By H. C. HOLLWAY-CALTHROP. Illustrated. Crown 8vo. 6s.

ARISTOPHANES.—THE BIRDS. Translated into English Verse, with Introduction, Notes, and Appendices. By Prof. B. H. KENNEDY, D.D. Crown 8vo. 6s.
—— HELP NOTES FOR THE USE OF STUDENTS. Crown 8vo. 1s. 6d.

ARISTOTLE ON FALLACIES; OR, THE SOPHISTICI ELENCHI. With Translation and Notes by E. POSTE, M.A. 8vo. 8s. 6d.

ARISTOTLE.—THE FIRST BOOK OF THE METAPHYSICS OF ARISTOTLE. Translated with marginal Analysis and Summary. By a Cambridge Graduate. 8vo. 5s.
—— THE POLITICS. Translated with an Analysis and Critical Notes by J. E. C. WELLDON, Litt. D. 2nd Edition. 10s. 6d.
—— THE RHETORIC. By the same Translator. Crown 8vo. 7s. 6d.

ARMY PRELIMINARY EXAMINATION, Specimens of Papers set at the, 1882-89. With Answers to the Mathematical Questions. Crown 8vo. 3s. 6d.

ARNAULD, ANGELIQUE. By FRANCES MARTIN. Crown 8vo. 4s. 6d.

ARNOLD (Matthew).—THE COMPLETE POETICAL WORKS. New Edition. 3 vols. Crown 8vo. 7s. 6d. each.—Vol. I. Early Poems, Narrative Poems, and Sonnets.—Vol. II. Lyric and Elegiac Poems.—Vol. III. Dramatic and Later Poems.
—— COMPLETE POETICAL WORKS. 1 vol. With Portrait. Crown 8vo. 7s. 6d.

LIST OF PUBLICATIONS.

ARNOLD (M.).—ESSAYS IN CRITICISM. 6th Edition. Crown 8vo. 9s.
—— ESSAYS IN CRITICISM. Second Series. With an Introductory Note by Lord COLERIDGE. Crown 8vo. 7s. 6d.
—— ISAIAH XL.—LXVI. WITH THE SHORTER PROPHECIES ALLIED TO IT. With Notes. Crown 8vo. 5s.
—— ISAIAH OF JERUSALEM. In the Authorised English Version, with Introduction, Corrections, and Notes. Crown 8vo. 4s. 6d.
—— A BIBLE-READING FOR SCHOOLS. The Great Prophecy of Israel's Restoration (Isaiah xl.-lxvi.) 4th Edition. 18mo. 1s.
—— HIGHER SCHOOLS AND UNIVERSITIES IN GERMANY. Crown 8vo. 6s.
—— DISCOURSES IN AMERICA. Cr. 8vo. 4s. 6d.
—— JOHNSON'S LIVES OF THE POETS, THE SIX CHIEF LIVES FROM. With Macaulay's "Life of Johnson." With Preface by MATTHEW ARNOLD. Crown 8vo. 4s. 6d.
—— EDMUND BURKE'S LETTERS, TRACTS AND SPEECHES ON IRISH AFFAIRS. Edited by MATTHEW ARNOLD. Crown 8vo. 6s.
—— REPORTS ON ELEMENTARY SCHOOLS, 1852-82. Edited by the Right Hon. Sir FRANCIS SANDFORD, K.C.B. Cr. 8vo. 3s. 6d.

ARNOLD (T.)—THE SECOND PUNIC WAR. By the late THOMAS ARNOLD, D.D. Edited by WILLIAM T. ARNOLD, M.A. With Eight Maps. Crown 8vo. 5s.

ARNOLD (W. T.).—THE ROMAN SYSTEM OF PROVINCIAL ADMINISTRATION. Crn. 8vo. 6s.

ART AT HOME SERIES. Edited by W. J. LOFTIE, B.A.
MUSIC IN THE HOUSE. By JOHN HULLAH. Fourth Edition. Crown 8vo. 2s. 6d.
THE DINING-ROOM. By Mrs. LOFTIE. With Illustrations. 2nd Edition. Crown 8vo. 2s. 6d.
THE BEDROOM AND BOUDOIR. By Lady BARKER. Crown 8vo. 2s. 6d.
AMATEUR THEATRICALS. By WALTER H. POLLOCK and Lady POLLOCK. Illustrated by KATE GREENAWAY. Crown 8vo. 2s. 6d.
NEEDLEWORK. By ELIZABETH GLAISTER. Illustrated. Crown 8vo. 2s. 6d.
THE LIBRARY. By ANDREW LANG, with a Chapter on English Illustrated Books, by AUSTIN DOBSON. Crown 8vo. 3s. 6d.

ARTEVELDE. JAMES AND PHILIP VAN ARTEVELDE. By W. J. ASHLEY. Cr. 8vo. 6s.

ATKINSON (J. B.).—AN ART TOUR TO NORTHERN CAPITALS OF EUROPE. 8vo. 12s.

ATKINSON (J. C.).—FORTY YEARS IN A MOORLAND PARISH. Crn. 8vo. 8s. 6d. net.

AUSTIN (Alfred).—POETICAL WORKS. New Collected Edit. In 6 vols. Cr. 8vo. 5s. each. Monthly Vols. from December, 1890:
Vol. I. THE TOWER OF BABEL.
Vol. II. SAVONAROLA, etc.
Vol. III. PRINCE LUCIFER.
Vol. IV. THE HUMAN TRAGEDY.
Vol. V. NARRATIVE POEMS.
Vol. VI. LYRICAL POEMS.
—— SOLILOQUIES IN SONG. Crown 8vo. 6s.
—— AT THE GATE OF THE CONVENT; AND OTHER POEMS. Crown 8vo. 6s.

AUSTIN (A.).—MADONNA'S CHILD. Crown 4to. 3s. 6d.
—— ROME OR DEATH. Crown 4to. 9s.
—— THE GOLDEN AGE. Crown 8vo. 5s.
—— THE SEASON. Crown 8vo. 5s.
—— LOVE'S WIDOWHOOD: AND OTHER POEMS. Crown 8vo. 6s.
—— ENGLISH LYRICS. Crown 8vo. 3s. 6d.

AUTENRIETH (Dr. G.).—AN HOMERIC DICTIONARY. Translated from the German, by R. P. KEEP, Ph.D. Crown 8vo. 6s.

BABRIUS. With Introductory Dissertations, Critical Notes, Commentary, and Lexicon, by W. G. RUTHERFORD, LL.D. 8vo. 12s. 6d.

"BACCHANTE." THE CRUISE OF H.M.S. "BACCHANTE," 1879-1882. Compiled from the private Journals, Letters and Note-books of PRINCE ALBERT VICTOR and PRINCE GEORGE OF WALES. By the Rev. Canon DALTON. 2 vols. Medium 8vo. 52s. 6d.

BACON (FRANCIS): ACCOUNT OF HIS LIFE AND WORKS. By E. A. ABBOTT. 8vo. 14s.

BAINES (Rev. Edward).—SERMONS. With a Preface and Memoir, by ALFRED BARRY, D.D., late Bishop of Sydney. Crn. 8vo. 6s.

BAKER (Sir Samuel White).—ISMAILIA. A Narrative of the Expedition to Central Africa for the Suppression of the Slave Trade, organised by ISMAIL, Khedive of Egypt. Crown 8vo. 6s.
—— THE NILE TRIBUTARIES OF ABYSSINIA, AND THE SWORD HUNTERS OF THE HAMRAN ARABS. Crown 8vo. 6s.
—— THE ALBERT N'YANZA GREAT BASIN OF THE NILE AND EXPLORATION OF THE NILE SOURCES. Crown 8vo. 6s.
—— CYPRUS AS I SAW IT IN 1879. 8vo. 12s. 6d.
—— CAST UP BY THE SEA; OR, THE ADVENTURES OF NED GRAY. With Illustrations by HUARD. Crown 8vo. 6s.
—— THE EGYPTIAN QUESTION. Letters to the Times and the Pall Mall Gazette. 8vo. 2s.
—— TRUE TALES FOR MY GRANDSONS. Illustrated by W. J. HENNESSY. Cr. 8vo. 3s. 6d.
—— WILD BEASTS AND THEIR WAYS: REMINISCENCES OF EUROPE, ASIA, AFRICA, AND AMERICA. Illustrated. Ex. cr. 8vo. 12s. 6d.

BALCH (Elizabeth). — GLIMPSES OF OLD ENGLISH HOMES. Illustrated. Gl. 4to. 14s.

BALDWIN (Prof. J. M.)—HANDBOOK OF PSYCHOLOGY: SENSES AND INTELLECT. 2nd Edition. 8vo. 12s. 6d.

BALFOUR (The Right Hon. A. J.).—A DEFENCE OF PHILOSOPHIC DOUBT. Being an Essay on the Foundations of Belief. 8vo. 12s.

BALFOUR (Prof. F. M.).—ELASMOBRANCH FISHES. With Plates. 8vo. 21s.
—— COMPARATIVE EMBRYOLOGY. With Illustrations. 2 vols. 2nd Edition. 8vo.—Vol. I. 18s.—Vol. II. 21s.
—— THE COLLECTED WORKS. Memorial Edition. Edited by M. FOSTER, F.R.S., and ADAM SEDGWICK, M.A. 4 vols. 8vo. 6l. 6s.
Vols. I. and IV. Special Memoirs. May be had separately. Price 73s. 6d. net.

BALL (Sir R. S.).—EXPERIMENTAL MECHANICS. Illustrated. New Ed. Cr. 8vo. 6s.

BALL (W. Platt).—ARE THE EFFECTS OF USE AND DISUSE INHERITED? An Examination of the View held by Spencer and Darwin. Crown 8vo. 3s. 6d.

BALL (W. W. R.).—THE STUDENT'S GUIDE TO THE BAR. 5th Edition, revised. Crown 8vo. 2s. 6d.

—— A SHORT ACCOUNT OF THE HISTORY OF MATHEMATICS. Crown 8vo. 10s. 6d.

BALLANCE (C. A.) and EDMUNDS (W.)—LIGATION IN CONTINUITY. 8vo.

BARKER (Lady).—FIRST LESSONS IN THE PRINCIPLES OF COOKING. 3rd Ed. 18mo. 1s.

—— A YEAR'S HOUSEKEEPING IN SOUTH AFRICA. Illustrated. Crown 8vo. 3s. 6d.

—— STATION LIFE IN NEW ZEALAND. Crown 8vo. 3s. 6d.

—— LETTERS TO GUY. Crown 8vo. 5s.

BARNES. LIFE OF WILLIAM BARNES, POET AND PHILOLOGIST. By his Daughter, LUCY BAXTER ("Leader Scott"). Cr. 8vo. 7s. 6d.

BARRY (Bishop).—FIRST WORDS IN AUSTRALIA: Sermons. Crown 8vo. 1s.

BARTHOLOMEW (J. G.).—LIBRARY REFERENCE ATLAS OF THE WORLD. With Index to 100,000 places. Folio. 2l. 12s. 6d. net. Also issued in Monthly Parts. Part I. March, 1891, 5s. net.

—— PHYSICAL AND POLITICAL SCHOOL ATLAS. With 80 maps. 4to. 7s. 6d.; half mor. 10s. 6d.

—— ELEMENTARY SCHOOL ATLAS. 4to. 1s.

BARWELL (Richard, F.R.C.S.).—THE CAUSES AND TREATMENT OF LATERAL CURVATURE OF THE SPINE. Crown 8vo. 5s.

—— ON ANEURISM, ESPECIALLY OF THE THORAX AND ROOT OF THE NECK. 3s. 6d.

BASTIAN (H. Charlton).—THE BEGINNINGS OF LIFE. 2 vols. Crown 8vo. 28s.

—— EVOLUTION AND THE ORIGIN OF LIFE. Crown 8vo. 6s. 6d.

—— ON PARALYSIS FROM BRAIN DISEASE IN ITS COMMON FORMS. Crown 8vo. 10s. 6d.

BATHER (Archdeacon).—ON SOME MINISTERIAL DUTIES, CATECHIZING, PREACHING, &c. Edited, with a Preface, by C. J. VAUGHAN, D.D. Fcp. 8vo. 4s. 6d.

BEASLEY (R. D.).—AN ELEMENTARY TREATISE ON PLANE TRIGONOMETRY. With numerous Examples. 9th Edition. Crown 8vo. 3s. 6d.

BEAUMARCHAIS. LE BARBIER DE SEVILLE, OU LE PRÉCAUTION INUTILE. Comedie en Quatre Actes. Edited by L. P. BLOUET, B.A., Univ. Gallic. Fcp. 8vo. 3s. 6d.

BEESLY (Mrs.).—STORIES FROM THE HISTORY OF ROME. Fcp. 8vo. 2s. 6d.

BEHAGHEL (OTTO).—THE GERMAN LANGUAGE. Translated by EMIL TRECHMANN, B.A., Ph.D. Globe 8vo.

BELCHER (Rev. H.).—SHORT EXERCISES IN LATIN PROSE COMPOSITION, AND EXAMINATION PAPERS IN LATIN GRAMMAR. 18mo. 1s. 6d.—KEY (for Teachers only). 3s. 6d.

BELCHER (Rev. H.).—SHORT EXERCISES IN LATIN PROSE COMPOSITION. Part II. On the Syntax of Sentences. With an Appendix. 18mo. 2s.

KEY (for Teachers only). 18mo. 3s.

BENHAM (Rev. W.).—A COMPANION TO THE LECTIONARY. Crown 8vo. 4s. 6d.

BERLIOZ (Hector): AUTOBIOGRAPHY OF. Transl. by RACHEL and ELEANOR HOLMES. 2 vols. Crown 8vo. 21s.

BERNARD (M.).—FOUR LECTURES ON SUBJECTS CONNECTED WITH DIPLOMACY. 8vo. 9s.

BERNARD (St.) THE LIFE AND TIMES OF ST. BERNARD, ABBOT OF CLAIRVAUX. By J. C. MORISON, M.A. Crown 8vo. 6s.

BERNERS (J.)—FIRST LESSONS ON HEALTH. 18mo. 1s.

BETHUNE-BAKER (J. F.).—THE INFLUENCE OF CHRISTIANITY ON WAR. 8vo. 5s.

—— THE STERNNESS OF CHRIST'S TEACHING, AND ITS RELATION TO THE LAW OF FORGIVENESS. Crown 8vo. 2s. 6d.

BETSY LEE: A FO'C'S'LE YARN. Extra fcp. 8vo. 3s. 6d.

BETTANY (G. T.).—FIRST LESSONS IN PRACTICAL BOTANY. 18mo. 1s.

BIGELOW (M. M.).—HISTORY OF PROCEDURE IN ENGLAND FROM THE NORMAN CONQUEST. The Norman Period, 1066-1204. 8vo. 16s.

BIKÉLAS (D.).—LOUKIS LARAS; OR, THE REMINISCENCES OF A CHIOTE MERCHANT DURING THE GREEK WAR OF INDEPENDENCE. Translated by J. GENNADIUS, Greek Minister in London. Crown 8vo. 7s. 6d.

BINNIE (the late Rev. William).—SERMONS. Crown 8vo. 6s.

BIRKS (Thomas Rawson, M.A.).—FIRST PRINCIPLES OF MORAL SCIENCE; OR, FIRST COURSE OF LECTURES DELIVERED IN THE UNIVERSITY OF CAMBRIDGE. Cr. 8vo. 8s. 6d.

—— MODERN UTILITARIANISM; OR, THE SYSTEMS OF PALEY, BENTHAM, AND MILL EXAMINED AND COMPARED. Crown 8vo. 6s. 6d.

—— THE DIFFICULTIES OF BELIEF IN CONNECTION WITH THE CREATION AND THE FALL, REDEMPTION AND JUDGMENT. 2nd Edition. Crown 8vo. 5s.

—— COMMENTARY ON THE BOOK OF ISAIAH, CRITICAL, HISTORICAL, AND PROPHETICAL; INCLUDING A REVISED ENGLISH TRANSLATION. 2nd Edition. 8vo. 12s. 6d.

—— THE NEW TESTAMENT. Essay on the Right Estimation of MS. Evidence in the Text of the New Testament. Cr. 8vo. 3s. 6d.

—— SUPERNATURAL REVELATION; OR, FIRST PRINCIPLES OF MORAL THEOLOGY. 8vo. 8s.

—— MODERN PHYSICAL FATALISM, AND THE DOCTRINE OF EVOLUTION. Including an Examination of Mr. Herbert Spencer's "First Principles." Crown 8vo. 6s.

—— JUSTIFICATION AND IMPUTED RIGHTEOUSNESS. Being a Review of Ten Sermons on the Nature and Effects of Faith by JAMES THOMAS O'BRIEN, D.D., late Bishop of Ossory, Ferns, and Leighlin. Cr. 8vo. 6s.

BJÖRNSON (B.). SYNNÖVE SOLBAKKEN. Translated by JULIE SUTTER. Cr. 8vo. 6s.

BLACK (William). See p. 28.

BLACKBURNE. LIFE OF THE RIGHT HON. FRANCIS BLACKBURNE, late Lord Chancellor of Ireland, by his son, EDWARD BLACKBURNE. With Portrait. 8vo. 12s.

BLACKIE (Prof. John Stuart.).—GREEK AND ENGLISH DIALOGUES FOR USE IN SCHOOLS AND COLLEGES. 3rd Edition. Fcp. 8vo. 2s. 6d.

—— GREEK PRIMER, COLLOQUIAL AND CONSTRUCTIVE. Globe 8vo.

—— HORÆ HELLENICÆ. 8vo. 12s.

—— THE WISE MEN OF GREECE : IN A SERIES OF DRAMATIC DIALOGUES. Cr. 8vo. 9s.

—— GOETHE'S FAUST. Translated into English Verse. 2nd Edition. Crown 8vo. 9s.

—— LAY SERMONS. Crown 8vo. 6s.

—— MESSIS VITAE : Gleanings of Song from a Happy Life. Crown 8vo. 4s. 6d.

—— WHAT DOES HISTORY TEACH? Two Edinburgh Lectures. Globe 8vo. 2s. 6d.

BLAKE (J. F.)—ASTRONOMICAL MYTHS. With Illustrations. Crown 8vo. 9s.

BLAKE. LIFE OF WILLIAM BLAKE. With Selections from his Poems and other Writings. Illustrated from Blake's own Works. By ALEXANDER GILCHRIST. 2nd Edition. 2 vols. cloth gilt. Medium 8vo. 2l. 2s.

BLAKISTON (J. R.).—THE TEACHER: HINTS ON SCHOOL MANAGEMENT. Cr. 8vo. 2s. 6d.

BLANFORD (H. F.).—THE RUDIMENTS OF PHYSICAL GEOGRAPHY FOR THE USE OF INDIAN SCHOOLS. 12th Edition. Illustrated. Globe 8vo. 2s. 6d.

—— A PRACTICAL GUIDE TO THE CLIMATES AND WEATHER OF INDIA, CEYLON AND BURMA, AND THE STORMS OF INDIAN SEAS. 8vo. 12s. 6d.

—— ELEMENTARY GEOGRAPHY OF INDIA, BURMA, AND CEYLON. Illus. Gl. 8vo. 2s. 6d.

BLANFORD (W. T.).—GEOLOGY AND ZOOLOGY OF ABYSSINIA. 8vo. 21s.

BLYTH (A. Wynter).—A MANUAL OF PUBLIC HEALTH. 8vo. 17s. net.

BÖHM-BAWERK (Prof.).—CAPITAL AND INTEREST. Translated by W. SMART, M.A. 8vo. 14s.

—— THE POSITIVE THEORY OF CAPITAL. Translated by W. SMART, M.A. 8vo.

BOISSEVAIN (G. M.).—THE MONETARY PROBLEM. 8vo, sewed. 3s. net.

BOLDREWOOD (Rolf). —A COLONIAL REFORMER. 3 vols. Cr. 8vo. 31s. 6d. See also p. 29.

BOLEYN (ANNE) : A Chapter of English History, 1527-1536. By PAUL FRIEDMANN. 2 vols. 8vo. 28s.

BONAR (James).—MALTHUS AND HIS WORK. 8vo. 12s. 6d.

BOOLE (George).—A TREATISE ON THE CALCULUS OF FINITE DIFFERENCES. Edited by J. F. MOULTON. 3rd Edition. Cr. 8vo. 10s. 6d.

—— THE MATHEMATICAL ANALYSIS OF LOGIC. 8vo. Sewed, 5s

BOTTOMLEY (J. T.). — FOUR-FIGURE MATHEMATICAL TABLES. Comprising Logarithmic and Trigonometrical Tables, and Tables of Squares, Square Roots and Reciprocals. 8vo. 2s. 6d.

BOUGHTON (G. H.) and ABBEY (E. A.).— SKETCHING RAMBLES IN HOLLAND. With Illustrations. Fcp. 4to. 21s.

BOUTMY (M.). -- STUDIES IN CONSTITUTIONAL LAW. Translated by Mrs. DICEY, with Preface by Prof. A. V. DICEY. Crown 8vo. [In the Press.

—— THE ENGLISH CONSTITUTION. Translated by Mrs. EADEN, with Introduction by Sir F. POLLOCK, Bart. Crown 8vo. 6s.

BOWEN (H. Courthope).—FIRST LESSONS IN FRENCH. 18mo. 1s.

BOWER (Prof. F. O.).—A COURSE OF PRACTICAL INSTRUCTION IN BOTANY. Cr. 8vo. 10s. 6d.

BRADSHAW (J. G.).—A COURSE OF EASY ARITHMETICAL EXAMPLES FOR BEGINNERS. Globe 8vo. 2s. With Answers. 2s. 6d.

BRAIN. A JOURNAL OF NEUROLOGY. Edited for the Neurological Society of London, by A. DE WATTEVILLE. Published Quarterly. 8vo. 3s. 6d. Yearly Vols. I. to XII. 8vo, cloth. 15s. each.

BREYMANN (Prof. H.).—A FRENCH GRAMMAR BASED ON PHILOLOGICAL PRINCIPLES. 3rd Edition. Extra fcp. 8vo. 4s. 6d.

—— FIRST FRENCH EXERCISE BOOK. 2nd Edition. Extra fcp. 8vo. 4s. 6d.

—— SECOND FRENCH EXERCISE BOOK. Extra fcp. 8vo. 2s. 6d.

BRIDGES (John A.).—IDYLLS OF A LOST VILLAGE. Crown 8vo. 7s. 6d.

BRIGHT (John).—SPEECHES ON QUESTIONS OF PUBLIC POLICY. Edited by THOROLD ROGERS. 2nd Edit. 2 vols. 8vo. 25s.— Cheap Edition. Extra fcp. 8vo. 3s. 6d.

—— PUBLIC ADDRESSES. Edited by THOROLD ROGERS. 8vo. 14s.

BRIGHT (H. A.)—THE ENGLISH FLOWER GARDEN. Crown 8vo. 3s. 6d.

—— A YEAR IN A LANCASHIRE GARDEN. New Edition. Crown 8vo. 3s. 6d.

BRIMLEY (George).—ESSAYS. Globe 8vo. 5s.

BRODIE (Sir Benjamin).—IDEAL CHEMISTRY Crown 8vo. 2s.

BROOKE, Sir Jas., THE RAJA OF SARAWAK (Life of). By GERTRUDE L. JACOB. 2 vols. 8vo. 25s.

BROOKE (Stopford A.).—PRIMER OF ENGLISH LITERATURE. 18mo. 1s.

Large Paper Edition. 8vo. 7s. 6d.

—— EARLY ENGLISH LITERATURE. 2 vols. 8vo. [Vol. I. in the Press.

—— RIQUET OF THE TUFT : A LOVE DRAMA. Extra crown 8vo. 6s.

—— POEMS. Globe 8vo. 6s.

—— MILTON. Fcp. 8vo. 1s. 6d.

Large Paper Edition. 8vo. 21s. net.

—— DOVE COTTAGE, WORDSWORTH'S HOME, FROM 1800—1808. Globe 8vo. 1s.

BROOKS (Rev. Phillips).—THE CANDLE OF THE LORD, AND OTHER SERMONS. Cr. 8vo. 6s.
—— SERMONS PREACHED IN ENGLISH CHURCHES. Crown 8vo. 6s.
—— TWENTY SERMONS. Crown 8vo. 6s.
—— TOLERANCE. Crown 8vo. 2s. 6d.
—— THE LIGHT OF THE WORLD, AND OTHER SERMONS. Crown 8vo. 3s. 6d.

BROOKSMITH (J.).——ARITHMETIC IN THEORY AND PRACTICE. Crown 8vo. 4s. 6d. KEY. Crown 8vo. 10s. 6d.

BROOKSMITH (J. and E. J.).—ARITHMETIC FOR BEGINNERS. Globe 8vo. 1s. 6d.

BROOKSMITH (E. J.).—WOOLWICH MATHEMATICAL PAPERS, for Admission in the Royal Military Academy, 1880—1888. Edited by E. J. Brooksmith, B.A. Crown 8vo. 6s.
—— SANDHURST MATHEMATICAL PAPERS, for Admission into the Royal Military College, 1881—89. Edited by E. J. BROOKSMITH, B.A. Crown 8vo. 3s. 6d.

BROWN (J. Allen).—PALÆOLITHIC MAN IN NORTH-WEST MIDDLESEX. 8vo. 7s. 6d.

BROWN (T. E.).—THE MANX WITCH: AND OTHER POEMS. Crown 8vo. 7s. 6d.

BROWNE (J. H. Balfour).—WATER SUPPLY. Crown 8vo. 2s. 6d.

BRUNTON (Dr. T. Lauder).—A TEXT-BOOK OF PHARMACOLOGY, THERAPEUTICS, AND MATERIA MEDICA. 3rd Edition. Medium 8vo. 21s.
—— DISORDERS OF DIGESTION: THEIR CONSEQUENCES AND TREATMENT. 8vo. 10s. 6d.
—— PHARMACOLOGY AND THERAPEUTICS; OR, MEDICINE PAST AND PRESENT. Cr. 8vo. 6s.
—— TABLES OF MATERIA MEDICA: A COMPANION TO THE MATERIA MEDICA MUSEUM. 8vo. 5s.
—— THE BIBLE AND SCIENCE. With Illustrations. Crown 8vo. 10s. 6d.
—— CROONIAN LECTURES ON THE CONNECTION BETWEEN CHEMICAL CONSTITUTION AND PHYSIOLOGICAL ACTION. Being an Introduction to Modern Therapeutics. 8vo.

BRYANS (Clement).—LATIN PROSE EXERCISES BASED UPON CAESAR'S "GALLIC WAR." With a Classification of Caesar's Phrases, and Grammatical Notes on Caesar's Chief Usages. Pott 8vo. 2s. 6d. KEY (for Teachers only). 4s. 6d.

BRYCE (James, M.P., D.C.L.).—THE HOLY ROMAN EMPIRE. 8th Edition. Crown 8vo. 7s. 6d.—*Library Edition.* 8vo. 14s.
—— TRANSCAUCASIA AND ARARAT. 3rd Edition. Crown 8vo. 9s.
—— THE AMERICAN COMMONWEALTH. 2nd Edition. 2 vols. Extra Crown 8vo. 25s.

BUCHHEIM (Dr.).—DEUTSCHE LYRIK. 18mo. 4s. 6d.
—— DEUTSCHE BALLADEN UND ROMANZEN. 18mo. [*In the Press.*

BUCKLAND (Anna).—OUR NATIONAL INSTITUTIONS. 18mo. 1s.

BUCKLEY (Arabella).—HISTORY OF ENGLAND FOR BEGINNERS. With Coloured Maps and Chronological and Genealogical Tables. Globe 8vo. 3s.

BUCKNILL (Dr.).—THE CARE OF THE INSANE. Crown 8vo. 3s. 6d.

BUCKTON (G. B.).—MONOGRAPH OF THE BRITISH CICADÆ, OR TETTIGIDÆ. In 8 parts, Quarterly. Part I. January, 1890. 8vo. I.—V. ready. 8s. each net.—Vol. I. 8vo. 33s. 6d. net.

BUMBLEBEE BOGO'S BUDGET. By a RETIRED JUDGE. Illustrations by ALICE HAVERS. Crown 8vo. 2s. 6d.

BURGON (Dean).—POEMS. Ex. fcp. 8vo. 4s. 6d.

BURKE (Edmund).—LETTERS, TRACTS, AND SPEECHES ON IRISH AFFAIRS. Edited by MATTHEW ARNOLD, with Preface. Cr. 8vo. 6s.
—— REFLECTIONS ON THE FRENCH REVOLUTION. Ed. by F. G. SELBY. Gl. 8vo. 5s.

BURN (Robert).—ROMAN LITERATURE IN RELATION TO ROMAN ART. With Illustrations. Extra Crown 8vo. 14s.

BURNS.—THE POETICAL WORKS. With a Biographical Memoir by ALEXANDER SMITH. In 2 vols. fcp. 8vo. 10s.

BURY (J. B.).—A HISTORY OF THE LATER ROMAN EMPIRE FROM ARCADIUS TO IRENE, A.D. 390—800. 2 vols. 8vo. 32s.

BUTL'R (Archer).—SERMONS, DOCTRINAL AND PRACTICAL. 11th Edition. 8vo. 8s.
—— SECOND SERIES OF SERMONS. 8vo. 7s.
—— LETTERS ON ROMANISM. 8vo. 10s. 6d.

BUTLER (George).—SERMONS PREACHED IN CHELTENHAM COLLEGE CHAPEL. 8vo. 7s. 6d.

BUTLER'S HUDIBRAS. Edited by ALFRED MILNES. Fcp. 8vo. Part I. 3s. 6d. Part II. and III. 4s. 6d.

CÆSAR. *See* pp. 31, 32.

CAIRNES (Prof. J. E.).—POLITICAL ESSAYS. 8vo. 10s. 6d.
—— SOME LEADING PRINCIPLES OF POLITICAL ECONOMY NEWLY EXPOUNDED. 8vo. 14s.
—— THE SLAVE POWER. 8vo. 10s. 6d.
—— THE CHARACTER AND LOGICAL METHOD OF POLITICAL ECONOMY. Crown 8vo. 6s.

CALDERON.—SELECT PLAYS OF CALDERON. Edited by NORMAN MACCOLL, M.A. Crown 8vo. 14s.

CALDERWOOD (Prof.)—HANDBOOK OF MORAL PHILOSOPHY. Crown 8vo. 6s.
—— THE RELATIONS OF MIND AND BRAIN. 2nd Edition. 8vo. 12s.
—— THE PARABLES OF OUR LORD. Crown 8vo. 6s.
—— THE RELATIONS OF SCIENCE AND RELIGION. Crown 8vo. 5s.
—— ON TEACHING. 4th Edition. Extra fcp. 8vo. 2s. 6d.

CAMBRIDGE. COOPER'S LE KEUX'S MEMORIALS OF CAMBRIDGE. Illustrated with 90 Woodcuts in the Text, 154 Plates on Steel and Copper by LE KEUX, STORER, &c., including 20 Etchings by R. FARREN. 3 vols. 4to half levant morocco. 10*l*. 10s.

LIST OF PUBLICATIONS.

CAMBRIDGE Senate-House Problems and Riders, with Solutions:
1848—51. Riders. By Jameson. 8vo. 7s. 6d.
1875. Problems and Riders. Edited by Prof. A. G. Greenhill. Crown 8vo. 8s. 6d.
1878. Solutions by the Mathematical Moderators and Examiners. Edited by J. W. L. Glaisher, M.A. 8vo. 12s.

CAMEOS FROM ENGLISH HISTORY. See p. 54, *under* Yonge.

CAMPBELL (Dr. John M'Leod).—The Nature of the Atonement. 6th Edition. Crown 8vo. 6s.
—— Reminiscences and Reflections. Ed., with an Introductory Narrative, by his Son, Donald Campbell, M.A. Crown 8vo. 7s. 6d.
—— Responsibility for the Gift of Eternal Life. Compiled from Sermons preached at Row, in the years 1829—31. Crown 8vo. 5s.
—— Thoughts on Revelation. 2nd Edit. Crown 8vo. 5s.

CAMPBELL (J. F.).—My Circular Notes. Cheaper issue. Crown 8vo. 6s.

CANDLER (H.).—Help to Arithmetic. 2nd Edition. Globe 8vo. 2s. 6d.

CANTERBURY (His Grace Edward White, Archbishop of).—Boy-Life: its Trial, its Strength, its Fulness. Sundays in Wellington College, 1859—73. 4th Edition. Crown 8vo. 6s.
—— The Seven Gifts. Addressed to the Diocese of Canterbury in his Primary Visitation. 2nd Edition. Crown 8vo. 6s.
—— Christ and His Times. Addressed to the Diocese of Canterbury in his Second Visitation. Crown 8vo. 6s.

CARLES (W. R.).—Life in Corea. 8vo. 12s. 6d.

CARLYLE (Thomas).—Reminiscences. Ed. by Charles Eliot Norton. 2 vols. Crown 8vo. 12s.
—— Early Letters of Thomas Carlyle. Edited by C. E. Norton. 2 vols. 1814—26. Crown 8vo. 18s.
—— Letters of Thomas Carlyle. Edited by C. E. Norton. 2 vols. 1826—36. Crown 8vo. 18s.
—— Goethe and Carlyle, Correspondence between. Edited by C. E. Norton. Crown 8vo. 9s.

CARNOT—THURSTON.—Reflections on the Motive Power of Heat, and on Machines fitted to Develop that Power. From the French of N. L. S. Carnot. Edited by R. H. Thurston, LL.D. Crown 8vo. 7s. 6d.

CARPENTER (Bishop W. Boyd).—Truth in Tale. Addresses, chiefly to Children. Cr. 8vo. 4s. 6d.
—— The Permanent Elements of Religion: Bampton Lectures, 1887. Cr. 8vo. 6s.

CARR (J. Comyns).—Papers on Art. Cr. 8vo. 8s. 6d.

CARROLL (Lewis).—Alice's Adventures in Wonderland. With 42 Illustrations by Tenniel. Crown 8vo. 6s. net.
People's Edition. With all the original Illustrations. Crown 8vo. 2s. 6d. net.
  A German Translation of the same. Crown 8vo, gilt. 6s. net.
  A French Translation of the same. Crown 8vo, gilt. 6s. net.
  An Italian Translation of the same. Crown 8vo, gilt. 6s. net.
—— Alice's Adventures Under-ground. Being a Facsimile of the Original MS. Book, afterwards developed into "Alice's Adventures in Wonderland." With 27 Illustrations by the Author. Crown 8vo. 4s. net.
—— Through the Looking-Glass and What Alice Found There. With 50 Illustrations by Tenniel. Cr. 8vo, gilt. 6s. net.
People's Edition. With all the original Illustrations. Crown 8vo. 2s. 6d. net.
People's Edition of "Alice's Adventures in Wonderland," and "Through the Looking-Glass." 1 vol. Crown 8vo. 4s. 6d. net.
—— The Game of Logic. Cr. 8vo. 3s. net.
—— Rhyme? and Reason? With 65 Illustrations by Arthur B. Frost, and 9 by Henry Holiday. Crown 8vo. 6s. net.
—— A Tangled Tale. Reprinted from the "Monthly Packet." With 6 Illustrations by Arthur B. Frost. Crn. 8vo. 4s. 6d. net.
—— Sylvie and Bruno. With 46 Illustrations by Harry Furniss. Cr. 8vo. 7s 6d. net.
—— The Nursery "Alice." Twenty Coloured Enlargements from Tenniel's Illustrations to "Alice's Adventures in Wonderland," with Text adapted to Nursery Readers. 4to. 4s. net.
—— The Hunting of The Snark, An Agony in Eight Fits. With 9 Illustrations by Henry Holiday. Cr. 8vo. 4s. 6d. net.

CARSTARES (Wm.): A Character and Career of the Revolutionary Epoch (1649—1715). By R. H. Story. 8vo. 12s.

CARTER (R. Brudenell, F.C.S.).—A Practical Treatise on Diseases of the Eye. 8vo. 16s.
—— Eyesight, Good and Bad. Cr. 8vo. 6s.
—— Modern Operations for Cataract. 8vo. 6s.

CASSEL (Dr. D.).—Manual of Jewish History and Literature. Translated by Mrs. Henry Lucas. Fcp. 8vo. 2s. 6d.

CAUCASUS: Notes on the. By "Wanderer." 8vo. 9s.

CAUTLEY (G. S.).—A Century of Emblems. With Illustrations by the Lady Marian Alford. Small 4to. 10s. 6d.

CAZENOVE (J. Gibson).—Concerning the Being and Attributes of God. 8vo. 5s.

CHALMERS (J. B.).—Graphical Determination of Forces in Engineering Structures. 8vo. 24s.

CHASSERESSE (D.).—Sporting Sketches. Illustrated. Crown 8vo. 3s. 6d.

CHATTERTON: A BIOGRAPHICAL STUDY. By Sir DANIEL WILSON, LL.D. Crown 8vo. 6s. 6d.

CHERRY (Prof. R. R.).—LECTURES ON THE GROWTH OF CRIMINAL LAW IN ANCIENT COMMUNITIES. 8vo. 5s. net.

CHEYNE (C. H. H.).—AN ELEMENTARY TREATISE ON THE PLANETARY THEORY. Crown 8vo. 7s. 6d.

CHEYNE (T. K.).—THE BOOK OF ISAIAH CHRONOLOGICALLY ARRANGED. Crown 8vo. 7s. 6d.

CHOICE NOTES ON THE FOUR GOSPELS, drawn from Old and New Sources. Crown 8vo. 4 vols. 4s. 6d. each. (St. Matthew and St. Mark in 1 vol. 9s.)

CHRISTIE (J.).—CHOLERA EPIDEMICS IN EAST AFRICA. 8vo. 15s.

CHRISTIE (J. R.).—ELEMENTARY TEST QUESTIONS IN PURE AND MIXED MATHEMATICS. Crown 8vo. 8s. 6d.

CHRISTMAS CAROL, A. Printed in Colours, with Illuminated Borders from MSS. of the Fourteenth and Fifteenth Centuries. 4to. 21s.

CHURCH (Very Rev. R. W.).—THE SACRED POETRY OF EARLY RELIGIONS. 2nd Edition. 12mo. 1s.

—— HUMAN LIFE AND ITS CONDITIONS. Cr. 8vo. 6s.

—— THE GIFTS OF CIVILISATION, and other Sermons. 2nd Edition. Crown 8vo. 7s. 6d.

—— DISCIPLINE OF THE CHRISTIAN CHARACTER, and other Sermons. Crown 8vo. 4s. 6d.

—— ADVENT SERMONS. 1885. Cr. 8vo. 4s. 6d.

—— MISCELLANEOUS WRITINGS. Collected Edition. 5 vols. Globe 8vo. 5s. each.
Vol. I. MISCELLANEOUS ESSAYS. II. DANTE: AND OTHER ESSAYS. III. ST. ANSELM. IV. SPENSER. V. BACON.

—— THE OXFORD MOVEMENT. 1833—45. 8vo. 12s. 6d. net.

CHURCH (Rev. A. J.).—LATIN VERSION OF SELECTIONS FROM TENNYSON. By Prof. CONINGTON, Prof. SEELEY, Dr. HESSEY, T. E. KEBBEL, &c. Edited by A. J. CHURCH, M.A. Extra fcp. 8vo. 6s.

—— STORIES FROM THE BIBLE. Illustrated. Crown 8vo. 5s.

CICERO. THE LIFE AND LETTERS OF MARCUS TULLIUS CICERO. By the Rev. G. E. JEANS, M.A. 2nd Edition. Crown 8vo. 10s. 6d.

—— THE ACADEMICA. The Text revised and explained by J. S. REID, M.L. 8vo. 15s.

—— THE ACADEMICS. Translated by J. S. REID, M.L. 8vo. 5s. 6d.

See also pp. 31, 32.

CLARK. MEMORIALS FROM JOURNALS AND LETTERS OF SAMUEL CLARK, M.A. Edited by his Wife. Crown 8vo. 7s. 6d.

CLARK (L.) and SADLER (H.).—THE STAR GUIDE. Royal 8vo. 5s.

CLARKE (C. B.).—A GEOGRAPHICAL READER AND COMPANION TO THE ATLAS. Cr. 8vo. 2s.

—— A CLASS-BOOK OF GEOGRAPHY. With 18 Coloured Maps. Fcp. 8vo. 3s.; swd., 2s. 6d.

—— SPECULATIONS FROM POLITICAL ECONOMY. Crown 8vo. 3s. 6d.

CLASSICAL WRITERS. Edited by JOHN RICHARD GREEN. Fcp. 8vo. 1s. 6d. each.
EURIPIDES. By Prof. MAHAFFY.
MILTON. By STOPFORD A. BROOKE.
LIVY. By the Rev. W. W. CAPES, M.A.
VERGIL. By Prof. NETTLESHIP, M.A.
SOPHOCLES. By Prof. L. CAMPBELL, M.A.
DEMOSTHENES. By Prof. BUTCHER, M.A.
TACITUS. By CHURCH and BRODRIBB.

CLAUSIUS (R.).—THE MECHANICAL THEORY OF HEAT. Translated by WALTER R. BROWNE. Crown 8vo. 10s. 6d.

CLERGYMAN'S SELF-EXAMINATION CONCERNING THE APOSTLES' CREED. Extra fcp. 8vo. 1s. 6d.

CLIFFORD (Prof. W. K.).—ELEMENTS OF DYNAMIC. An Introduction to the Study of Motion and Rest in Solid and Fluid Bodies. Crown 8vo. Part I. Kinematic. Books I.—III. 7s. 6d. Book IV. and Appendix, 6s.

—— LECTURES AND ESSAYS. Ed. by LESLIE STEPHEN and Sir F. POLLOCK. Cr. 8vo. 8s. 6d.

—— SEEING AND THINKING. With Diagrams. Crown 8vo. 3s. 6d.

—— MATHEMATICAL PAPERS. Edited by R. TUCKER. With an Introduction by H. J. STEPHEN SMITH, M.A. 8vo. 30s.

CLIFFORD (Mrs. W. K.).—ANYHOW STORIES. With Illustrations by DOROTHY TENNANT. Crown 8vo. 1s. 6d.; paper covers, 1s.

CLOUGH (A. H.).—POEMS. New Edition. Crown 8vo. 7s. 6d.

—— PROSE REMAINS. With a Selection from his Letters, and a Memoir by his Wife. Crown 8vo. 7s. 6d.

COAL: ITS HISTORY AND ITS USES. By Profs. GREEN, MIALL, THORPE, RÜCKER, and MARSHALL. 8vo. 12s. 6d.

COBDEN (Richard.).—SPEECHES ON QUESTIONS OF PUBLIC POLICY. Ed. by J. BRIGHT and J. E. THOROLD ROGERS. Globe 8vo. 3s. 6d.

COCKSHOTT (A.) and WALTERS (F. B.). —A TREATISE ON GEOMETRICAL CONICS. Crown 8vo. 5s.

COHEN (Dr. Julius B.).—THE OWENS COLLEGE COURSE OF PRACTICAL ORGANIC CHEMISTRY. Fcp. 8vo. 2s. 6d.

COLENSO (Bp.).—THE COMMUNION SERVICE FROM THE BOOK OF COMMON PRAYER, WITH SELECT READINGS FROM THE WRITINGS OF THE REV. F. D. MAURICE. Edited by BISHOP COLENSO. 6th Edition. 16mo. 2s. 6d.

COLERIDGE.—THE POETICAL AND DRAMATIC WORKS OF SAMUEL TAYLOR COLERIDGE. 4 vols. Fcp. 8vo. 31s. 6d.
Also an Edition on Large Paper, 2l. 12s. 6d.

COLLECTS OF THE CHURCH OF ENGLAND. With a Coloured Floral Design to each Collect. Crown 8vo. 12s.

COLLIER (Hon. John).—A PRIMER OF ART. 18mo. 1s.

COLSON (F. H.).—FIRST GREEK READER. Stories and Legends. With Notes, Vocabulary, and Exercises. Globe 8vo. 3s.

COMBE. LIFE OF GEORGE COMBE. By CHARLES GIBBON. 2 vols. 8vo. 32s.

—— EDUCATION: ITS PRINCIPLES AND PRACTICE AS DEVELOPED BY GEORGE COMBE. Edited by WILLIAM JOLLY. 8vo. 15s.

CONGREVE (Rev. John).—HIGH HOPES AND PLEADINGS FOR A REASONABLE FAITH, NOBLER THOUGHTS, LARGER CHARITY. Crown 8vo. 5s.

CONSTABLE (Samuel). GEOMETRICAL EXERCISES FOR BEGINNERS. Cr. 8vo. 3s. 6d.

COOK (E. T.).—A POPULAR HANDBOOK TO THE NATIONAL GALLERY. Including, by special permission, Notes collected from the Works of Mr. RUSKIN. 3rd Edition. Crown 8vo, half morocco. 14s.

Also an Edition on Large Paper, limited to 250 copies. 2 vols. 8vo.

COOKE (Josiah P., jun.).—PRINCIPLES OF CHEMICAL PHILOSOPHY. New Ed. 8vo. 16s.

—— RELIGION AND CHEMISTRY. Crown 8vo. 7s. 6d.

—— ELEMENTS OF CHEMICAL PHYSICS. 4th Edition. Royal 8vo. 21s.

COOKERY. MIDDLE CLASS BOOK. Compiled for the Manchester School of Cookery. Fcp. 8vo. 1s. 6d.

CO-OPERATION IN THE UNITED STATES: HISTORY OF. Edited by H. B. ADAMS. 8vo. 15s.

COPE (E. D.).—THE ORIGIN OF THE FITTEST. Essays on Evolution. 8vo. 12s. 6d.

COPE (E. M.).—AN INTRODUCTION TO ARISTOTLE'S RHETORIC. 8vo. 14s.

CORBETT (Julian).—THE FALL OF ASGARD: A Tale of St. Olaf's Day. 2 vols. 12s.

—— FOR GOD AND GOLD. Crown 8vo. 6s.

—— KOPHETUA THE THIRTEENTH. 2 vols. Globe 8vo. 12s.

CORE (T. H.).—QUESTIONS ON BALFOUR STEWART'S "LESSONS IN ELEMENTARY PHYSICS." Fcp. 8vo. 2s.

CORFIELD Dr. W. H.).—THE TREATMENT AND UTILISATION OF SEWAGE. 3rd Edition, Revised by the Author, and by LOUIS C. PARKES, M.D. 8vo. 16s.

CORNELL UNIVERSITY STUDIES IN CLASSICAL PHILOLOGY. Edited by I. FLAGG, W. G. HALE, and B. I. WHEELER. I. The C U M-Constructions: their History and Functions. Part I. Critical. 1s. 8d. net. Part II. Constructive. By W. G. HALE. 3s. 4d. net. II. Analogy and the Scope of its Application in Language. By B. I. WHEELER. 1s. 3d. net.

COSSA.—GUIDE TO THE STUDY OF POLITICAL ECONOMY. From the Italian of Dr. LUIGI COSSA. Crown 8vo. 4s. 6d.

COTTERILL (Prof. James H.).—APPLIED MECHANICS: An Introduction to the Theory of Structures and Machines. 2nd Edition. Med. 8vo. 18s.

COTTERILL (Prof. J. H.) and SLADE (J. H.). — LESSONS IN APPLIED MECHANICS. Fcp. 8vo. 5s. 6d.

COTTON (Bishop).—SERMONS PREACHED TO ENGLISH CONGREGATIONS IN INDIA. Crown 8vo. 7s. 6d.

COUES (Elliott).—KEY TO NORTH AMERICAN BIRDS. Illustrated. 8vo. 2l. 2s.

—— HANDBOOK OF FIELD AND GENERAL ORNITHOLOGY. Illustrated. 8vo. 10s. net.

COX (G. V.).—RECOLLECTIONS OF OXFORD. 2nd Edition. Crown 8vo. 6s.

CRAIK (Mrs.).—POEMS. New and Enlarged Edition. Extra fcp. 8vo. 6s.

—— CHILDREN'S POETRY. Ex. fcp. 8vo. 4s. 6d.

—— SONGS OF OUR YOUTH. Small 4to. 6s.

—— CONCERNING MEN: AND OTHER PAPERS. Crown 8vo. 4s. 6d.

—— ABOUT MONEY: AND OTHER THINGS. Crown 8vo. 6s.

—— SERMONS OUT OF CHURCH. Cr. 8vo. 6s.

—— AN UNKNOWN COUNTRY. Illustrated by F. NOEL PATON. Royal 8vo. 7s. 6d.

—— ALICE LEARMONT: A FAIRY TALE. With Illustrations. 4s. 6d.

—— AN UNSENTIMENTAL JOURNEY THROUGH CORNWALL. Illustrated. 4to. 12s. 6d.

—— OUR YEAR: A CHILD'S BOOK IN PROSE AND VERSE. Illustrated. 2s. 6d.

—— LITTLE SUNSHINE'S HOLIDAY. Globe 8vo. 2s. 6d.

—— THE ADVENTURES OF A BROWNIE. Illustrated by Mrs. ALLINGHAM. 4s. 6d.

—— THE LITTLE LAME PRINCE AND HIS TRAVELLING CLOAK. A Parable for Old and Young. With 24 Illustrations by J. McL. RALSTON. Crown 8vo. 4s. 6d.

—— THE FAIRY BOOK: THE BEST POPULAR FAIRY STORIES. 18mo. 4s. 6d.

See also p. 29.

CRAIK (Henry).—THE STATE IN ITS RELATION TO EDUCATION. Crown 8vo. 3s. 6d.

CRANE (Lucy).—LECTURES ON ART AND THE FORMATION OF TASTE. Cr. 8vo. 6s.

CRANE (Walter).—THE SIRENS THREE. A Poem. Written and Illustrated by WALTER CRANE. Royal 8vo. 10s. 6d.

CRAVEN (Mrs. Dacre).—A GUIDE TO DISTRICT NURSES. Crown 8vo. 2s. 6d.

CRAWFORD (F. Marion).—A CIGARETTE MAKER'S ROMANCE. Crown 8vo. 6s.

—— KHALED. 2 vols. Globe 8vo.

See also p. 29.

CROSS (Rev. J. A.).—BIBLE READINGS SELECTED FROM THE PENTATEUCH AND THE BOOK OF JOSHUA. 2nd Ed. Globe 8vo. 2s. 6d.

CROSSLEY (E.), GLEDHILL (J.), and WILSON (J. M.).—A HANDBOOK OF DOUBLE STARS. 8vo. 21s.—CORRECTIONS TO THE SAME. 8vo. 1s.

CUMMING (Linnæus).—ELECTRICITY. An Introduction to the Theory of Electricity. With numerous Examples. Cr. 8vo. 8s. 6d.

CUNNINGHAM (Rev. John). — THE GROWTH OF THE CHURCH IN ITS ORGANISATION AND INSTITUTIONS. Being the Croall Lectures for 1886. 8vo. 9s.

CUNNINGHAM (Rev. W.).— THE EPISTLE OF ST. BARNABAS. A Dissertation, including a Discussion of its Date and Authorship. Together with the Greek Text, the Latin Version, and a New English Translation and Commentary. Crown 8vo. 7s. 6d.

—— CHRISTIAN CIVILISATION, WITH SPECIAL REFERENCE TO INDIA. Crown 8vo. 5s.

—— THE CHURCHES OF ASIA: A METHODICAL SKETCH OF THE SECOND CENTURY. Crown 8vo. 6s.

CUNYNGHAME (Gen. Sir A. T.).—MY COMMAND IN SOUTH AFRICA, 1874—78. 8vo. 12s. 6d.

CURTEIS (Rev. G. H.).—DISSENT IN ITS RELATION TO THE CHURCH OF ENGLAND. Bampton Lectures for 1871. Cr. 8vo. 7s. 6d.

——THE SCIENTIFIC OBSTACLES TO CHRISTIAN BELIEF. The Boyle Lectures, 1884. Cr. 8vo. 6s.

CUTHBERTSON (Francis). — EUCLIDIAN GEOMETRY. Extra fcp. 8vo. 4s. 6d.

DAGONET THE JESTER. Cr. 8vo. 4s. 6d.

DAHN (Felix). FELICITAS. Translated by M. A. C. E. Crown 8vo. 4s. 6d.

"DAILY NEWS."—CORRESPONDENCE OF THE WAR BETWEEN RUSSIA AND TURKEY, 1877. TO THE FALL OF KARS. Cr. 8vo. 6s.

——CORRESPONDENCE OF THE RUSSO-TURKISH WAR. FROM THE FALL OF KARS TO THE CONCLUSION OF PEACE. Crown 8vo. 6s.

DALE (A. W. W.).—THE SYNOD OF ELVIRA, AND CHRISTIAN LIFE IN THE FOURTH CENTURY. Crown 8vo. 10s. 6d.

DALTON (Rev. T.).—RULES AND EXAMPLES IN ARITHMETIC. New Edition. 18mo. 2s. 6d.

—— RULES AND EXAMPLES IN ALGEBRA. Part I. New Edit. 18mo. 2s. Part II. 2s. 6d. KEY TO ALGEBRA. Part I. Crn. 8vo. 7s. 6d.

DAMIEN (Father.): A JOURNEY FROM CASHMERE TO HIS HOME IN HAWAII. By EDWARD CLIFFORD. Portrait. Crown 8vo. 2s. 6d.

DANIELL (Alfred). A TEXT-BOOK OF THE PRINCIPLES OF PHYSICS. With Illustrations. 2nd Edition. Medium 8vo. 21s.

DANTE.—THE PURGATORY OF DANTE ALIGHIERI. Edited, with Translations and Notes, by A. J. BUTLER. Cr. 8vo. 12s. 6d.

—— THE PARADISO OF DANTE. Edited, with a Prose Translation and Notes, by A. J. BUTLER. 2nd Edit. Crown 8vo. 12s. 6d.

—— DE MONARCHIA. Translated by F. J. CHURCH. 8vo. 4s. 6d.

—— DANTE: AND OTHER ESSAYS. By DEAN CHURCH. Globe 8vo. 5s.

—— READINGS ON THE PURGATORIO OF DANTE. Chiefly based on the Commentary of Benvenuto Da Imola. By the Hon. W. W. VERNON, M.A. With an Introduction by DEAN CHURCH. 2 vols. Crn. 8vo. 24s.

DARWIN (CHAS.): MEMORIAL NOTICES, reprinted from Nature. By T. H. HUXLEY, G. J. ROMANES, ARCHIBALD GEIKIE, and W. THISELTON DYER. With a Portrait. Crown 8vo. 2s. 6d.

DAVIES (Rev. J. Llewellyn).—THE GOSPEL AND MODERN LIFE. 2nd Edition, to which is added MORALITY ACCORDING TO THE SACRAMENT OF THE LORD'S SUPPER. Extra fcp. 8vo. 6s.

—— WARNINGS AGAINST SUPERSTITION. Ex. fcp. 8vo. 2s. 6d.

—— THE CHRISTIAN CALLING. Ex. fcp. 8vo. 6s.

—— THE EPISTLES OF ST. PAUL TO THE EPHESIANS, THE COLOSSIANS, AND PHILEMON. With Introductions and Notes. 2nd Edition. 8vo. 7s. 6d.

—— SOCIAL QUESTIONS FROM THE POINT OF VIEW OF CHRISTIAN THEOLOGY. 2nd Ed. Crown 8vo. 6s.

—— ORDER AND GROWTH AS INVOLVED IN THE SPIRITUAL CONSTITUTION OF HUMAN SOCIETY. Crown 8vo.

DAWKINS (Prof. W. Boyd).—EARLY MAN IN BRITAIN AND HIS PLACE IN THE TERTIARY PERIOD. Medium 8vo. 25s.

DAWSON (Sir J. W.).—ACADIAN GEOLOGY, THE GEOLOGICAL STRUCTURE, ORGANIC REMAINS, AND MINERAL RESOURCES OF NOVA SCOTIA, NEW BRUNSWICK, AND PRINCE EDWARD ISLAND. 3rd Ed. 8vo. 21s.

DAWSON (James).—AUSTRALIAN ABORIGINES. Small 4to. 14s.

DAY (H. G.).—PROPERTIES OF CONIC SECTIONS PROVED GEOMETRICALLY. Crown 8vo. 3s. 6d.

DAY (Rev. Lal Behari).—BENGAL PEASANT LIFE. Crown 8vo. 6s.

—— FOLK TALES OF BENGAL. Cr. 8vo. 4s. 6d.

DAY (R. E.).—ELECTRIC LIGHT ARITHMETIC. Pott 8vo. 2s.

DAYS WITH SIR ROGER DE COVERLEY. From the Spectator. With Illustrations by HUGH THOMSON. Fcp. 4to. 6s.

DEÁK (FRANCIS): HUNGARIAN STATESMAN. A Memoir. 8vo. 12s. 6d.

DEAKIN (R.).—RIDER PAPERS ON EUCLID Books I. and II. 18mo. 1s.

DELAMOTTE (Prof. P. H.).—A BEGINNER'S DRAWING-BOOK. Progressively arranged. With Plates. 3rd Edit. Crn. 8vo. 3s. 6d.

DEMOCRACY: AN AMERICAN NOVEL. Crown 8vo. 4s. 6d.

DE MORGAN (Mary).—THE NECKLACE OF PRINCESS FIORIMONDE, AND OTHER STORIES. Illustrated by WALTER CRANE. Extra fcp. 8vo. 3s. 6d. Also a Large Paper Edition, with the Illustrations on India Paper. 100 copies only printed.

DEMOSTHENES.—See p. 32.

DE VERE (Aubrey). ESSAYS CHIEFLY ON POETRY. 2 vols. Globe 8vo. 12s.

—— ESSAYS, CHIEFLY LITERARY AND ETHICAL. Globe 8vo. 6s.

DICEY (Prof. A. V.).—LECTURES INTRODUCTORY TO THE STUDY OF THE LAW OF THE CONSTITUTION. 3rd Edition. 8vo. 12s. 6d.

LIST OF PUBLICATIONS.

DICEY (Prof. A. V.).—LETTERS ON UNIONIST DELUSIONS. Crown 8vo. 2s. 6d.
—— THE PRIVY COUNCIL. Crown 8vo. 3s. 6d.

DICKENS (Charles). — THE POSTHUMOUS PAPERS OF THE PICKWICK CLUB. With Notes and numerous Illustrations. Edited by CHARLES DICKENS the younger. 2 vols. Extra crown 8vo. 21s.

DICKSON (R.) and EDMOND (J. P.).— ANNALS OF SCOTTISH PRINTING, FROM THE INTRODUCTION OF THE ART IN 1507 TO THE BEGINNING OF THE SEVENTEENTH CENTURY. Dutch hand-made paper. Demy 4to, buckram, 2l. 2s. net.—Royal 4to, 2 vols. half Japanese vellum, 4l. 4s. net.

DIDEROT AND THE ENCYCLOPÆDISTS. By JOHN MORLEY. 2 vols. Globe 8vo. 10s.

DIGGLE (Rev. J. W.).—GODLINESS AND MANLINESS. A Miscellany of Brief Papers touching the Relation of Religion to Life. Crown 8vo. 6s.

DILETTANTI SOCIETY'S PUBLICATIONS.—ANTIQUITIES OF IONIA. Vols. I. II. and III. 2l. 2s. each, or 5l. 5s. the set, net. Vol. IV., folio, half mor., 3l. 13s. 6d. net.
—— PENROSE (Francis C.). An Investigation of the Principles of Athenian Architecture. Illustrated by numerous engravings. New Edition. Enlarged. Folio. 7l. 7s. net.
—— SPECIMENS OF ANCIENT SCULPTURE: EGYPTIAN, ETRUSCAN, GREEK, AND ROMAN. Selected from different Collections in Great Britain by the Society of Dilettanti. Vol. II. Folio. 5l. 5s. net.

DILKE (Sir C. W.). GREATER BRITAIN. A RECORD OF TRAVEL IN ENGLISH-SPEAKING COUNTRIES DURING 1866-67. (America, Australia, India.) 9th Edition. Crown 8vo. 6s.
—— PROBLEMS OF GREATER BRITAIN. Maps. 4th Edition. Extra crown 8vo. 12s. 6d.

DILLWYN (E. A.).—JILL. Crown 8vo. 6s.
—— JILL AND JACK. 2 vols. Globe 8vo. 12s.

DODGSON (C. L.). EUCLID. Books I. and II. With Words substituted for the Algebraical Symbols used in the first edition. 4th Edition. Crown 8vo. 2s.
—— EUCLID AND HIS MODERN RIVALS. 2nd Edition. Cr. 8vo. 6s.
—— SUPPLEMENT TO FIRST EDITION OF "EUCLID AND HIS MODERN RIVALS." Cr. 8vo. Sewed, 1s.
—— CURIOSA MATHEMATICA. Part I. A New Theory of Parallels. 3rd Ed. Cr. 8vo. 2s.

DONALDSON (Prof. James).—THE APOSTOLICAL FATHERS. A CRITICAL ACCOUNT OF THEIR GENUINE WRITINGS, AND OF THEIR DOCTRINES. 2nd Ed. Cr. 8vo. 7s. 6d.

DONISTHORPE (Wordsworth). — INDIVIDUALISM: A SYSTEM OF POLITICS. 8vo. 14s.

DOYLE (Sir F. H.).—THE RETURN OF THE GUARDS: AND OTHER POEMS. Cr. 8vo. 7s. 6d.

DREW (W. H.).—A GEOMETRICAL TREATISE ON CONIC SECTIONS. 8th Ed. Cr. 8vo. 5s.

DRUMMOND (Prof. James).—INTRODUCTION TO THE STUDY OF THEOLOGY. Crown 8vo. 5s.

DRYDEN: ESSAYS OF. Edited by Prof. C. D. YONGE. Fcp. 8vo. 2s. 6d.

DUFF (Right Hon. Sir M. E. Grant). NOTES OF AN INDIAN JOURNEY. 8vo. 10s. 6d.
—— MISCELLANIES, POLITICAL AND LITERARY. 8vo. 10s. 6d.

DÜNTZER (H.).—LIFE OF GOETHE. Translated by T. W. LYSTER. With Illustrations. 2 vols. Crown 8vo. 21s.
—— LIFE OF SCHILLER. Translated by P. E. PINKERTON. Illustrations. Cr. 8vo. 10s. 6d.

DUPUIS (Prof. N. F.).— ELEMENTARY SYNTHETIC GEOMETRY OF THE POINT, LINE, AND CIRCLE IN THE PLANE. Gl. 8vo. 4s. 6d.

DYER (J. M.).- EXERCISES IN ANALYTICAL GEOMETRY. Crown 8vo. 4s. 6d.

DYER (Louis).—STUDIES OF THE GODS IN GREECE AT CERTAIN SANCTUARIES RECENTLY EXCAVATED. Extra crown 8vo.

DYNAMICS, SYLLABUS OF ELEMENTARY. Part I. LINEAR DYNAMICS. With an Appendix on the Meanings of the Symbols in Physical Equations. Prepared by the Association for the Improvement of Geometrical Teaching. 4to, sewed. 1s.

EADIE (Prof. John).—THE ENGLISH BIBLE: AN EXTERNAL AND CRITICAL HISTORY OF THE VARIOUS ENGLISH TRANSLATIONS OF SCRIPTURE. 2 vols. 8vo. 28s.
—— ST. PAUL'S EPISTLES TO THE THESSALONIANS, COMMENTARY ON THE GREEK TEXT. 8vo. 12s.
—— LIFE OF JOHN EADIE, D.D., LL.D. By JAMES BROWN, D.D. 2nd Ed. Cr. 8vo. 7s. 6d.

EAGLES (T. H.).--CONSTRUCTIVE GEOMETRY OF PLANE CURVES. Crown 8vo. 12s.

EASTLAKE (Lady).—FELLOWSHIP: LETTERS ADDRESSED TO MY SISTER-MOURNERS. Cr. 8vo. 2s. 6d.

EBERS (Dr. George).—THE BURGOMASTER'S WIFE. Translated by CLARA BELL. Crown 8vo. 4s. 6d.
—— ONLY A WORD. Translated by CLARA BELL. Crown 8vo. 4s. 6d.

ECCE HOMO. A SURVEY OF THE LIFE AND WORK OF JESUS CHRIST. 20th Ed. Cr. 8vo. 6s.

ECONOMIC JOURNAL (THE). Edited by F. Y. EDGEWORTH. No. 1, Ap. 1891. 8vo. 5s.

ECONOMICS, THE QUARTERLY JOURNAL OF. Vol. II. Parts II. III. IV. 2s. 6d. each; Vol. III. 4 parts, 2s. 6d. each; Vol. IV. 4 parts, 2s. 6d. each. Vol. V. Part I. 2s. 6d. net.

EDGAR (J. H.) and PRITCHARD (G. S.).— NOTE-BOOK ON PRACTICAL SOLID OR DESCRIPTIVE GEOMETRY, CONTAINING PROBLEMS WITH HELP FOR SOLUTION. 4th Edition, Enlarged. By ARTHUR G. MEEZE. Globe 8vo. 4s. 6d.

EDWARDS (Joseph). — AN ELEMENTARY TREATISE ON THE DIFFERENTIAL CALCULUS. Crown 8vo. 10s. 6d.

EDWARDS-MOSS (Sir J. E.).—A SEASON IN SUTHERLAND. Crown 8vo. 1s. 6d.

EICKE (K. M.).—FIRST LESSONS IN LATIN. Extra fcp. 8vo. 2s.

EIMER (G. H. T.).—ORGANIC EVOLUTION AS THE RESULT OF THE INHERITANCE OF ACQUIRED CHARACTERS ACCORDING TO THE LAWS OF ORGANIC GROWTH. Translated by J. T. CUNNINGHAM, M.A. 8vo. 12s. 6d.

ELDERTON (W. A.).—MAPS AND MAP DRAWING. Pott 8vo. 1s.

ELLERTON (Rev. John).—THE HOLIEST MANHOOD, AND ITS LESSONS FOR BUSY LIVES. Crown 8vo. 6s.

ELLIOTT. LIFE OF HENRY VENN ELLIOTT, OF BRIGHTON. By JOSIAH BATEMAN, M.A. 3rd Edition. Extra fcp. 8vo. 6s.

ELLIS (A. J.).—PRACTICAL HINTS ON THE QUANTITATIVE PRONUNCIATION OF LATIN. Extra fcp. 8vo. 4s. 6d.

ELLIS (Tristram).—SKETCHING FROM NATURE. Illustr. by H. STACY MARKS, R.A., and the Author. 2nd Edition. Cr. 8vo. 3s. 6d.

EMERSON. THE LIFE OF RALPH WALDO EMERSON. By J. L. CABOT. 2 vols. Crown 8vo. 18s.

—— THE COLLECTED WORKS OF RALPH WALDO EMERSON. 6 vols. (1) MISCELLANIES. With an Introductory Essay by JOHN MORLEY. (2) ESSAYS. (3) POEMS. (4) ENGLISH TRAITS; AND REPRESENTATIVE MEN. (5) CONDUCT OF LIFE; AND SOCIETY AND SOLITUDE. (6) LETTERS; AND SOCIAL AIMS, &c. Globe 8vo. 5s. each.

ENGLAND (E. B.).—EXERCISES IN LATIN SYNTAX AND IDIOM. Arranged with reference to Roby's School Latin Grammar. Crn. 8vo. 2s. 6d.—KEY. Crn. 8vo. 2s. 6d.

ENGLISH CITIZEN (THE).—A Series of Short Books on his Rights and Responsibilities. Edited by HENRY CRAIK, C.B. Crown 8vo. 3s. 6d. each.

CENTRAL GOVERNMENT. By H. D. TRAILL.
THE ELECTORATE AND THE LEGISLATURE. By SPENCER WALPOLE.
THE POOR LAW. By the Rev. T. W. FOWLE.
THE NATIONAL BUDGET; THE NATIONAL DEBT; TAXES AND RATES. By A. J. WILSON.
THE STATE IN RELATION TO LABOUR. By W. STANLEY JEVONS, LL.D., F.R.S.
THE STATE AND THE CHURCH. By the Hon. ARTHUR ELLIOTT, M.P.
FOREIGN RELATIONS. By SPENCER WALPOLE.
THE STATE IN ITS RELATION TO TRADE. By Sir T. H. FARRER, Bart.
LOCAL GOVERNMENT. By M. D. CHALMERS.
THE STATE IN ITS RELATION TO EDUCATION. By HENRY CRAIK, C.B.
THE LAND LAWS. By Sir F. POLLOCK, Bart. 2nd Edition.
COLONIES AND DEPENDENCIES. Part I. INDIA. By J. S. COTTON, M.A. II. THE COLONIES. By E. J. PAYNE.
JUSTICE AND POLICE. By F. W. MAITLAND.
THE PUNISHMENT AND PREVENTION OF CRIME. By Colonel Sir EDMUND DU CANE.
THE NATIONAL DEFENCES. By Colonel MAURICE, R.A. (In the Press.)

ENGLISH CLASSICS. With Introductions and Notes. Globe 8vo.
BACON.—ESSAYS. Edited by F. G. SELBY, M.A. 3s.; sewed, 2s. 6d.
BURKE.—REFLECTIONS ON THE FRENCH REVOLUTION. By the same. 3s.

ENGLISH CLASSICS—continued.
GOLDSMITH.—THE TRAVELLER AND THE DESERTED VILLAGE. Edited by ARTHUR BARRETT, B.A. 1s. 9d.; sewed, 1s. 6d.—THE TRAVELLER (separately), sewed, 1s.
HELPS; ESSAYS WRITTEN IN THE INTERVALS OF BUSINESS. Edit. by F. J. ROWE and W. T. WEBB. 1s. 9d.; sewed, 1s. 6d.
MILTON—PARADISE LOST, BOOKS I. and II. Edited by M. MACMILLAN, B.A. 1s. 9d.; sewed, 1s. 6d.—BOOKS I. and II. (separately), 1s. 3d. each; sewed, 1s. each.
— L'ALLEGRO, IL PENSEROSO, LYCIDAS, ARCADES, SONNETS, ETC. Edit. by WM. BELL, M.A. 1s. 9d.; sewed, 1s. 6d.
— COMUS. By the same. 1s. 3d.; swd. 1s.
— SAMSON AGONISTES. Edited by H. M. PERCIVAL, M.A. 2s.; sewed, 1s. 9d.
SCOTT.—THE LAY OF THE LAST MINSTREL. By G. H. STUART, M.A., and E. H. ELLIOT, B.A. Canto I. 9d.; Cantos I.-III. 1s. 3d.; sewed, 1s. Cantos IV.-VI. 1s. 3d.; sewed, 1s.
— MARMION. Edited by MICHAEL MACMILLAN, B.A. 3s.; sewed, 2s. 6d.
— ROKEBY. By the same. 3s.; swd. 2s. 6d.
— THE LADY OF THE LAKE. Edited by G. H. STUART, M.A. 2s. 6d.; sewed, 2s.
SHAKESPEARE—THE TEMPEST. Edited by K. DEIGHTON. 1s. 9d.; sewed, 1s. 6d.
— MUCH ADO ABOUT NOTHING. By the same. 2s.; sewed, 1s. 9d.
— A MIDSUMMER NIGHT'S DREAM. By the same. 1s. 9d.; sewed, 1s. 6d.
— THE MERCHANT OF VENICE. By the same. 1s. 9d.; sewed, 1s. 6d.
— AS YOU LIKE IT. By the same.
— TWELFTH NIGHT. By the same. 1s. 9d.; sewed, 1s. 6d.
— THE WINTER'S TALE. By the same. 2s.; sewed, 1s. 9d.
— KING JOHN. By the same. 1s. 9d.; sewed, 1s. 6d.
— RICHARD II. By the same. 1s. 9d.; sewed, 1s. 6d.
— HENRY V. By the same. 1s. 9d.; swd. 1s. 6d.
— RICHARD III. Edited by C. H. TAWNEY, M.A. 2s. 6d.; sewed, 2s.
— CORIOLANUS. Edited by K. DEIGHTON. 2s. 6d.; sewed, 2s.
— JULIUS CÆSAR. By the same. 1s. 9d.; sewed, 1s. 6d.
— MACBETH. By the same. 1s. 9d.; swd. 1s. 6d.
— HAMLET. By the same. 2s. 6d.; sewed, 2s.
— KING LEAR. By the same.
— OTHELLO. By the same. 2s.; swd. 1s. 9d.
— ANTONY AND CLEOPATRA. By the same.
— CYMBELINE. By the same. 2s. 6d.; swd. 2s.
SOUTHEY.—LIFE OF NELSON. By MICHAEL MACMILLAN, B.A. 3s.; sewed, 2s. 6d.
TENNYSON.—SELECTIONS. By F. J. ROWE, M.A., and W. T. WEBB, M.A. 3s. 6d.
— THE COMING OF ARTHUR, AND THE PASSING OF ARTHUR. By F. J. ROWE. 2s.
— ENOCH ARDEN. Edit. by W. T. WEBB

ENGLISH HISTORY, READINGS IN.—Selected and Edited by JOHN RICHARD GREEN. 3 Parts. Fcp. 8vo. 1s. 6d. each.

Part I. Hengist to Cressy. II. Cressy to Cromwell. III. Cromwell to Balaklava.

ENGLISH ILLUSTRATED MAGAZINE (THE).—Profusely Illustrated. Published Monthly. Number I. October, 1883. 6d. net. Vol. I. 1884. 7s. 6d. Vols. II.—VII. Super royal 8vo, extra cloth, coloured edges. 8s. each. [Cloth Covers for binding Volumes, 1s. 6d. each.]

—— Proof Impressions of Engravings originally published in *The English Illustrated Magazine*. 1884. In Portfolio 4to. 21s.

ENGLISH MEN OF ACTION.—Crown 8vo. With Portraits. 2s. 6d. each.

The following Volumes are Ready:

GENERAL GORDON. By Col. Sir W. BUTLER.
HENRY V. By the Rev. A. J. CHURCH.
LIVINGSTONE. By THOMAS HUGHES.
LORD LAWRENCE. By Sir RICHARD TEMPLE.
WELLINGTON. By GEORGE HOOPER.
DAMPIER. By W. CLARK RUSSELL.
MONK. By JULIAN CORBETT.
STRAFFORD. By H. D. TRAILL.
WARREN HASTINGS. By Sir ALFRED LYALL.
PETERBOROUGH. By W. STEBBING.
CAPTAIN COOK. By WALTER BESANT.
SIR HENRY HAVELOCK. By A. FORBES.
CLIVE. By Colonel Sir CHARLES WILSON.
SIR CHARLES NAPIER. By Col. Sir WM. BUTLER.
DRAKE. By JULIAN CORBETT.
WARWICK, THE KING-MAKER. By C. W. OMAN.

The undermentioned are in the Press or in Preparation:

MONTROSE. By MOWBRAY MORRIS.
RODNEY. By DAVID HANNAY.
SIR JOHN MOORE. By Colonel MAURICE.
BRUCE. By Sir SAMUEL BAKER.
SIMON DE MONTFORT. By G. W. PROTHERO.

ENGLISH MEN OF LETTERS.—Edited by JOHN MORLEY. Crown 8vo. 2s. 6d. each. Cheap Edition. 1s. 6d.; sewed, 1s.

JOHNSON. By LESLIE STEPHEN.
SCOTT. By R. H. HUTTON.
GIBBON. By J. COTTER MORISON.
HUME. By T. H. HUXLEY.
GOLDSMITH. By WILLIAM BLACK.
SHELLEY. By J. A. SYMONDS.
DEFOE. By W. MINTO.
BURNS. By Principal SHAIRP.
SPENSER. By R. W. CHURCH.
THACKERAY. By ANTHONY TROLLOPE.
MILTON. By MARK PATTISON.
BURKE. By JOHN MORLEY.
HAWTHORNE. By HENRY JAMES.
SOUTHEY. By Prof. DOWDEN.
BUNYAN. By J. A. FROUDE.
CHAUCER. By Prof. A. W. WARD.
COWPER. By GOLDWIN SMITH.
POPE. By LESLIE STEPHEN.
BYRON. By Prof. NICHOL.
DRYDEN. By G. SAINTSBURY.
LOCKE. By Prof. FOWLER.
WORDSWORTH. By F. W. H. MYERS.
LANDOR. By SIDNEY COLVIN.
DE QUINCEY. By Prof. MASSON.
CHARLES LAMB. By Rev. ALFRED AINGER.

ENGLISH MEN OF LETTERS—*contd.*

BENTLEY. By Prof. JEBB.
DICKENS. By A. W. WARD.
GRAY. By EDMUND GOSSE.
SWIFT. By LESLIE STEPHEN.
STERNE. By H. D. TRAILL.
MACAULAY. By J. COTTER MORISON.
FIELDING. By AUSTIN DOBSON.
SHERIDAN. By Mrs OLIPHANT.
ADDISON. By W. J. COURTHOPE.
BACON. By R. W. CHURCH.
COLERIDGE. By H. D. TRAILL.
SIR PHILIP SIDNEY. By J. A. SYMONDS.
KEATS. By SIDNEY COLVIN.

ENGLISH POETS. Selections, with Critical Introductions by various Writers, and a General Introduction by MATTHEW ARNOLD. Edited by T. H. WARD, M.A. 2nd Edition. 4 vols. Crown 8vo. 7s. 6d. each.

Vol. I. CHAUCER TO DONNE. II. BEN JONSON TO DRYDEN. III. ADDISON TO BLAKE. IV. WORDSWORTH TO ROSSETTI.

ENGLISH STATESMEN (TWELVE). Crown 8vo. 2s. 6d. each.

WILLIAM THE CONQUEROR. By EDWARD A. FREEMAN, D.C.L., LL.D. [*Ready.*
HENRY II. By Mrs. J. R. GREEN. [*Ready.*
EDWARD I. By F. YORK POWELL.
HENRY VII. By JAMES GAIRDNER. [*Ready.*
CARDINAL WOLSEY. By Bishop CREIGHTON. [*Ready.*
ELIZABETH. By E. S. BEESLY.
OLIVER CROMWELL. By FREDERIC HARRISON. [*Ready.*
WILLIAM III. By H. D. TRAILL. [*Ready.*
WALPOLE. By JOHN MORLEY. [*Ready.*
CHATHAM. By JOHN MORLEY.
PITT. By JOHN MORLEY.
PEEL. By J. R. THURSFIELD. [*Ready*

ESSEX FIELD CLUB MEMOIRS. Vol. I. REPORT ON THE EAST ANGLIAN EARTHQUAKE OF 22ND APRIL, 1884. By RAPHAEL MELDOLA, F.R.S., and WILLIAM WHITE, F.E.S. Maps and Illustrations. 8vo. 3s. 6d.

ETON COLLEGE, HISTORY OF, 1440—1884. By H. C. MAXWELL LYTE, C.B. Illustrations. 2nd Edition. Med. 8vo. 21s.

EURIPIDES.—MEDEA. Edited by A. W. VERRALL, Litt.D. 8vo. 7s. 6d.

—— IPHIGENEIA IN AULIS. Edited, with Introduction, Notes, and Commentary, by E. B. ENGLAND, M.A. 8vo.

—— ION. Translated by Rev. M. A. BAYFIELD, M.A. Crown 8vo. 2s. net. With Music, 4to. 4s. 6d. net.

See also pp. 31, 32.

EUROPEAN HISTORY, NARRATED IN A SERIES OF HISTORICAL SELECTIONS FROM THE BEST AUTHORITIES. Edited and arranged by E. M. SEWELL and C. M. YONGE. 2 vols. 3rd Edition. Crown 8vo. 6s. each.

EVANS (Sebastian).—BROTHER FABIAN'S MANUSCRIPT, AND OTHER POEMS. Fcp. 8vo, cloth. 6s.

—— IN THE STUDIO: A DECADE OF POEMS. Extra fcp. 8vo. 5s.

EVERETT (Prof. J. D.).—UNITS AND PHYSICAL CONSTANTS. 2nd Ed. Globe 8vo. 5s.

FAIRFAX. LIFE OF ROBERT FAIRFAX OF STEETON, Vice-Admiral, Alderman, and Member for York, A.D. 1666—1725. By CLEMENTS R. MARKHAM, C.B. 8vo. 12s. 6d.

FAITH AND CONDUCT: AN ESSAY ON VERIFIABLE RELIGION. Crown 8vo. 7s. 6d.

FARRAR (Archdeacon).—THE FALL OF MAN, AND OTHER SERMONS. 5th Ed. Cr. 8vo. 6s.

—— THE WITNESS OF HISTORY TO CHRIST. Hulsean Lectures for 1870. 7th Ed. Cr. 8vo. 5s.

—— SEEKERS AFTER GOD. THE LIVES OF SENECA, EPICTETUS, AND MARCUS AURELIUS. 12th Edition. Crown 8vo. 6s.

—— THE SILENCE AND VOICES OF GOD. University and other Sermons. 7th Ed. Cr. 8vo. 6s.

—— IN THE DAYS OF THY YOUTH. Sermons on Practical Subjects, preached at Marlborough College. 9th Edition. Cr. 8vo. 9s.

—— ETERNAL HOPE. Five Sermons, preached in Westminster Abbey. 28th Thousand. Crown 8vo. 6s.

—— SAINTLY WORKERS. Five Lenten Lectures. 3rd Edition. Crown 8vo. 6s.

—— EPHPHATHA; OR, THE AMELIORATION OF THE WORLD. Sermons preached at Westminster Abbey. Crown 8vo. 6s.

—— MERCY AND JUDGMENT. A few Last Words on Christian Eschatology. 2nd Ed. Crown 8vo. 10s. 6d.

—— THE MESSAGES OF THE BOOKS. Being Discourses and Notes on the Books of the New Testament. 8vo. 14s.

—— SERMONS AND ADDRESSES DELIVERED IN AMERICA. Crown 8vo. 7s. 6d.

—— THE HISTORY OF INTERPRETATION. Being the Bampton Lectures, 1885. 8vo. 16s.

FASNACHT (G. Eugène).—THE ORGANIC METHOD OF STUDYING LANGUAGES. I. FRENCH. Extra fcp. 8vo. 3s. 6d.

—— A SYNTHETIC FRENCH GRAMMAR FOR SCHOOLS. Crown 8vo. 3s. 6d.

—— FRENCH READINGS FOR CHILDREN. Illustrated. Globe 8vo.

FAWCETT (Rt. Hon. Henry).—MANUAL OF POLITICAL ECONOMY. 7th Edition, revised. Crown 8vo. 12s.

—— AN EXPLANATORY DIGEST OF PROFESSOR FAWCETT'S MANUAL OF POLITICAL ECONOMY. By CYRIL A. WATERS. Cr. 8vo. 2s. 6d.

—— SPEECHES ON SOME CURRENT POLITICAL QUESTIONS. 8vo. 10s. 6d.

—— FREE TRADE AND PROTECTION. 6th Edition. Crown 8vo. 3s. 6d.

FAWCETT (Mrs. H.).—POLITICAL ECONOMY FOR BEGINNERS, WITH QUESTIONS. 7th Edition. 18mo. 2s. 6d.

—— SOME EMINENT WOMEN OF OUR TIMES. Short Biographical Sketches. Cr. 8vo. 2s. 6d.

FAWCETT (Rt. Hon. Henry and Mrs. H.).—ESSAYS AND LECTURES ON POLITICAL AND SOCIAL SUBJECTS. 8vo. 10s. 6d.

FAY (Amy.).—MUSIC-STUDY IN GERMANY. Preface by Sir GEO. GROVE. Cr. 8vo. 4s. 6d.

FEARNLEY (W.).—A MANUAL OF ELEMENTARY PRACTICAL HISTOLOGY. Cr. 8vo. 7s. 6d.

FEARON (D. R.).—SCHOOL INSPECTION. 6th Edition. Crown 8vo. 2s. 6d.

FERREL (Prof. W.).—A POPULAR TREATISE ON THE WINDS. 8vo. 18s.

FERRERS (Rev. N. M.).—A TREATISE ON TRILINEAR CO-ORDINATES, THE METHOD OF RECIPROCAL POLARS, AND THE THEORY OF PROJECTIONS. 4th Ed. Cr. 8vo. 6s. 6d.

—— SPHERICAL HARMONICS AND SUBJECTS CONNECTED WITH THEM. Crown 8vo. 7s. 6d.

FESSENDEN (C.).—ELEMENTS OF PHYSICS FOR PUBLIC SCHOOLS. Globe 8vo.

FINCK (Henry T.).—ROMANTIC LOVE AND PERSONAL BEAUTY. 2 vols. Cr. 8vo. 18s.

FIRST LESSONS IN BUSINESS MATTERS. By A BANKER'S DAUGHTER. 2nd Edition. 18mo. 1s.

FISHER (Rev. Osmond).—PHYSICS OF THE EARTH'S CRUST. 2nd Edition. 8vo. 12s.

FISKE (John).—OUTLINES OF COSMIC PHILOSOPHY, BASED ON THE DOCTRINE OF EVOLUTION. 2 vols. 8vo. 25s.

—— DARWINISM, AND OTHER ESSAYS. Crown 8vo. 7s. 6d.

—— MAN'S DESTINY VIEWED IN THE LIGHT OF HIS ORIGIN. Crown 8vo. 3s. 6d.

—— AMERICAN POLITICAL IDEAS VIEWED FROM THE STAND-POINT OF UNIVERSAL HISTORY. Crown 8vo. 4s.

—— THE CRITICAL PERIOD IN AMERICAN HISTORY, 1783—89. Ex. Cr. 8vo. 10s. 6d.

—— THE BEGINNINGS OF NEW ENGLAND; OR, THE PURITAN THEOCRACY IN ITS RELATIONS TO CIVIL AND RELIGIOUS LIBERTY. Crown 8vo. 7s. 6d.

—— CIVIL GOVERNMENT IN THE UNITED STATES CONSIDERED WITH SOME REFERENCE TO ITS ORIGIN. Crown 8vo. 6s. 6d.

FISON (L.) and HOWITT (A. W.).—KAMILAROI and KURNAI GROUP. Group-Marriage and Relationship and Marriage by Elopement. 8vo. 15s.

FITCH (J. G.).—NOTES ON AMERICAN SCHOOLS AND TRAINING COLLEGES. Globe 8vo. 2s. 6d.

FITZGERALD (Edward): LETTERS AND LITERARY REMAINS OF. Ed. by W. ALDIS WRIGHT, M.A. 3 vols. Crown 8vo. 31s. 6d.

—— THE RUBÁIYÁT OF OMAR KHÁYYÁM. Extra Crown 8vo. 10s. 6d.

FITZ GERALD (Caroline).—VENETIA VICTRIX, AND OTHER POEMS. Ex. fcp. 8vo. 3s. 6d.

FLEAY (Rev. F. G.).—A SHAKESPEARE MANUAL. Extra fcp. 8vo. 4s. 6d.

FLEISCHER (Dr. Emil).—A SYSTEM OF VOLUMETRIC ANALYSIS. Translated by M. M. PATTISON MUIR, F.R.S.E. Cr. 8vo. 7s. 6d.

FLOWER (Prof. W. H.).—AN INTRODUCTION TO THE OSTEOLOGY OF THE MAMMALIA. With numerous Illustrations. 3rd Edition, revised with the assistance of HANS GADOW, Ph.D., M.A. Crown 8vo. 10s. 6d.

FLÜCKIGER (F. A.) and HANBURY (D.).—PHARMACOGRAPHIA. A History of the principal Drugs of Vegetable Origin met with in Great Britain and India. 2nd Edition, revised. 8vo. 21s.

FO'C'SLE YARNS, including "Betsy Lee," and other Poems. Crown 8vo. 7s. 6d.

LIST OF PUBLICATIONS.

FORBES (Archibald). SOUVENIRS OF SOME CONTINENTS. Crown 8vo. 6s.

FORBES (Edward): MEMOIR OF. By GEORGE WILSON, M.D., and ARCHIBALD GEIKIE, F.R.S., &c. Demy 8vo. 14s.

FORSYTH (A. R.).—A TREATISE ON DIFFERENTIAL EQUATIONS. Demy 8vo. 14s.

FOSTER (Prof. Michael).—A TEXT-BOOK OF PHYSIOLOGY. Illustrated. 5th Edition. 8vo. Part I., Book I. Blood—The Tissues of Movement, the Vascular Mechanism. 10s. 6d. - Part II., Book II. The Tissues of Chemical Action, with their Respective Mechanisms Nutrition. 10s. 6d. Part III., Book III. The Central Nervous System. 7s. 6d.—Book IV. The Tissues and Mechanisms of Reproduction.

—— PRIMER OF PHYSIOLOGY. 18mo. 1s.

FOSTER (Prof. Michael) and BALFOUR (F. M.) (the late).—THE ELEMENTS OF EMBRYOLOGY. Edited by ADAM SEDGWICK, M.A., and WALTER HEAPE. Illustrated. 3rd Ed., revised and enlarged. Cr. 8vo. 10s. 6d.

FOSTER (Michael) and LANGLEY (J. N.).—A COURSE OF ELEMENTARY PRACTICAL PHYSIOLOGY AND HISTOLOGY. 6th Edition, enlarged. Crown 8vo. 7s. 6d.

FOTHERGILL (Dr. J. Milner).—THE PRACTITIONER'S HANDBOOK OF TREATMENT; OR, THE PRINCIPLES OF THERAPEUTICS. 3rd Edition, enlarged. 8vo. 16s.

—— THE ANTAGONISM OF THERAPEUTIC AGENTS, AND WHAT IT TEACHES. Cr. 8vo. 6s.

—— FOOD FOR THE INVALID, THE CONVALESCENT, THE DYSPEPTIC, AND THE GOUTY. 2nd Edition. Crown 8vo. 3s. 6d.

FOWLE (Rev. T. W.).—A NEW ANALOGY BETWEEN REVEALED RELIGION AND THE COURSE AND CONSTITUTION OF NATURE. Crown 8vo. 6s.

FOWLER (Rev. Thomas).—PROGRESSIVE MORALITY; AN ESSAY IN ETHICS. Crown 8vo. 5s.

FOWLER (W. W.).—TALES OF THE BIRDS. Illustrated. Crown 8vo. 3s. 6d.

—— A YEAR WITH THE BIRDS. Illustrated. Crown 8vo. 3s. 6d.

FOX (Dr. Wilson).—ON THE ARTIFICIAL PRODUCTION OF TUBERCLE IN THE LOWER ANIMALS. With Plates. 4to. 5s. 6d.

—— ON THE TREATMENT OF HYPERPYREXIA, AS ILLUSTRATED IN ACUTE ARTICULAR RHEUMATISM BY MEANS OF THE EXTERNAL APPLICATION OF COLD. 8vo. 2s. 6d.

FRAMJI (Dosabhai).—HISTORY OF THE PARSIS; INCLUDING THEIR MANNERS, CUSTOMS, RELIGION, AND PRESENT POSITION. Illustrated. 2 vols. Med. 8vo. 36s.

FRANKLAND (Prof. Percy).—A HANDBOOK OF AGRICULTURAL CHEMICAL ANALYSIS. Crown 8vo. 7s. 6d.

FRASER — HUGHES. — JAMES FRASER, SECOND BISHOP OF MANCHESTER: A Memoir. By T. HUGHES. Crown 8vo. 6s.

FRASER.—SERMONS. By the Right Rev. JAMES FRASER, D.D., Second Bishop of Manchester. Edited by Rev. JOHN W. DIGGLE. 2 vols. Crown 8vo. 6s. each.

FRASER-TYTLER. — SONGS IN MINOR KEYS. By C. C. FRASER-TYTLER (Mrs. EDWARD LIDDELL). 2nd Ed. 18mo. 6s.

FRATERNITY; A Romance. 2 vols. Cr. 8vo. 21s.

FRAZER (J. G.).—THE GOLDEN BOUGH; A Study in Comparative Religion. 2 vols. 8vo. 28s.

FREDERICK (Mrs.).—HINTS TO HOUSEWIVES ON SEVERAL POINTS, PARTICULARLY ON THE PREPARATION OF ECONOMICAL AND TASTEFUL DISHES. Crown 8vo. 1s.

FREEMAN (Prof. E. A.).—HISTORY OF THE CATHEDRAL CHURCH OF WELLS. Crown 8vo. 3s. 6d.

—— OLD ENGLISH HISTORY. With 5 Col. Maps. 9th Edition, revised. Extra fcp. 8vo. 6s.

—— HISTORICAL ESSAYS. First Series. 4th Edition. 8vo. 10s. 6d.

—— HISTORICAL ESSAYS. Second Series. 3rd Edition. With Additional Essays. 8vo. 10s. 6d.

—— HISTORICAL ESSAYS. Third Series. 8vo. 12s.

—— THE GROWTH OF THE ENGLISH CONSTITUTION FROM THE EARLIEST TIMES. 5th Edition. Crown 8vo. 5s.

—— GENERAL SKETCH OF EUROPEAN HISTORY. With Maps, &c. 18mo. 3s. 6d.

—— COMPARATIVE POLITICS. Lectures at the Royal Institution. To which is added "The Unity of History." 8vo. 14s.

—— HISTORICAL AND ARCHITECTURAL SKETCHES; CHIEFLY ITALIAN. Illustrated by the Author. Crown 8vo. 10s. 6d.

—— SUBJECT AND NEIGHBOUR LANDS OF VENICE. Illustrated. Crown 8vo. 10s. 6d.

—— ENGLISH TOWNS AND DISTRICTS. A Series of Addresses and Essays. 8vo. 14s.

—— THE OFFICE OF THE HISTORICAL PROFESSOR. Inaugural Lecture at Oxford. Crown 8vo. 2s.

—— DISESTABLISHMENT AND DISENDOWMENT. WHAT ARE THEY? 4th Edition. Crown 8vo. 1s.

—— GREATER GREECE AND GREATER BRITAIN: GEORGE WASHINGTON THE EXPANDER OF ENGLAND. With an Appendix on IMPERIAL FEDERATION. Cr. 8vo. 3s. 6d.

—— THE METHODS OF HISTORICAL STUDY. Eight Lectures at Oxford. 8vo. 10s. 6d.

—— THE CHIEF PERIODS OF EUROPEAN HISTORY. Six Lectures read in the University of Oxford, with an Essay on GREEK CITIES UNDER ROMAN RULE. 8vo. 10s. 6d.

—— FOUR OXFORD LECTURES, 1887. FIFTY YEARS OF EUROPEAN HISTORY—TEUTONIC CONQUEST IN GAUL AND BRITAIN. 8vo. 5s.

FRENCH COURSE.—See p. 34.

FRIEDMANN (Paul).—ANNE BOLEYN. A Chapter of English History, 1527—36. 2 vols. 8vo. 28s.

FROST (Percival).—AN ELEMENTARY TREATISE ON CURVE TRACING. 8vo. 12s.

—— THE FIRST THREE SECTIONS OF NEWTON'S PRINCIPIA. 4th Edition. 8vo. 12s.

—— SOLID GEOMETRY. 3rd Edition. 8vo. 16s.

—— HINTS FOR THE SOLUTION OF PROBLEMS IN THE THIRD EDITION OF SOLID GEOMETRY. 8vo. 8s. 6d.

FURNIVALL (F. J.).—LE MORTE ARTHUR. Edited from the Harleian MS. 2252, in the British Museum. Fcp. 8vo. 7s. 6d.

GAIRDNER (Jas.).—HENRY VII. Crown 8vo. 2s. 6d.

GALTON (Francis). — METEOROGRAPHICA; OR, METHODS OF MAPPING THE WEATHER. 4to. 9s.

—— ENGLISH MEN OF SCIENCE: THEIR NATURE AND NURTURE. 8vo. 8s. 6d.

—— INQUIRIES INTO HUMAN FACULTY AND ITS DEVELOPMENT. 8vo. 16s.

—— RECORD OF FAMILY FACULTIES. Consisting of Tabular Forms and Directions for Entering Data. 4to. 2s. 6d.

—— LIFE HISTORY ALBUM: Being a Personal Note-book, combining the chief advantages of a Diary, Photograph Album, a Register of Height, Weight, and other Anthropometrical Observations, and a Record of Illnesses. 4to. 3s. 6d.—Or, with Cards of Wools for Testing Colour Vision. 4s. 6d.

—— NATURAL INHERITANCE. 8vo. 9s.

GAMGEE (Prof. Arthur).—A TEXT-BOOK OF THE PHYSIOLOGICAL CHEMISTRY OF THE ANIMAL BODY, including an account of the Chemical Changes occurring in Disease. Vol. I. Med. 8vo. 18s.

GANGUILLET (E.) and KUTTER (W. R.).—A GENERAL FORMULA FOR THE UNIFORM FLOW OF WATER IN RIVERS AND OTHER CHANNELS. Translated by RUDOLPH HERING and JOHN C. TRAUTWINE, Jun. 8vo. 17s.

GARDNER (Percy). SAMOS AND SAMIAN COINS. An Essay. 8vo. 7s. 6d.

GARNETT (R.).—IDYLLS AND EPIGRAMS. Chiefly from the Greek Anthology. Fcp. 8vo. 2s. 6d.

GASKOIN (Mrs. Herman). — CHILDREN'S TREASURY OF BIBLE STORIES. 18mo. 1s. each. —Part I. Old Testament; II. New Testament; III. Three Apostles.

GEDDES (Prof. William D.).—THE PROBLEM OF THE HOMERIC POEMS. 8vo. 14s.

—— FLOSCULI GRÆCI BOREALES, SIVE ANTHOLOGIA GRÆCA ABERDONENSIS CONTEXUIT GULIELMUS D. GEDDES. Cr. 8vo. 6s.

—— THE PHAEDO OF PLATO. Edited, with Introduction and Notes. 2nd Edition. 8vo. 8s. 6d.

GEIKIE (Archibald).—PRIMER OF PHYSICAL GEOGRAPHY. With Illustrations. 18mo. 1s.

—— PRIMER OF GEOLOGY. Illust. 18mo. 1s.

—— ELEMENTARY LESSONS IN PHYSICAL GEOGRAPHY. With Illustrations. Fcp. 8vo. 4s. 6d.—QUESTIONS ON THE SAME. 1s. 6d.

—— OUTLINES OF FIELD GEOLOGY. With numerous Illustrations. Crown 8vo. 3s. 6d.

GEIKIE (A.).—TEXT-BOOK OF GEOLOGY. Illustrated. 2nd Edition. 7th Thousand. Medium 8vo. 28s.

—— CLASS-BOOK OF GEOLOGY. Illustrated. 2nd Edition. Crown 8vo. 4s. 6d.

—— GEOLOGICAL SKETCHES AT HOME AND ABROAD. With Illustrations. 8vo. 10s. 6d.

—— THE SCENERY OF SCOTLAND. Viewed in connection with its Physical Geology. 2nd Edition. Crown 8vo. 12s. 6d.

—— THE TEACHING OF GEOGRAPHY. A Practical Handbook for the use of Teachers. Globe 8vo. 2s.

—— GEOGRAPHY OF THE BRITISH ISLES. 18mo. 1s.

GEOMETRY, SYLLABUS OF PLANE. Corresponding to Euclid I.—VI. Prepared by the Association for the Improvement of Geometrical Teaching. New Edit. Cr. 8vo. 1s.

GEOMETRY, SYLLABUS OF MODERN PLANE. Association for the Improvement of Geometrical Teaching. Crown 8vo, sewed. 1s.

GIBBINS (H. de B.).— COMMERCIAL HISTORY OF EUROPE. 18mo. 2s. 6d.

GILES (P.).—A SHORT MANUAL OF PHILOLOGY FOR CLASSICAL STUDENTS. Crown 8vo. [In the Press.

GILMAN (N. P.). — PROFIT-SHARING BETWEEN EMPLOYER AND EMPLOYÉ. A Study in the Evolution of the Wages System. Crown 8vo. 7s. 6d.

GILMORE (Rev. John).—STORM WARRIORS; OR, LIFEBOAT WORK ON THE GOODWIN SANDS. Crown 8vo. 3s. 6d.

GLADSTONE (Rt. Hon. W. E.).—HOMERIC SYNCHRONISM. An Inquiry into the Time and Place of Homer. Crown 8vo. 6s.

—— PRIMER OF HOMER. 18mo. 1s.

—— LANDMARKS OF HOMERIC STUDY, TOGETHER WITH AN ESSAY ON THE POINTS OF CONTACT BETWEEN THE ASSYRIAN TABLETS AND THE HOMERIC TEXT. Cr. 8vo. 2s. 6d.

GLADSTONE (J. H.).—SPELLING REFORM FROM AN EDUCATIONAL POINT OF VIEW. 3rd Edition. Crown 8vo. 1s. 6d.

GLADSTONE (J. H.) and TRIBE (A.).—THE CHEMISTRY OF THE SECONDARY BATTERIES OF PLANTÉ AND FAURE. Crown 8vo. 2s. 6d.

GLOBE EDITIONS. Gl. 8vo. 3s. 6d. each. THE COMPLETE WORKS OF WILLIAM SHAKESPEARE. Edited by W. G. CLARK and W. ALDIS WRIGHT.

MORTE D'ARTHUR. Sir Thomas Malory's Book of King Arthur and of his Noble Knights of the Round Table. The Edition of Caxton, revised for modern use. By Sir E. STRACHEY, Bart.

THE POETICAL WORKS OF SIR WALTER SCOTT. With Essay by Prof. PALGRAVE.

THE POETICAL WORKS AND LETTERS OF ROBERT BURNS. Edited, with Life and Glossarial Index, by ALEXANDER SMITH.

THE ADVENTURES OF ROBINSON CRUSOE. With Introduction by HENRY KINGSLEY.

GOLDSMITH'S MISCELLANEOUS WORKS. Edited by Prof. MASSON.

POPE'S POETICAL WORKS. Edited, with Memoir and Notes, by Prof. WARD.

LIST OF PUBLICATIONS.

GLOBE EDITIONS—*continued.*

SPENSER'S COMPLETE WORKS. Edited by R. MORRIS. Memoir by J. W. HALES.

DRYDEN'S POETICAL WORKS. A revised Text and Notes. By W. D. CHRISTIE.

COWPER'S POETICAL WORKS. Edited by the Rev. W. BENHAM, B.D.

VIRGIL'S WORKS. Rendered into English by JAMES LONSDALE and S. LEE.

HORACE'S WORKS. Rendered into English by JAMES LONSDALE and S. LEE.

MILTON'S POETICAL WORKS. Edited, with Introduction, &c., by Prof. MASSON.

GLOBE READERS, THE.—A New Series of Reading Books for Standards I.—VI. Selected, arranged, and Edited by A. F. MURISON, sometime English Master at Aberdeen Grammar School. With Original Illustrations. Globe 8vo.

Primer I.	(48 pp.)	3d.
Primer II.	(48 pp.)	3d.
Book I.	(132 pp.)	6d.
Book II.	(136 pp.)	9d.
Book III.	(232 pp.)	1s. 3d.
Book IV.	(328 pp.)	1s. 9d.
Book V.	(408 pp.)	2s.
Book VI.	(436 pp.)	2s. 6d.

GLOBE READERS, THE SHORTER.—A New Series of Reading Books for Standards I.—VI. Edited by A. F. MURISON. Gl. 8vo.

Primer I.	(48 pp.)	3d.
Primer II.	(48 pp.)	3d.
Standard I.	(90 pp.)	6d.
Standard II.	(124 pp.)	9d.
Standard III.	(178 pp.)	1s.
Standard IV.	(182 pp.)	1s.
Standard V.	(216 pp.)	1s. 3d.
Standard VI.	(228 pp.)	1s. 6d.

** This Series has been abridged from the "Globe Readers" to meet the demand for smaller reading books.

GLOBE READINGS FROM STANDARD AUTHORS. Globe 8vo.

COWPER'S TASK: An Epistle to Joseph Hill, Esq.; TIROCINIUM, or a Review of the Schools; and the HISTORY OF JOHN GILPIN. Edited, with Notes, by Rev. WILLIAM BENHAM, B.D. 1s.

GOLDSMITH'S VICAR OF WAKEFIELD. With a Memoir of Goldsmith by Prof. MASSON. 1s.

LAMB'S (CHARLES) TALES FROM SHAKSPEARE. Edited, with Preface, by Rev. ALFRED AINGER, M.A. 2s.

SCOTT'S (SIR WALTER) LAY OF THE LAST MINSTREL; and the LADY OF THE LAKE. Edited by Prof. F. T. PALGRAVE. 1s.

— MARMION; and THE LORD OF THE ISLES. By the same Editor. 1s.

THE CHILDREN'S GARLAND FROM THE BEST POETS. Selected and arranged by COVENTRY PATMORE. 2s.

A BOOK OF GOLDEN DEEDS OF ALL TIMES AND ALL COUNTRIES. Gathered and narrated anew by CHARLOTTE M. YONGE. 2s.

GODFRAY (Hugh).—AN ELEMENTARY TREATISE ON LUNAR THEORY. 2nd Edition. Crown 8vo. 5s. 6d.

GODFRAY (H.).—A TREATISE ON ASTRONOMY, FOR THE USE OF COLLEGES AND SCHOOLS. 8vo. 12s. 6d.

GOETHE—CARLYLE.—CORRESPONDENCE BETWEEN GOETHE AND CARLYLE. Edited by C. E. NORTON. Crown 8vo. 9s.

GOETHE'S LIFE. By Prof. HEINRICH DÜNTZER. Translated by T. W. LYSTER. 2 vols. Crown 8vo. 21s.

GOETHE.—FAUST. Translated into English Verse by JOHN STUART BLACKIE. 2nd Edition. Crown 8vo. 9s.

— FAUST, Part I. Edited, with Introduction and Notes; followed by an Appendix on Part II., by JANE LEE. 18mo. 4s. 6d.

— REYNARD THE FOX. Trans. into English Verse by A. D. AINSLIE. Crn. 8vo. 7s. 6d.

— GÖTZ VON BERLICHINGEN. Edited by H. A. BULL, M.A. 18mo. 2s.

GOLDEN TREASURY SERIES.—Uniformly printed in 18mo, with Vignette Titles by Sir J. E. MILLAIS, Sir NOEL PATON, T. WOOLNER, W. HOLMAN HUNT, ARTHUR HUGHES, &c. Engraved on Steel. Bound in extra cloth. 4s. 6d. each.

THE GOLDEN TREASURY OF THE BEST SONGS AND LYRICAL POEMS IN THE ENGLISH LANGUAGE. Selected and arranged, with Notes, by Prof. F. T. PALGRAVE.

THE CHILDREN'S GARLAND FROM THE BEST POETS. Selected by COVENTRY PATMORE.

THE BOOK OF PRAISE. From the best English Hymn Writers. Selected by ROUNDELL, EARL OF SELBORNE.

THE FAIRY BOOK: THE BEST POPULAR FAIRY STORIES. Selected by the Author of "John Halifax, Gentleman."

THE BALLAD BOOK. A Selection of the Choicest British Ballads. Edited by WILLIAM ALLINGHAM.

THE JEST BOOK. The Choicest Anecdotes and Sayings. Arranged by MARK LEMON.

BACON'S ESSAYS, AND COLOURS OF GOOD AND EVIL. With Notes and Glossarial Index by W. ALDIS WRIGHT, M.A.

THE PILGRIM'S PROGRESS FROM THIS WORLD TO THAT WHICH IS TO COME. By JOHN BUNYAN.

THE SUNDAY BOOK OF POETRY FOR THE YOUNG. Selected by C. F. ALEXANDER.

A BOOK OF GOLDEN DEEDS OF ALL TIMES AND ALL COUNTRIES. By the Author of "The Heir of Redclyffe."

THE ADVENTURES OF ROBINSON CRUSOE. Edited by J. W. CLARK, M.A.

THE REPUBLIC OF PLATO. Translated by J. LL. DAVIES, M.A., and D. J. VAUGHAN.

THE SONG BOOK. Words and Tunes Selected and arranged by JOHN HULLAH.

LA LYRE FRANÇAISE. Selected and arranged, with Notes, by G. MASSON.

TOM BROWN'S SCHOOL DAYS. By AN OLD BOY.

A BOOK OF WORTHIES. By the Author of "The Heir of Redclyffe."

GUESSES AT TRUTH. By TWO BROTHER.

GOLDEN TREASURY SERIES—*contd.*

THE CAVALIER AND HIS LADY. Selections from the Works of the First Duke and Duchess of Newcastle. With an Introductory Essay by EDWARD JENKINS.

SCOTTISH SONG. Compiled by MARY CARLYLE AITKEN.

DEUTSCHE LYRIK. The Golden Treasury of the best German Lyrical Poems. Selected by Dr. BUCHHEIM.

CHRYSOMELA. A Selection from the Lyrical Poems of Robert Herrick. By Prof. F. T. PALGRAVE.

POEMS OF PLACES—ENGLAND AND WALES. Edited by H. W. LONGFELLOW. 2 vols.

SELECTED POEMS OF MATTHEW ARNOLD.

THE STORY OF THE CHRISTIANS AND MOORS IN SPAIN. By CHARLOTTE M. YONGE.

LAMB'S TALES FROM SHAKSPEARE. Edited by Rev. ALFRED AINGER, M.A.

SHAKESPEARE'S SONGS AND SONNETS. Ed. with Notes, by Prof. F. T. PALGRAVE.

POEMS OF WORDSWORTH. Chosen and Edited by MATTHEW ARNOLD.
Large Paper Edition. 9s.

POEMS OF SHELLEY. Ed. by S. A. BROOKE.
Large Paper Edition. 12s. 6d.

THE ESSAYS OF JOSEPH ADDISON. Chosen and Edited by JOHN RICHARD GREEN.

POETRY OF BYRON. Chosen and arranged by MATTHEW ARNOLD.
Large Paper Edition. 9s.

SIR THOMAS BROWNE'S RELIGIO MEDICI; LETTER TO A FRIEND, &c., AND CHRISTIAN MORALS. Ed. by W. A. GREENHILL, M.D.

THE SPEECHES AND TABLE-TALK OF THE PROPHET MOHAMMAD. Translated by STANLEY LANE-POOLE.

SELECTIONS FROM WALTER SAVAGE LANDOR. Edited by SIDNEY COLVIN.

SELECTIONS FROM COWPER'S POEMS. With an Introduction by Mrs. OLIPHANT.

LETTERS OF WILLIAM COWPER. Edited, With Introduction, by Rev. W. BENHAM.

THE POETICAL WORKS OF JOHN KEATS. Edited by Prof. F. T. PALGRAVE.

LYRICAL POEMS OF LORD TENNYSON. Selected and Annotated by Prof. FRANCIS T. PALGRAVE.
Large Paper Edition. 9s.

IN MEMORIAM. By LORD TENNYSON, Poet Laureate.
Large Paper Edition. 9s.

THE TRIAL AND DEATH OF SOCRATES. Being the Euthyphron, Apology, Crito, and Phaedo of Plato. Translated by F. J. CHURCH.

A BOOK OF GOLDEN THOUGHTS. By HENRY ATTWELL.

PLATO.—PHAEDRUS, LYSIS, AND PROTAGORAS. A New Translation, by J. WRIGHT.

THEOCRITUS, BION, AND MOSCHUS. Rendered into English Prose by ANDREW LANG.
Large Paper Edition. 9s.

BALLADS, LYRICS, AND SONNETS. From the Works of HENRY W. LONGFELLOW.

GOLDEN TREASURY SERIES—*contd.*

DEUTSCHE BALLADEN UND ROMANZEN. The Golden Treasury of the Best German Ballads and Romances. Selected and arranged by Dr. BUCHHEIM. [*In the Press.*

GOLDEN TREASURY SERIES. Re-issue in uniform binding with Vignette Titles. Monthly volumes from May, 1891. 2s. 6d. each net.

THE GOLDEN TREASURY OF THE BEST SONGS AND LYRICAL POEMS IN THE ENGLISH LANGUAGE. Selected and arranged, with Notes, by Prof. F. T. PALGRAVE.

THE CHILDREN'S GARLAND FROM THE BEST POETS. Selected by COVENTRY PATMORE.

THE PILGRIM'S PROGRESS FROM THIS WORLD TO THAT WHICH IS TO COME. By JOHN BUNYAN.

THE BOOK OF PRAISE. From the best English Hymn Writers. Selected by ROUNDELL, EARL OF SELBORNE.

BACON'S ESSAYS, AND COLOURS OF GOOD AND EVIL. With Notes and Glossarial Index by W. ALDIS WRIGHT, M.A.

THE FAIRY BOOK: THE BEST POPULAR FAIRY STORIES. Selected by Mrs. CRAIK.

THE JEST BOOK. The Choicest Anecdotes and Sayings. Arranged by MARK LEMON.

THE BALLAD BOOK. A Selection of the Choicest British Ballads. Edited by WILLIAM ALLINGHAM.

THE SUNDAY BOOK OF POETRY FOR THE YOUNG. Selected by C. F. ALEXANDER.

A BOOK OF GOLDEN DEEDS OF ALL TIMES AND ALL COUNTRIES. By C. M. YONGE.

THE ADVENTURES OF ROBINSON CRUSOE. Edited by J. W. CLARK, M.A.

THE REPUBLIC OF PLATO. Translated by J. LL. DAVIES, M.A., and D. J. VAUGHAN.

Other Volumes to follow.

GOLDEN TREASURY PSALTER. THE STUDENT'S EDITION. Being an Edition with briefer Notes of "The Psalms Chronologically Arranged by Four Friends." 18mo. 3s. 6d.

GOLDSMITH.—ESSAYS OF OLIVER GOLDSMITH. Edited by C. D. YONGE, M.A. Fcp. 8vo. 2s. 6d.

—— THE TRAVELLER AND THE DESERTED VILLAGE. With Notes by J. W. HALES, M.A. Crown 8vo. 6d.

—— THE VICAR OF WAKEFIELD. With 182 Illustrations by HUGH THOMSON, and Preface by AUSTIN DOBSON. Crown 8vo. 6s.
Also with uncut edges, paper label. 6s.
See also ENGLISH CLASSICS, p. 12.

GONE TO TEXAS. LETTERS FROM OUR BOYS. Edited, with Preface, by THOMAS HUGHES, Q.C. Crown 8vo. 4s. 6d.

GOODALE (G. L.).—PHYSIOLOGICAL BOTANY. Part I. OUTLINES OF THE HISTORY OF PHÆNOGAMOUS PLANTS; II. VEGETABLE PHYSIOLOGY. 6th Edition. 8vo. 10s. 6d.

GOODWIN (Prof. W. W.).—SYNTAX OF THE GREEK MOODS AND TENSES. 8vo. 14s.

—— A GREEK GRAMMAR. Crown 8vo. 6s.

—— A SCHOOL GREEK GRAMMAR. Crown 8vo. 3s. 6d.

LIST OF PUBLICATIONS. 19

GORDON (General). A SKETCH. By REGINALD H. BARNES. Crown 8vo. 1s.

—— LETTERS OF GENERAL C. G. GORDON TO HIS SISTER, M. A. GORDON. 4th Edition. Crown 8vo. 3s. 6d.

GORDON (Lady Duff).—LAST LETTERS FROM EGYPT, TO WHICH ARE ADDED LETTERS FROM THE CAPE. 2nd Edition. Cr. 8vo. 9s.

GOSCHEN (Rt. Hon. George J.).—REPORTS AND SPEECHES ON LOCAL TAXATION. 8vo. 5s.

GOSSE (E.).—A HISTORY OF EIGHTEENTH CENTURY LITERATURE (1660—1780). Crn. 8vo. 7s. 6d.

GOW (Dr. James).—A COMPANION TO SCHOOL CLASSICS. Illustrated. 2nd Ed. Cr. 8vo. 6s.

GOYEN (P.).—HIGHER ARITHMETIC AND ELEMENTARY MENSURATION, for the Senior Classes of Schools and Candidates preparing for Public Examinations. Globe 8vo. 5s.

GRAHAM (David).—KING JAMES I. An Historical Tragedy. Globe 8vo. 7s.

GRAHAM (John W.).—NEÆRA: A TALE OF ANCIENT ROME. Crown 8vo. 6s.

GRAHAM (R. H.)—GEOMETRY OF POSITION. Crown 8vo. 7s. 6d.

GRAND'HOMME. — CUTTING OUT AND DRESSMAKING. From the French of Mdlle. E. GRAND'HOMME. 18mo. 1s.

GRAY (Prof. Andrew).—THE THEORY AND PRACTICE OF ABSOLUTE MEASUREMENTS IN ELECTRICITY AND MAGNETISM. 2 vols. Crown 8vo. Vol. I. 12s. 6d.

—— ABSOLUTE MEASUREMENTS IN ELECTRICITY AND MAGNETISM. 2nd Edit., revised. Fcp. 8vo. 5s. 6d.

GRAY (Prof. Asa).—STRUCTURAL BOTANY; OR, ORGANOGRAPHY ON THE BASIS OF MORPHOLOGY. 8vo. 10s. 6d.

—— THE SCIENTIFIC PAPERS OF ASA GRAY. Selected by CHARLES S. SARGENT. 2 vols. 8vo. 21s.

GRAY (Tho.).—WORKS. Edited by E. GOSSE. In 4 vols. Globe 8vo. 20s.—Vol. I. POEMS, JOURNALS, AND ESSAYS.—II. LETTERS.—III. LETTERS.—IV. NOTES ON ARISTOPHANES; AND PLATO.

GREAVES (John).—A TREATISE ON ELEMENTARY STATICS. 2nd Ed. Cr. 8vo. 6s. 6d.

—— STATICS FOR BEGINNERS. Gl. 8vo. 3s. 6d.

GREEK TESTAMENT. THE NEW TESTAMENT IN THE ORIGINAL GREEK. The Text revised by Bishop WESTCOTT, D.D., and Prof. F. J. A. HORT, D.D. 2 vols. Crn. 8vo. 10s. 6d. each.—Vol. I. Text; II. Introduction and Appendix.

THE NEW TESTAMENT IN THE ORIGINAL GREEK, FOR SCHOOLS. The Text Revised by Bishop WESTCOTT, D.D., and F. J. A. HORT, D.D. 12mo. 4s. 6d.—18mo, roan, red edges. 5s. 6d.; morocco, gilt, 6s. 6d.

SCHOOL READINGS IN THE GREEK TESTAMENT. Being the Outlines of the Life of our Lord as given by St. Mark, with additions from the Text of the other Evangelists. Edited, with Notes and Vocabulary, by A. CALVERT, M.A. Fcp. 8vo. 2s. 6d.

THE GREEK TESTAMENT AND THE ENGLISH VERSION, A COMPANION TO. By PHILIP SCHAFF, D.D. Crown 8vo. 12s.

GREEK TESTAMENT—*continued.*

THE GOSPEL ACCORDING TO ST. MATTHEW. Greek Text as Revised by Bishop WESTCOTT and Dr. HORT. With Introduction and Notes by Rev. A. SLOMAN, M.A. Fcp. 8vo. 2s. 6d.

THE GOSPEL ACCORDING TO ST. LUKE. The Greek Text as revised by Bp. WESTCOTT and Dr. HORT. With Introduction and Notes by Rev. J. BOND, M.A. Fcp. 8vo. 2s. 6d.

THE ACTS OF THE APOSTLES. Being the Greek Text as Revised by Bishop WESTCOTT and Dr. HORT. With Explanatory Notes by T. E. PAGE, M.A. Fcp. 8vo. 3s. 6d.

GREEN (John Richard).—A SHORT HISTORY OF THE ENGLISH PEOPLE. With Coloured Maps, Genealogical Tables, and Chronological Annals. New Edition, thoroughly revised. Cr. 8vo. 8s. 6d. 151st Thousand. Also the same in Four Parts. With the corresponding portion of Mr. Tait's "Analysis." 3s. each. Part I 607—1265. II. 1204—1553. III. 1540—1689. IV. 1660—1873.

—— HISTORY OF THE ENGLISH PEOPLE. In 4 vols. 8vo.—Vol. I. With 8 Coloured Maps. 16s.—II. 16s.—III. With 4 Maps. 16s.—IV. With Maps and Index. 16s.

—— THE MAKING OF ENGLAND. With Maps. 8vo. 16s.

—— THE CONQUEST OF ENGLAND. With Maps and Portrait. 8vo. 18s.

—— READINGS IN ENGLISH HISTORY. In 3 Parts. Fcp. 8vo. 1s. 6d. each.

GREEN (J. R.) and GREEN (Alice S.).—A SHORT GEOGRAPHY OF THE BRITISH ISLANDS. With 28 Maps. Fcp. 8vo. 3s. 6d.

GREEN (Mrs. J. R.).—HENRY II. Crown 8vo. 2s. 6d.

GREEN (W. S.).—AMONG THE SELKIRK GLACIERS. Crown 8vo. 7s. 6d.

GREENHILL (Prof. A. G.).—DIFFERENTIAL AND INTEGRAL CALCULUS. Cr. 8vo. 10s.6d.

GREENWOOD (Jessy E.).—THE MOON MAIDEN: AND OTHER STORIES. Crown 8vo. 3s. 6d.

GRIFFITHS (W. H.).—LESSONS ON PRESCRIPTIONS AND THE ART OF PRESCRIBING. New Edition. 18mo. 3s. 6d.

GRIMM'S FAIRY TALES. A Selection from the Household Stories. Translated from the German by LUCY CRANE, and done into Pictures by WALTER CRANE. Crown 8vo. 6s.

GROVE (Sir George).—A DICTIONARY OF MUSIC AND MUSICIANS, A.D. 1450—1889. Edited by Sir GEORGE GROVE, D.C.L. In 4 vols. 8vo, 21s. each. With Illustrations in Music Type and Woodcut.—Also published in Parts. Parts I.—XIV. XIX.—XXII. 3s. 6d. each; XV. XVI. 7s.; XVII. XVIII. 7s.; XXIII.—XXV., Appendix, Edited by J. A. FULLER MAITLAND, M.A. 9s. [Cloth cases for binding the volumes, 1s. each.]

—— A COMPETE INDEX TO THE ABOVE. By Mrs. E. WODEHOUSE. 8vo. 7s. 6d.

—— PRIMER OF GEOGRAPHY. Maps. 18mo.

GUEST (Dr. E.).—ORIGINES CELTICÆ (A Fragment) and other Contributions to the History of Britain. Maps. 2 vols. 8vo. 32s.

GUEST (M. J.).—LECTURES ON THE HISTORY OF ENGLAND. Crown 8vo. 6s.

GUIDE TO THE UNPROTECTED, In Every-day Matters relating to Property and Income. 5th Ed. Extra fcp. 8vo. 3s. 6d.

GUILLEMIN (Amédée).—THE FORCES OF NATURE. A Popular Introduction to the Study of Physical Phenomena. 455 Woodcuts. Royal 8vo. 21s.

—— THE APPLICATIONS OF PHYSICAL FORCES. With Coloured Plates and Illustrations. Royal 8vo. 21s.

—— ELECTRICITY AND MAGNETISM. A Popular Treatise. Translated and Edited, with Additions and Notes, by Prof. SYLVANUS P. THOMPSON. Royal 8vo. [In the Press.

GUIZOT.—GREAT CHRISTIANS OF FRANCE. ST. LOUIS AND CALVIN. Crown 8vo. 6s.

GUNTON (George).—WEALTH AND PROGRESS. Crown 8vo. 6s.

HADLEY (Prof. James).—ESSAYS, PHILOLOGICAL AND CRITICAL. 8vo. 16s.

HADLEY—ALLEN.—A GREEK GRAMMAR FOR SCHOOLS AND COLLEGES. By Prof. JAMES HADLEY. Revised and in part Rewritten by Prof. FREDERIC DE FOREST ALLEN. Crown 8vo. 6s.

HALES (Prof. J. W.).—LONGER ENGLISH POEMS, with Notes, Philological and Explanatory, and an Introduction on the Teaching of English. 12th Ed. Ext. fcp. 8vo. 4s. 6d.

HALL (H. S.) and KNIGHT (S. R.).—ELEMENTARY ALGEBRA FOR SCHOOLS. 6th Ed., revised. Gl. 8vo. 3s. 6d. With Answers, 4s. 6d.
KEY. Crown 8vo. 8s. 6d.

—— ALGEBRAICAL EXERCISES AND EXAMINATION PAPERS to accompany "Elementary Algebra." 2nd Edition. Globe 8vo. 2s. 6d.

—— HIGHER ALGEBRA. A Sequel to "Elementary Algebra for Schools." 3rd Edition. Crown 8vo. 7s. 6d.
KEY. Crown 8vo. 10s. 6d.

—— ARITHMETICAL EXERCISES AND EXAMINATION PAPERS. Globe 8vo. 2s. 6d.

HALL (H. S.) and STEVENS (F. H.).—A TEXT-BOOK OF EUCLID'S ELEMENTS. Globe 8vo. Complete, 4s. 6d.
Book I. 1s.
Books I. and II. 1s. 6d.
Books I.—IV. 3s.
Books III. and IV. 2s.
Books III.—VI. 3s.
Books V. VI. and XI. 2s. 6d.
Book XI. 1s.

HALLWARD (R. F.).—FLOWERS OF PARADISE. Music, Verse, Design, Illustration. Royal 4to. 6s.

HALSTED (G. B.).—THE ELEMENTS OF GEOMETRY. 8vo. 12s. 6d.

HAMERTON (P. G.).—THE INTELLECTUAL LIFE. 4th Edition. Crown 8vo. 10s. 6d.

—— ETCHING AND ETCHERS. 3rd Edition, revised. With 48 Plates. Colombier 8vo.

—— THOUGHTS ABOUT ART. New Edition. Crown 8vo. 8s. 6d.

HAMERTON (P. G.).—HUMAN INTERCOURSE. 4th Edition. Crown 8vo. 8s. 6d.

—— FRENCH AND ENGLISH: A COMPARISON. Crown 8vo. 10s. 6d.

HAMILTON (Prof. D. J.).—ON THE PATHOLOGY OF BRONCHITIS, CATARRHAL PNEUMONIA, TUBERCLE, AND ALLIED LESIONS OF THE HUMAN LUNG. 8vo. 8s. 6d.

—— A TEXT-BOOK OF PATHOLOGY, SYSTEMATIC AND PRACTICAL. Illustrated. Vol. I. 8vo. 25s.

HANBURY (Daniel).—SCIENCE PAPERS, CHIEFLY PHARMACOLOGICAL AND BOTANICAL. Medium 8vo. 14s.

HANDEL: LIFE OF. By W. S. ROCKSTRO. Crown 8vo. 10s. 6d.

HARDWICK (Ven. Archdeacon).—CHRIST AND OTHER MASTERS. 6th Edition. Crown 8vo. 10s. 6d.

—— A HISTORY OF THE CHRISTIAN CHURCH. Middle Age. 6th Edition. Edit. by Bishop STUBBS. Crown 8vo. 10s. 6d.

—— A HISTORY OF THE CHRISTIAN CHURCH DURING THE REFORMATION. 9th Edition. Revised by Bishop STUBBS. Cr. 8vo. 10s. 6d.

HARDY (Arthur Sherburne).—BUT YET A WOMAN. A Novel. Crown 8vo. 4s. 6d.

—— THE WIND OF DESTINY. 2 vols. Globe 8vo. 12s.

HARDY (H. J.).—A LATIN READER FOR THE LOWER FORMS IN SCHOOLS. Globe 8vo. 2s. 6d.

HARDY (Thomas).—See p. 29.

HARE (Julius Charles).—THE MISSION OF THE COMFORTER. New Edition. Edited by Dean PLUMPTRE. Crown 8vo. 7s. 6d.

—— THE VICTORY OF FAITH. Edited by Dean PLUMPTRE, with Introductory Notices by Prof. MAURICE and by Dean STANLEY. Cr. 8vo. 6s. 6d.

—— GUESSES AT TRUTH. By Two Brothers, AUGUSTUS WILLIAM HARE and JULIUS CHARLES HARE. With a Memoir and Two Portraits. 18mo. 4s. 6d.

HARMONIA. By the Author of "Estelle Russel." 3 vols. Crown 8vo. 31s. 6d.

HARPER (Father Thomas).—THE METAPHYSICS OF THE SCHOOL. In 5 vols. Vols. I. and II. 8vo. 18s. each; Vol. III., Part I. 12s.

HARRIS (Rev. G. C.).—SERMONS. With a Memoir by CHARLOTTE M. YONGE, and Portrait. Extra fcp. 8vo. 6s.

HARRISON (Frederic).—THE CHOICE OF BOOKS. Globe 8vo. 6s.
Large Paper Edition. Printed on handmade paper. 15s.

HARRISON (Miss Jane) and VERRALL (Mrs.). MYTHOLOGY AND MONUMENTS OF ANCIENT ATHENS. Illustrated. Cr. 8vo. 16s.

HARTE (Bret).—See p. 29.

HARTLEY (Prof. W. Noel).—A COURSE OF QUANTITATIVE ANALYSIS FOR STUDENTS. Globe 8vo. 5s.

HARWOOD (George).—DISESTABLISHMENT; OR, A DEFENCE OF THE PRINCIPLE OF A NATIONAL CHURCH. 8vo. 12s.

—— THE COMING DEMOCRACY. Cr. 8vo. 6s.

LIST OF PUBLICATIONS. 21

HARWOOD (George).—FROM WITHIN. Cr. 8vo. 6s.

HAYWARD (R. B.).—THE ELEMENTS OF SOLID GEOMETRY. Globe 8vo. 3s.

HEARD (Rev. W. A.).—A SECOND GREEK EXERCISE BOOK. Globe 8vo. 2s. 6d.

HELLENIC STUDIES, THE JOURNAL OF.—8vo. Vol. I. With Plates of Illustrations. 30s.—Vol. II. 30s. With Plates of Illustrations. Or in 2 Parts, 15s. each.—Vol. III. 2 Parts. With Plates of Illustrations. 15s. each.—Vol. IV. 2 Parts. With Plates. Part I. 15s. Part II. 21s. Or complete, 30s.—Vol. V. With Plates. 30s.—Vol. VI. With Plates. Part I. 15s. Part II. 15s. Or complete, 30s.—Vol. VII. Part I. 15s. Part II. 15s. Or complete, 30s.—Vol. VIII. Part I. 15s. Part II. 15s.—Vol. IX. 2 Parts. 15s. each.—Vol. X. 30s.—Vol. XI. Pt. I. 15s. net.

The Journal will be sold at a reduced price to Libraries wishing to subscribe, but official application must in each case be made to the Council. Information on this point, and upon the conditions of Membership, may be obtained on application to the Hon. Sec., Mr. George Macmillan, 29, Bedford Street, Covent Garden.

HENSLOW (Rev. G.).—THE THEORY OF EVOLUTION OF LIVING THINGS, AND THE APPLICATION OF THE PRINCIPLES OF EVOLUTION TO RELIGION. Crown 8vo. 6s.

HERODOTUS.—THE HISTORY. Translated into English, with Notes and Indices, by G. C. MACAULAY, M.A. 2 vols. Cr. 8vo. 18s.

—— BOOKS I.—III. Edited by A. H. SAYCE, M.A. 8vo. 16s.
See also p. 32.

HERTEL (Dr.).—OVERPRESSURE IN HIGH SCHOOLS IN DENMARK. With Introduction by Sir J. CRICHTON-BROWNE. Cr. 8vo. 3s. 6d.

HERVEY (Rt. Rev. Lord Arthur).—THE GENEALOGIES OF OUR LORD AND SAVIOUR JESUS CHRIST. 8vo. 10s. 6d.

HICKS (W. M.).—ELEMENTARY DYNAMICS OF PARTICLES AND SOLIDS. Cr. 8vo. 6s. 6d.

HILL (Florence D.).—CHILDREN OF THE STATE. Ed. by FANNY FOWKE. Cr. 8vo. 6s.

HILL (Octavia).—OUR COMMON LAND, AND OTHER ESSAYS. Extra fcp. 8vo. 3s. 6d.

—— HOMES OF THE LONDON POOR. Sewed. Crown 8vo. 1s.

HIORNS (Arthur H.).—PRACTICAL METALLURGY AND ASSAYING. A Text-Book for the use of Teachers, Students, and Assayers. With Illustrations. Globe 8vo. 6s.

—— A TEXT-BOOK OF ELEMENTARY METALLURGY FOR THE USE OF STUDENTS. Gl. 8vo. 4s.

—— IRON AND STEEL MANUFACTURE. A Text-Book for Beginners. Illustr. Gl. 8vo. 3s. 6d.

—— MIXED METALS OR METALLIC ALLOYS. Globe 8vo. 6s.

HISTORICAL COURSE FOR SCHOOLS. Ed. by EDW. A. FREEMAN, D.C.L. 18mo.
Vol. I. GENERAL SKETCH OF EUROPEAN HISTORY. By E. A. FREEMAN. With Maps, &c. 3s. 6d.
II. HISTORY OF ENGLAND. By EDITH THOMPSON. Coloured Maps. 2s. 6d.
III. HISTORY OF SCOTLAND. By MARGARET MACARTHUR. 2s.

HISTORICAL COURSE FOR SCHOOLS —*continued.*
IV. HISTORY OF ITALY. By the Rev. W. HUNT, M.A. Maps. 3s. 6d.
V. HISTORY OF GERMANY. By JAMES SIME, M.A. 3s.
VI. HISTORY OF AMERICA. By J. A. DOYLE. With Maps. 4s. 6d.
VII. HISTORY OF EUROPEAN COLONIES. By E. J. PAYNE, M.A. Maps. 4s. 6d.
VIII. HISTORY OF FRANCE. By CHARLOTTE M. YONGE. Maps. 3s. 6d.

HOBART.—ESSAYS AND MISCELLANEOUS WRITINGS OF VERE HENRY, LORD HOBART. With a Biographical Sketch. Edited by MARY, LADY HOBART. 2 vols. 8vo. 25s.

HOBDAY (E.).—VILLA GARDENING. A Handbook for Amateur and Practical Gardeners. Extra crown 8vo. 6s.

HODGSON (F.).—MYTHOLOGY FOR LATIN VERSIFICATION. 6th Edition. Revised by F. C. HODGSON, M.A. 18mo. 3s.

HODGSON.—MEMOIR OF REV. FRANCIS HODGSON, B.D., SCHOLAR, POET, AND DIVINE. By his Son, the Rev. JAMES T. HODGSON, M.A. 2 vols. Crown 8vo. 18s.

HÖFFDING (Dr. H.).—OUTLINES OF PSYCHOLOGY. Translated by M. E. LOWNDES. Crown 8vo. 6s.

HOFMANN (Prof. A. W.).—THE LIFE WORK OF LIEBIG IN EXPERIMENTAL AND PHILOSOPHIC CHEMISTRY. 8vo. 5s.

HOGAN, M.P. Globe 8vo. 2s.

HOLE (Rev. C.).—GENEALOGICAL STEMMA OF THE KINGS OF ENGLAND AND FRANCE. On a Sheet. 1s.

—— A BRIEF BIOGRAPHICAL DICTIONARY. 2nd Edition. 18mo. 4s. 6d.

HOLLAND (Prof. T. E.).—THE TREATY RELATIONS OF RUSSIA AND TURKEY, FROM 1774 TO 1853. Crown 8vo. 2s.

HOLMES (O. W., Jun.).—THE COMMON LAW. 8vo. 12s.

HOMER.—THE ODYSSEY OF HOMER DONE INTO ENGLISH PROSE. By S. H. BUTCHER, M.A., and A. LANG, M.A. 7th Edition. Crown 8vo. 6s.

—— THE ODYSSEY OF HOMER. Books I.—XII. Translated into English Verse by the EARL OF CARNARVON. Crown 8vo. 7s. 6d.

—— THE ILIAD. Edited, with English Notes and Introduction, by WALTER LEAF, Litt.D. 2 vols. 8vo. 14s. each.—Vol. I. Bks. I.—XII; Vol. II. Bks. XIII.—XXIV.

—— ILIAD. Translated into English Prose. By ANDREW LANG, WALTER LEAF, and ERNEST MYERS. Crown 8vo. 12s. 6d.

—— PRIMER OF HOMER. By Rt. Hon. W. E. GLADSTONE, M.P. 18mo. 1s.
See also pp. 31, 32.

HON. MISS FERRARD, THE. By the Author of "Hogan, M.P." Globe 8vo. 2s.

HOOKER (Sir J. D.).—THE STUDENT'S FLORA OF THE BRITISH ISLANDS. Edition. Globe 8vo. 10s. 6d.

—— PRIMER OF BOTANY. 18mo. 1s.

HOOKER (Sir Joseph D.) and BALL (J.).—JOURNAL OF A TOUR IN MAROCCO AND THE GREAT ATLAS. 8vo. 21s.

HOOLE (C. H.).—THE CLASSICAL ELEMENT IN THE NEW TESTAMENT. Considered as a Proof of its Genuineness. 8vo. 10s. 6d.

HOOPER (W. H.) and PHILLIPS (W. C.).—A MANUAL OF MARKS ON POTTERY AND PORCELAIN. 16mo. 4s. 6d.

HOPE (Frances J.).—NOTES AND THOUGHTS ON GARDENS AND WOODLANDS. Cr. 8vo. 6s.

HOPKINS (Ellice).—AUTUMN SWALLOWS: A Book of Lyrics. Extra fcp. 8vo. 6s.

HOPPUS (Mary).—A GREAT TREASON: A Story of the War of Independence. 2 vols. Crown 8vo. 9s.

HORACE.—THE WORKS OF HORACE RENDERED INTO ENGLISH PROSE. By J. LONSDALE and S. LEE. Globe 8vo. 3s. 6d.

—— STUDIES, LITERARY AND HISTORICAL, IN THE ODES OF HORACE. By A. W. VERRALL, Litt.D. 8vo. 8s. 6d.

—— THE ODES OF HORACE IN A METRICAL PARAPHRASE. By R. M. HOVENDEN, B.A. Extra fcap. 8vo. 4s. 6d.

—— LIFE AND CHARACTER: AN EPITOME OF HIS SATIRES AND EPISTLES. By R. M. HOVENDEN, B.A. Ext. fcp. 8vo. 4s. 6d.

—— WORD FOR WORD FROM HORACE: The Odes Literally Versified. By W. T. THORNTON, C.B. Crown 8vo. 7s. 6d.

See also pp. 31, 32.

HORT.—TWO DISSERTATIONS. I. On MONOΓENHΣ ΘEOΣ in Scripture and Tradition. II. On the "Constantinopolitan" Creed and other Eastern Creeds of the Fourth Century. By FENTON JOHN ANTHONY HORT, D.D. 8vo. 7s. 6d.

HORTON (Hon. S. Dana).—THE SILVER POUND AND ENGLAND'S MONETARY POLICY SINCE THE RESTORATION. With a History of the Guinea. 8vo. 14s.

HOWELL (George).—THE CONFLICTS OF CAPITAL AND LABOUR. 2nd Ed. Cr 8vo. 7s.6d.

HOWES (Prof. G. B.). AN ATLAS OF PRACTICAL ELEMENTARY BIOLOGY. With a Preface by Prof. HUXLEY. 4to. 14s.

HOZIER (Lieut.-Colonel H. M.).—THE SEVEN WEEKS' WAR. 3rd Edition. Crown 8vo. 6s.

—— THE INVASIONS OF ENGLAND. 2 vols. 8vo. 28s.

HÜBNER (Baron von).—A RAMBLE ROUND THE WORLD. Crown 8vo. 6s.

HUGHES (Thomas). ALFRED THE GREAT. Crown 8vo. 6s.

—— TOM BROWN'S SCHOOL DAYS. By AN OLD BOY. Illustrated Edition. Crown 8vo. 6s.—Golden Treasury Edition. 4s. 6d.—Uniform Edition. 3s.6d.—People's Edition. 2s.—People's Sixpenny Edition, Illustrated. Med. 4to. 6d.—Uniform with Sixpenny Kingsley. Medium 8vo. 6d.

—— TOM BROWN AT OXFORD. Crown 8vo. 6s.—Uniform Edition. 3s. 6d.

—— MEMOIR OF DANIEL MACMILLAN. With Portrait. Cr. 8vo. 4s. 6d.—Cheap Edition. Sewed. Crown 8vo. 1s.

HUGHES (T.).—RUGBY, TENNESSEE. Crn. 8vo. 4s. 6d.

—— GONE TO TEXAS. Edited by THOMAS HUGHES, Q.C. Crown 8vo. 4s. 6d.

—— THE SCOURING OF THE WHITE HORSE, AND THE ASHEN FAGGOT. Uniform Edit. 3s. 6d.

—— JAMES FRASER, Second Bishop of Manchester. A Memoir, 1818—85. Cr. 8vo. 6s.

—— FIFTY YEARS AGO: Rugby Address, 1891. 8vo, sewed. 6d. net.

HULL (E.).—A TREATISE ON ORNAMENTAL AND BUILDING STONES OF GREAT BRITAIN AND FOREIGN COUNTRIES. 8vo. 12s.

HULLAH (M. E.).—HANNAH TARNE. A Story for Girls. Globe 8vo. 2s. 6d.

HUMPHRY (Prof. Sir G. M.).—THE HUMAN SKELETON (INCLUDING THE JOINTS). With 260 Illustrations drawn from Nature. Med. 8vo. 14s.

—— THE HUMAN FOOT AND THE HUMAN HAND. With Illustrations. Fcp. 8vo. 4s. 6d.

—— OBSERVATIONS IN MYOLOGY. 8vo. 6s.

—— OLD AGE. The Results of Information received respecting nearly nine hundred persons who had attained the age of eighty years, including seventy-four centenarians. Crown 8vo. 4s. 6d.

HUNT (W.).—TALKS ABOUT ART. With a Letter from Sir J. E. MILLAIS, Bart., R.A. Crown 8vo. 3s. 6d.

HUSS (Hermann).—A SYSTEM OF ORAL INSTRUCTION IN GERMAN. Crown 8vo. 5s.

HUTTON (R. H.).—ESSAYS ON SOME OF THE MODERN GUIDES OF ENGLISH THOUGHT IN MATTERS OF FAITH. Globe 8vo. 6s.

—— ESSAYS. 2 vols. Globe 8vo. 6s. each.—Vol. I. Literary Essays; II. Theological Essays.

HUXLEY (Thomas Henry).—LESSONS IN ELEMENTARY PHYSIOLOGY. With numerous Illustrations. New Edit. Fcp. 8vo. 4s. 6d.

—— LAY SERMONS, ADDRESSES, AND REVIEWS. 9th Edition. 8vo. 7s. 6d.

—— ESSAYS SELECTED FROM LAY SERMONS, ADDRESSES, AND REVIEWS. 3rd Edition. Crown 8vo. 1s.

—— CRITIQUES AND ADDRESSES. 8vo. 10s. 6d.

—— PHYSIOGRAPHY. AN INTRODUCTION TO THE STUDY OF NATURE. 13th Ed. Cr.8vo. 6s.

—— AMERICAN ADDRESSES, WITH A LECTURE ON THE STUDY OF BIOLOGY. 8vo. 6s. 6d.

—— SCIENCE AND CULTURE, AND OTHER ESSAYS. 8vo. 10s. 6d.

—— SOCIAL DISEASES AND WORSE REMEDIES: LETTERS TO THE "TIMES" ON MR. BOOTH'S SCHEMES. With a Preface and Introductory Essay. 2nd Ed. Cr. 8vo, sewed. 1s. net.

HUXLEY'S PHYSIOLOGY, QUESTIONS ON, FOR SCHOOLS. By T. ALCOCK, M.D. 5th Edition. 18mo. 1s. 6d.

HUXLEY (T. H.) and MARTIN (H. N.).—A COURSE OF PRACTICAL INSTRUCTION IN ELEMENTARY BIOLOGY. New Edition, Revised and Extended by Prof. G. B. HOWES and D. H. SCOTT, M.A., Ph.D. With Preface by T. H. HUXLEY, F.R.S. Cr. 8vo. 10s. 6d.

LIST OF PUBLICATIONS. 23

IBBETSON (W. J.).—An Elementary Treatise on the Mathematical Theory of Perfectly Elastic Solids. 8vo. 21s.

ILLINGWORTH (Rev. J. R.).—Sermons Preached in a College Chapel. Crown 8vo. 5s.

IMITATIO CHRISTI, Libri IV. Printed in Borders after Holbein, Dürer, and other old Masters, containing Dances of Death, Acts of Mercy, Emblems, &c. Cr. 8vo. 7s. 6d.

INDIAN TEXT-BOOKS.—Primer of English Grammar. By R. Morris, LL.D. 18mo. 1s.; sewed, 10d.

Primer of Astronomy. By J. N. Lockyer. 18mo. 1s.; sewed, 10d.

Easy Selections from Modern English Literature. For the use of the Middle Classes in Indian Schools. With Notes. By Sir Roper Lethbridge. Cr. 8vo. 1s. 6d.

Selections from Modern English Literature. For the use of the Higher Classes in Indian Schools. By Sir Roper Lethbridge, M.A. Crown 8vo. 3s. 6d.

Series of Six English Reading Books for Indian Children. By P. C. Sircar. Revised by Sir Roper Lethbridge. Cr. 8vo. Book I. 5d.; Nagari Characters, 5d.; Persian Characters, 5d.; Book II. 6d.; Book III. 8d.; Book IV. 1s.; Book V. 1s. 2d.; Book VI. 1s. 3d.

High School Reader. By Eric Robertson. Crown 8vo. 2s.

Notes on the High School Reader. By the same. Crown 8vo. 1s.

The Orient Readers. Books I.—VI. By the same.

A Geographical Reader and Companion to the Atlas. By C. B. Clarke, F.R.S. Crown 8vo. 2s.

A Class-Book of Geography. By the same. Fcap. 8vo. 3s.; sewed, 2s. 6d.

The World's History. Compiled under direction of Sir Roper Lethbridge. Crown 8vo. 1s.

Easy Introduction to the History of India. By Sir Roper Lethbridge. Crown 8vo. 1s. 6d.

History of England. Compiled under direction of Sir Roper Lethbridge. Crown 8vo. 1s. 6d.

Easy Introduction to the History and Geography of Bengal. By Sir Roper Lethbridge. Crown 8vo. 1s. 6d.

Arithmetic. With Answers. By Barnard Smith. 18mo. 2s.

Algebra. By I. Todhunter. 18mo, sewed. 2s. 3d.

Euclid. First Four Books. With Notes, &c. By I. Todhunter. 18mo. 2s.

Elementary Mensuration and Land Surveying. By the same Author. 18mo. 2s.

Euclid. Books I.—IV. By H. S. Hall and F. H. Stevens. Gl. 8vo. 3s.; sewed, 2s. 6d.

Physical Geography. By H. F. Blanford. Crown 8vo. 2s. 6d.

Elementary Geometry and Conic Sections. By J. M. Wilson. Ex. fcp. 8vo. 6s.

INGRAM (T. Dunbar).—A History of the Legislative Union of Great Britain and Ireland. 8vo. 10s. 6d.

—— Two Chapters of Irish History: I. The Irish Parliament of James II.; II. The Alleged Violation of the Treaty of Limerick. 8vo. 6s.

IRVING (Joseph).—Annals of Our Time. A Diurnal of Events, Social and Political, Home and Foreign. From the Accession of Queen Victoria to Jubilee Day, being the First Fifty Years of Her Majesty's Reign. In 2 vols. 8vo.—Vol. I. June 20th, 1837, to February 28th, 1871. Vol. II. February 24th, 1871, to June 24th, 1887. 18s. each. The Second Volume may also be had in Three Parts: Part I. February 24th, 1871, to March 19th, 1874, 4s. 6d. Part II. March 20th, 1874, to July 22nd, 1878, 4s. 6d. Part III. July 23rd, 1878, to June 24th, 1887, 9s.

IRVING (Washington).—Old Christmas. From the Sketch Book. With 100 Illustrations by Randolph Caldecott. Crown 8vo, gilt edges. 6s.
Also with uncut edges, paper label. 6s.
People's Edition. Medium 4to. 6d.

—— Bracebridge Hall. With 120 Illustrations by Randolph Caldecott. Cloth elegant, gilt edges. Crown 8vo. 6s.
Also with uncut edges, paper label. 6s.
People's Edition. Medium 4to. 6d.

—— Old Christmas and Bracebridge Hall. Illustrations by Randolph Caldecott. *Edition de Luxe.* Royal 8vo. 21s.

ISMAY'S CHILDREN. By the Author of "Hogan, M.P." Globe 8vo. 2s.

JACKSON (Rev. Blomfield).—First Steps to Greek Prose Composition. 12th Edit. 18mo. 1s. 6d.
Key (supplied to Teachers only). 3s. 6d.

—— Second Steps to Greek Prose Composition. 18mo. 2s. 6d.
Key (supplied to Teachers only). 3s. 6d.

JACOB (Rev. J. A.).—Building in Silence, and other Sermons. Extra fcp. 8vo. 6s.

JAMES (Hen.).—Novels and Tales. Pocket Edition. 18mo. 14 vols. 2s. each vol.; The Portrait of a Lady. 3 vols.—Roderick Hudson. 2 vols.—The American. 2 vols. —Washington Square. 1 vol.—The Europeans. 1 vol.—Confidence. 1 vol. —The Siege of London; Madame de Mauves. 1 vol.—An International Episode; The Pension Beaurepas; The Point of View. 1 vol.—Daisy Miller, a Study; Four Meetings; Longstaff's Marriage; Benvolio. 1 vol.—The Madonna of the Future; A Bundle of Letters; The Diary of a Man of Fifty; Eugene Pickering. 1 vol.

—— French Poets and Novelists. New Edition. Crown 8vo. 4s. 6d.

—— Tales of Three Cities. Cr. 8vo. 4s. 6d.

—— Portraits of Places. Cr. 8vo. 7s. 6d.

—— Partial Portraits. Crown 8vo. 6s.
See also pp. 29, 30.

JAMES (Rev. Herbert).—The Country Clergyman and his Work. Cr. 8vo. 6s.

JAMES (Right Hon. Sir William Milbourne).—The British in India. 8vo. 12s. 6d.

JAMES (Wm.).—THE PRINCIPLES OF PSYCHOLOGY. 2 vols. 8vo. 25s. net.

JARDINE (Rev. Robert).—THE ELEMENTS OF THE PSYCHOLOGY OF COGNITION. Third Edition. Crown 8vo. 6s. 6d.

JEANS (Rev. G. E.).—HAILEYBURY CHAPEL, AND OTHER SERMONS. Fcp. 8vo. 3s. 6d.

JEBB (Prof. R. C.).—THE ATTIC ORATORS, FROM ANTIPHON TO ISAEOS. 2 vols. 8vo. 25s.

—— MODERN GREECE. Two Lectures. Crown 8vo. 5s.

JELLETT (Rev. Dr.).—THE ELDER SON, AND OTHER SERMONS. Crown 8vo. 6s.

—— THE EFFICACY OF PRAYER. 3rd Edition. Crown 8vo. 5s.

JENNINGS (A. C.).—CHRONOLOGICAL TABLES OF ANCIENT HISTORY. With Index. 8vo. 5s.

JENNINGS (A. C.) and LOWE (W. H.).—THE PSALMS, WITH INTRODUCTIONS AND CRITICAL NOTES. 2 vols. 2nd Edition. Crown 8vo. 10s. 6d. each.

JEVONS (W. Stanley).—THE PRINCIPLES OF SCIENCE: A TREATISE ON LOGIC AND SCIENTIFIC METHOD. Crown 8vo. 12s. 6d.

JEVONS (W. S.).—ELEMENTARY LESSONS IN LOGIC: DEDUCTIVE AND INDUCTIVE. 18mo. 3s. 6d.

—— THE THEORY OF POLITICAL ECONOMY. 3rd Edition. 8vo. 10s. 6d.

—— STUDIES IN DEDUCTIVE LOGIC. 2nd Edition. Crown 8vo. 6s.

—— INVESTIGATIONS IN CURRENCY AND FINANCE. Edited, with an Introduction, by H. S. FOXWELL, M.A. Illustrated by 20 Diagrams. 8vo. 21s.

—— METHODS OF SOCIAL REFORM. 8vo. 10s. 6d.

—— THE STATE IN RELATION TO LABOUR. Crown 8vo. 3s. 6d.

—— LETTERS AND JOURNAL. Edited by HIS WIFE. 8vo. 14s.

—— PURE LOGIC, AND OTHER MINOR WORKS. Edited by R. ADAMSON, M.A., and HARRIET A. JEVONS. With a Preface by Prof. ADAMSON. 8vo. 10s. 6d.

JEX-BLAKE (Dr. Sophia).—THE CARE OF INFANTS: A Manual for Mothers and Nurses. 18mo. 1s.

JOHNSON (W. E.).—A TREATISE ON TRIGONOMETRY. Crown 8vo. 8s. 6d.

JOHNSON (Prof. W. Woolsey).—CURVE TRACING IN CARTESIAN CO-ORDINATES. Crown 8vo. 4s. 6d.

—— A TREATISE ON ORDINARY AND DIFFERENTIAL EQUATIONS. Crown 8vo. 15s.

—— AN ELEMENTARY TREATISE ON THE INTEGRAL CALCULUS. Crown 8vo. 9s.

JOHNSON'S LIVES OF THE POETS. The Six Chief Lives. Edited by MATTHEW ARNOLD. Crown 8vo. 4s. 6d.

JONES (D. E.).—EXAMPLES IN PHYSICS. Containing 1000 Problems, with Answers and numerous solved Examples. Fcp. 8vo. 3s. 6d.

—— ELEMENTARY LESSONS IN HEAT, LIGHT, AND SOUND. Globe 8vo. 2s. 6d.

JONES (F.).—THE OWENS COLLEGE JUNIOR COURSE OF PRACTICAL CHEMISTRY. With Preface by Sir HENRY E. ROSCOE. New Edition. 18mo. 2s. 6d.

—— QUESTIONS ON CHEMISTRY. A Series of Problems and Exercises in Inorganic and Organic Chemistry. 18mo. 3s.

JONES (Rev. C. A.) and CHEYNE (C. H.).—ALGEBRAICAL EXERCISES. Progressively arranged. 18mo. 2s. 6d.

—— SOLUTIONS OF SOME OF THE EXAMPLES IN THE ALGEBRAICAL EXERCISES OF MESSRS. JONES AND CHEYNE. By the Rev. W. FAILES. Crown 8vo. 7s. 6d.

JUVENAL. THIRTEEN SATIRES OF JUVENAL. With a Commentary by Prof. J. E. B. MAYOR, M.A. 4th Edition. Vol. I. Crown 8vo. 10s. 6d.—Vol. II. Crown 8vo. 10s. 6d. Supplement to Third Edition, containing the Principal Changes made in the Fourth Edition. 5s.

—— THIRTEEN SATIRES. Translated into English after the Text of J. E. B. MAYOR by ALEX. LEEPER, M.A. Cr. 8vo. 3s. 6d.

See also p. 32.

KANT.—KANT'S CRITICAL PHILOSOPHY FOR ENGLISH READERS. By JOHN P. MAHAFFY, D.D., and JOHN H. BERNARD, B.D. New Edition. 2 vols. Crown 8vo. Vol. I. THE KRITIK OF PURE REASON EXPLAINED AND DEFENDED. 7s. 6d.—Vol. II. THE "PROLEGOMENA." Translated, with Notes and Appendices. 6s.

KANT—MAX MÜLLER.—CRITIQUE OF PURE REASON BY IMMANUEL KANT. Translated by F. MAX MÜLLER. With Introduction by LUDWIG NOIRÉ. 2 vols. 8vo. 16s. each.—Sold separately. Vol. I. HISTORICAL INTRODUCTION, by LUDWIG NOIRÉ, etc., etc.; Vol. II. CRITIQUE OF PURE REASON.

KAVANAGH (Rt. Hon. A. McMURROUGH): A Biography compiled by his Cousin, SARAH L. STEELE. With Portrait. 8vo. 14s. net.

KAY (Rev. W.).—A COMMENTARY ON ST. PAUL'S TWO EPISTLES TO THE CORINTHIANS. Greek Text, with Commentary. 8vo. 9s.

KEARY (Annie).—NATIONS AROUND. Crn. 8vo. 4s. 6d. *See also* pp. 28, 29.

KEARY (Eliza).—THE MAGIC VALLEY; OR, PATIENT ANTOINE. With Illustrations by "E.V.B." Globe 8vo. 2s. 6d.

KEARY (A. and E.).—THE HEROES OF ASGARD. Tales from Scandinavian Mythology. Globe 8vo. 2s. 6d.

KEATS. LETTERS OF KEATS. Edited by SIDNEY COLVIN. Globe 8vo.

KELLAND (P.) and TAIT (P. G.).—INTRODUCTION TO QUATERNIONS, WITH NUMEROUS EXAMPLES. 2nd Edition. Cr. 8vo. 7s. 6d.

KELLOGG (Rev. S. H.).—THE LIGHT OF ASIA AND THE LIGHT OF THE WORLD. Cr. 8vo. 7s. 6d.

KENNEDY (Prof. Alex. W. B.).—THE MECHANICS OF MACHINERY. With Illustrations. Crown 8vo. 12s. 6d.

KERNEL AND THE HUSK (THE): LETTERS ON SPIRITUAL CHRISTIANITY. By the Author of "Philochristus." Crown 8vo. 5s.

LIST OF PUBLICATIONS. 25

KEYNES (J. N.).—STUDIES AND EXERCISES IN FORMAL LOGIC. 2nd Ed. Cr. 8vo. 10s. 6d.

—— THE SCOPE AND METHOD OF POLITICAL ECONOMY. Crown 8vo. 7s. net.

KIEPERT (H.).—MANUAL OF ANCIENT GEOGRAPHY. Crown 8vo. 5s.

KILLEN (W. D.).—ECCLESIASTICAL HISTORY OF IRELAND, FROM THE EARLIEST DATE TO THE PRESENT TIME. 2 vols. 8vo. 25s.

KINGSLEY (Charles): HIS LETTERS, AND MEMORIES OF HIS LIFE. Edited by HIS WIFE. 2 vols. Crown 8vo. 12s.—*Cheap Edition*, 6s.

—— NOVELS AND POEMS. *Eversley Edition.* 13 vols. Globe 8vo. 5s. each.

WESTWARD HO! 2 vols.—TWO YEARS AGO. 2 vols.—HYPATIA. 2 vols.—YEAST. 1 vol.—ALTON LOCKE. 2 vols.—HEREWARD THE WAKE. 2 vols.—POEMS. 2 vols.

—— *Complete Edition* OF THE WORKS OF CHARLES KINGSLEY. Cr. 8vo. 3s. 6d. each.

WESTWARD HO! With a Portrait.
HYPATIA. | YEAST.
ALTON LOCKE. | TWO YEARS AGO.
HEREWARD THE WAKE. | POEMS.
THE HEROES; OR, GREEK FAIRY TALES FOR MY CHILDREN.
THE WATER BABIES: A FAIRY TALE FOR A LAND-BABY.
MADAM HOW AND LADY WHY; OR, FIRST LESSONS IN EARTH-LORE FOR CHILDREN.
AT LAST: A CHRISTMAS IN THE WEST INDIES.
PROSE IDYLLS. | PLAYS AND PURITANS.
THE ROMAN AND THE TEUTON. With Preface by Professor MAX MÜLLER.
SANITARY AND SOCIAL LECTURES.
HISTORICAL LECTURES AND ESSAYS.
SCIENTIFIC LECTURES AND ESSAYS.
LITERARY AND GENERAL LECTURES.
THE HERMITS.
GLAUCUS; OR, THE WONDERS OF THE SEASHORE. With Coloured Illustrations.
VILLAGE AND TOWN AND COUNTRY SERMONS.
THE WATER OF LIFE, AND OTHER SERMONS.
SERMONS ON NATIONAL SUBJECTS, AND THE KING OF THE EARTH.
SERMONS FOR THE TIMES.
GOOD NEWS OF GOD.
THE GOSPEL OF THE PENTATEUCH, AND DAVID.
DISCIPLINE, AND OTHER SERMONS.
WESTMINSTER SERMONS.
ALL SAINTS' DAY, AND OTHER SERMONS.

—— A *Sixpenny Edition* OF CHARLES KINGSLEY'S NOVELS. Med. 8vo. 6d. each.

WESTWARD HO!—HYPATIA.—YEAST.—ALTON LOCKE.—TWO YEARS AGO.—HEREWARD THE WAKE.

—— THE WATER BABIES: A FAIRY TALE FOR A LAND BABY. New Edition, with 100 New Pictures by LINLEY SAMBOURNE; engraved by J. SWAIN. Fcp. 4to. 12s. 6d.

—— THE HEROES; OR, GREEK FAIRY TALES FOR MY CHILDREN. Extra cloth, gilt edges. *Presentation Edition.* Crown 8vo. 7s. 6d.

—— GLAUCUS; OR, THE WONDERS OF THE SEA SHORE. With Coloured Illustrations, extra cloth, gilt edges. *Presentation Edition.* Crown 8vo. 7s. 6d.

KINGSLEY (C.).—HEALTH AND EDUCATION. Crown 8vo. 6s.

—— POEMS. *Pocket Edition.* 18mo. 1s. 6d.

—— SELECTIONS FROM SOME OF THE WRITINGS OF CHARLES KINGSLEY. Crown 8vo. 6s.

—— OUT OF THE DEEP: WORDS FOR THE SORROWFUL. From the Writings of CHARLES KINGSLEY. Extra fcp. 8vo. 3s. 6d.

—— DAILY THOUGHTS. Selected from the Writings of CHARLES KINGSLEY. By HIS WIFE. Crown 8vo. 6s.

—— FROM DEATH TO LIFE. Fragments of Teaching to a Village Congregation. With Letters on the "Life after Death." Edited by HIS WIFE. Fcp. 8vo. 2s. 6d.

—— TRUE WORDS FOR BRAVE MEN. Crown 8vo. 2s. 6d.

KINGSLEY (Henry).—TALES OF OLD TRAVEL. Crown 8vo. 3s. 6d.

KIPLING (Rudyard).—PLAIN TALES FROM THE HILLS. Crown 8vo. 6s.

—— THE LIGHT THAT FAILED. Cr. 8vo. 6s.

KITCHENER (F. E.).—GEOMETRICAL NOTE-BOOK. Containing Easy Problems in Geometrical Drawing, preparatory to the Study of Geometry. 4to. 2s.

KLEIN (Dr. E.).—MICRO-ORGANISMS AND DISEASE. An Introduction into the Study of Specific Micro-Organisms. With 121 Engravings. 3rd Edition. Crown 8vo. 6s.

—— THE BACTERIA IN ASIATIC CHOLERA Crown 8vo. 5s.

KNOX (A.).—DIFFERENTIAL CALCULUS FOR BEGINNERS. Fcp. 8vo. 3s. 6d.

KTESIAS.—THE FRAGMENTS OF THE PERSIKA OF KTESIAS. Edited, with Introduction and Notes, by J. GILMORE, M.A. 8vo. 8s. 6d.

KUENEN (Prof. A.).—AN HISTORICO-CRITICAL INQUIRY INTO THE ORIGIN AND COMPOSITION OF THE HEXATEUCH (PENTATEUCH AND BOOK OF JOSHUA). Translated by PHILIP H. WICKSTEED, M.A. 8vo. 14s.

KYNASTON (Herbert, D.D.).—SERMONS PREACHED IN THE COLLEGE CHAPEL, CHELTENHAM. Crown 8vo. 6s.

—— PROGRESSIVE EXERCISES IN THE COMPOSITION OF GREEK IAMBIC VERSE. Extra fcp. 8vo. 5s.

KEY (supplied to Teachers only). 4s. 6d.

—— EXEMPLARIA CHELTONIENSIA. Sive quae discipulis suis Carmina identidem Latine reddenda proposuit ipse reddidit ex cathedra dictavit HERBERT KYNASTON, M.A. Extra fcp. 8vo. 5s.

LABBERTON (R. H.).—NEW HISTORICAL ATLAS AND GENERAL HISTORY. 4to. 15s.

LAFARGUE (Philip).—THE NEW JUDGMENT OF PARIS: A Novel. 2 vols. Gl. 8vo. 12s.

LAMB.—COLLECTED WORKS. Edited, with Introduction and Notes, by the Rev. ALFRED AINGER, M.A. Globe 8vo. 5s. each volume.
I. ESSAYS OF ELIA.—II. PLAYS, POEMS, AND MISCELLANEOUS ESSAYS.—III. MRS. LEICESTER'S SCHOOL; THE ADVENTURES OF ULYSSES; AND OTHER ESSAYS.—IV. TALES FROM SHAKSPEARE.—V. and VI. LETTERS. Newly arranged, with additions.

LAMB. THE LIFE OF CHARLES LAMB. By Rev. ALFRED AINGER, M.A. Uniform with above. Globe 8vo. 5s.
—— TALES FROM SHAKSPEARE. 18mo. 4s. 6d. *Globe Readings Edition.* For Schools. Globe 8vo. 2s.

LANCIANI (Prof. R.).—ANCIENT ROME IN THE LIGHT OF RECENT DISCOVERIES. 4to. 24s.

LAND OF DARKNESS (THE). With some further Chapters in the Experiences of The Little Pilgrim. By the Author of "A Little Pilgrim in the Unseen." Cr. 8vo. 5s.

LANDAUER (J.) — BLOWPIPE ANALYSIS. Authorised English Edition by JAMES TAYLOR and WM. E. KAY. Ext. fcp. 8vo. 4s. 6d.

LANG (Andrew).—THE LIBRARY. With a Chapter on Modern Illustrated Books, by AUSTIN DOBSON. Crown 8vo. 3s. 6d.

LANG (Prof. Arnold).—TEXT-BOOK OF COMPARATIVE ANATOMY. Translated by H. M. BERNARD, M.A., F.Z.S., and MATILDA BERNARD. With Preface by Professor E. HAECKEL. 2 vols. Illustrated. 8vo

LANKESTER (Prof. E. Ray).— THE ADVANCEMENT OF SCIENCE: OCCASIONAL ESSAYS AND ADDRESSES. 8vo. 10s. 6d.
—— COMPARATIVE LONGEVITY IN MAN AND THE LOWER ANIMALS. Crn. 8vo. 4s. 6d.

LASLETT (Thomas).—TIMBER AND TIMBER TREES, NATIVE AND FOREIGN. Cr. 8vo. 8s. 6d.

LEAHY (Sergeant).—THE ART OF SWIMMING IN THE ETON STYLE. With Preface by Mrs. OLIPHANT. Crown 8vo. 2s.

LECTURES ON ART. By REGD. STUART POOLE, Professor W. B. RICHMOND, E. J. POYNTER, R.A., J. T. MICKLETHWAITE, and WILLIAM MORRIS. Crown 8vo. 4s. 6d.

LEPROSY INVESTIGATION COMMITTEE, JOURNAL OF THE. Ed. by P. S. ABRAHAM, M.A. Nos. I. II. 2s. 6d. each net.

LETHBRIDGE (Sir Roper).—A SHORT MANUAL OF THE HISTORY OF INDIA. With Maps. Crown 8vo. 5s.
For other Works by this Author, see *Indian Text-Books Series*, p. 23.

LEVETT R.) and DAVISON (A. F.).— ELEMENTS OF TRIGONOMETRY. Crown 8vo.

LEWIS (Richard).—HISTORY OF THE LIFE-BOAT AND ITS WORK. Crown 8vo. 5s.

LIGHTFOOT (Bishop). — ST. PAUL'S EPISTLE TO THE GALATIANS. A Revised Text, with Introduction, Notes, and Dissertations. 10th Edition. 8vo. 12s.
—— ST. PAUL'S EPISTLE TO THE PHILIPPIANS. A Revised Text, with Introduction, Notes and Dissertations. 9th Edition. 8vo. 12s.
—— ST. PAUL'S EPISTLES TO THE COLOSSIANS AND TO PHILEMON. A Revised Text with Introductions, etc. 9th Edition. 8vo. 12s.
—— THE APOSTOLIC FATHERS. Part I. ST. CLEMENT OF ROME. A Revised Text, with Introductions, Notes, Dissertations, and Translations. 2 vols. 8vo. 32s.
—— THE APOSTOLIC FATHERS. Part II. ST. IGNATIUS TO ST. POLYCARP. Revised Texts, with Introductions, Notes, Dissertations, and Translations. 2nd Edit. 3 vols. 8vo. 48s.

LIGHTFOOT (Bishop). — THE APOSTOLIC FATHERS. Abridged Edition. With Short Introductions, Greek Text, and English Translation. 8vo.
—— ESSAYS ON THE WORK ENTITLED "SUPERNATURAL RELIGION." 8vo. 10s. 6d.
—— A CHARGE DELIVERED TO THE CLERGY OF THE DIOCESE OF DURHAM, NOV. 25TH, 1886. Demy 8vo. 2s.
—— LEADERS IN THE NORTHERN CHURCH. 2nd Edition. Crown 8vo. 6s.
—— ORDINATION ADDRESSES AND COUNSELS TO CLERGY. Crown 8vo. 6s.
—— CAMBRIDGE SERMONS. Crown 8vo. 6s.
—— SERMONS PREACHED IN ST. PAUL'S CATHEDRAL. Crown 8vo. 6s.
—— SERMONS PREACHED ON SPECIAL OCCASIONS. Crown 8vo.
—— ON THE REVISION OF THE NEW TESTAMENT. Crown 8vo.

LIGHTWOOD (J. M.)—THE NATURE OF POSITIVE LAW. 8vo. 12s. 6d.

LINDSAY (Dr. J. A.).—THE CLIMATIC TREATMENT OF CONSUMPTION. Cr. 8vo. 5s.

LITTLE PILGRIM IN THE UNSEEN. 24th Thousand. Crown 8vo. 2s. 6d.

LIVY.—BOOKS XXI.—XXV. THE SECOND PUNIC WAR. Translated by A. J. CHURCH, M.A., and W. J. BRODRIBB, M.A. With Maps. Cr. 8vo. 7s. 6d. *See also* pp. 31, 32.

LOCK (Rev. J. B.)— ARITHMETIC FOR SCHOOLS. 4th Edition, revised. Globe 8vo. Complete with Answers, 4s. 6d. Without Answers, 4s. 6d.
—— KEY TO "ARITHMETIC FOR SCHOOLS." By the Rev. R. G. WATSON. Cr. 8vo. 10s. 6d.
—— ARITHMETIC FOR BEGINNERS. A School Class-Book of COMMERCIAL ARITHMETIC. Globe 8vo. 2s. 6d.
—— KEY TO "ARITHMETIC FOR BEGINNERS." By Rev. R. G. WATSON. Crown 8vo. 8s. 6d.
—— A SHILLING BOOK OF ARITHMETIC FOR ELEMENTARY SCHOOLS. 18mo. 1s.—With Answers, 1s. 6d.
—— TRIGONOMETRY. Globe 8vo. Part I. ELEMENTARY TRIGONOMETRY. 4s. 6d.—Part II. HIGHER TRIGONOMETRY. 4s. 6d. Complete, 7s. 6d.
—— KEY TO "ELEMENTARY TRIGONOMETRY." By H. CARR, B.A. Crown 8vo. 8s. 6d.
—— TRIGONOMETRY FOR BEGINNERS. As far as the Solution of Triangles. Gl. 8vo. 2s. 6d.
—— KEY TO "TRIGONOMETRY FOR BEGINNERS." Crown 8vo. 6s. 6d.
—— TRIGONOMETRY OF ONE ANGLE. Globe 8vo. 2s. 6d.
—— ELEMENTARY STATICS. Gl. 8vo. 4s. 6d.
—— DYNAMICS FOR BEGINNERS. 3rd Edit. Globe 8vo. 4s. 6d.

LOCKYER (J. Norman, F.R.S.).—ELEMENTARY LESSONS IN ASTRONOMY. Illustrations and Diagram. New Edit. 18mo. 5s. 6d.
—— PRIMER OF ASTRONOMY. 18mo. 1s.
—— OUTLINES OF PHYSIOGRAPHY: THE MOVEMENTS OF THE EARTH. Cr. 8vo. 1s. 6d.
—— THE CHEMISTRY OF THE SUN. 8vo. 14s.

LIST OF PUBLICATIONS. 27

LOCKYER (J. Norman, F.R.S.).—THE METEORITIC HYPOTHESIS OF THE ORIGIN OF COSMICAL SYSTEMS. 8vo. 17s. net.

— **LOCKYER'S ASTRONOMY,** QUESTIONS ON. By J. FORBES-ROBERTSON. 18mo. 1s. 6d.

LOCKYER—SEABROKE.—STAR-GAZING PAST AND PRESENT. By J. NORMAN LOCKYER, F.R.S., with the assistance of G. M. SEABROKE, F.R.A.S. Roy. 8vo. 21s.

LODGE (Prof. Oliver J.).—MODERN VIEWS OF ELECTRICITY. Crown 8vo. 6s. 6d.

LOEWY (B.).—QUESTIONS AND EXAMPLES IN EXPERIMENTAL PHYSICS, SOUND, LIGHT, HEAT, ELECTRICITY, AND MAGNETISM. Fcp. 8vo. 2s.

— A GRADUATED COURSE OF NATURAL SCIENCE, EXPERIMENTAL AND THEORETICAL, FOR SCHOOLS AND COLLEGES. Part I. FIRST YEAR'S COURSE FOR ELEMENTARY SCHOOLS AND THE JUNIOR CLASSES OF TECHNICAL SCHOOLS AND COLLEGES. Globe 8vo. 2s.

LONGINUS.—ON THE SUBLIME. Translated by H. L. HAVELL, B.A. With Introduction by ANDREW LANG. Crown 8vo. 4s. 6d.

LOWE (W. H.).—THE HEBREW STUDENT'S COMMENTARY ON ZECHARIAH, HEBREW AND LXX. 8vo. 10s. 6d.

LOWELL (James Russell).—COMPLETE POETICAL WORKS. 18mo. 4s. 6d.

— DEMOCRACY, AND OTHER ADDRESSES. Crown 8vo. 5s.

— HEARTSEASE AND RUE. Crown 8vo. 5s.

— POLITICAL ESSAYS. Ext. cr. 8vo. 7s. 6d.

— COMPLETE WORKS. 10 vols. Crn. 8vo. 6s. each.
Vols. I.—IV. LITERARY ESSAYS; Vol. V. POLITICAL ESSAYS; Vol. VI. LITERARY AND POLITICAL ADDRESSES; Vols. VII.—X. POETICAL WORKS.

LUBBOCK (Sir John, Bart.).—THE ORIGIN AND METAMORPHOSES OF INSECTS. With Illustrations. Crown 8vo. 3s. 6d.

— ON BRITISH WILD FLOWERS CONSIDERED IN THEIR RELATION TO INSECTS. With Illustrations. Crown 8vo. 4s. 6d.

— FLOWERS, FRUITS, AND LEAVES. With Illustrations. Crown 8vo. 4s. 6d.

— SCIENTIFIC LECTURES. With Illustrations. 2nd Edition, revised. 8vo. 8s. 6d.

— POLITICAL AND EDUCATIONAL ADDRESSES. 8vo. 8s. 6d.

— THE PLEASURES OF LIFE. New Edition. Gl. 8vo. 1s. 6d.; swd., 1s. 60th Thousand. *Library Edition.* Globe 8vo. 3s. 6d.
Part II. Globe 8vo. 1s. 6d.; sewed, 1s. *Library Edition.* Globe 8vo. 3s. 6d.

— Two Parts in one vol. Gl. 8vo. 2s. 6d.

— FIFTY YEARS OF SCIENCE: Address to the British Association, 1881. 5th Edition. Crown 8vo. 2s. 6d.

LUCAS (F.).—SKETCHES OF RURAL LIFE. Poems. Globe 8vo. 5s.

LUCIAN.—*See* p. 31.

LUCRETIUS.—*See* p. 32.

LUPTON (J. H.).—AN INTRODUCTION TO LATIN ELEGIAC VERSE COMPOSITION. Globe 8vo. 2s. 6d.

— LATIN RENDERING OF THE EXERCISES IN PART II. (XXV.-C.) TO LUPTON'S "INTRODUCTION TO LATIN ELEGIAC VERSE COMPOSITION." Globe 8vo. 3s. 6d.

— AN INTRODUCTION TO LATIN LYRIC VERSE COMPOSITION. Globe 8vo. 3s.—Key, 4s. 6d.

LUPTON (Sydney).—CHEMICAL ARITHMETIC. With 1200 Examples. Fcp. 8vo. 4s. 6d.

— NUMERICAL TABLES AND CONSTANTS IN ELEMENTARY SCIENCE. Ex. fcp. 8vo. 2s. 6d.

LYSIAS.—*See* p. 33.

LYTE (H. C. Maxwell).—ETON COLLEGE, HISTORY OF, 1440—1884. With Illustrations. 2nd Edition. 8vo. 21s.

—.THE UNIVERSITY OF OXFORD, A HISTORY OF, FROM THE EARLIEST TIMES TO THE YEAR 1530. 8vo. 16s.

LYTTON (Rt. Hon. Earl of).—THE RING OF AMASIS: A ROMANCE. Crown 8vo. 3s. 6d.

M'CLELLAND (W. J.).—GEOMETRY OF THE CIRCLE. Crown 8vo.

M'CLELLAND (W. J.) and PRESTON (T.).—A TREATISE ON SPHERICAL TRIGONOMETRY. With numerous Examples. Crown 8vo. 8s. 6d.—Or Part I. 4s. 6d.; Part II. 5s.

McCOSH (Rev. Dr. James).—THE METHOD OF THE DIVINE GOVERNMENT, PHYSICAL AND MORAL. 8vo. 10s. 6d.

— THE SUPERNATURAL IN RELATION TO THE NATURAL. Crown 8vo. 7s. 6d.

— THE INTUITIONS OF THE MIND. New Edition. 8vo. 10s. 6d.

— AN EXAMINATION OF MR. J. S. MILL'S PHILOSOPHY. 8vo. 10s. 6d.

— THE LAWS OF DISCURSIVE THOUGHT. A Text-Book of Formal Logic. Crn. 8vo. 5s.

— CHRISTIANITY AND POSITIVISM. Lectures on Natural Theology and Apologetics. Crown 8vo. 7s. 6d.

— THE SCOTTISH PHILOSOPHY, FROM HUTCHESON TO HAMILTON, BIOGRAPHICAL, EXPOSITORY, CRITICAL. Royal 8vo. 16s.

— THE EMOTIONS. 8vo. 9s.

— REALISTIC PHILOSOPHY DEFENDED IN A PHILOSOPHIC SERIES. 2 vols. Vol. I. EXPOSITORY. Vol. II. HISTORICAL AND CRITICAL. Crown 8vo. 14s.

— PSYCHOLOGY. Crown 8vo. I. THE COGNITIVE POWERS. 6s. 6d.—II. THE MOTIVE POWERS. 6s. 6d.

— FIRST AND FUNDAMENTAL TRUTHS. Being a Treatise on Metaphysics. 8vo. 9s.

— THE PREVAILING TYPES OF PHILOSOPHY: CAN THEY LOGICALLY REACH REALITY? 8vo. 3s. 6d.

MACDONALD (George).—ENGLAND'S ANTIPHON. Crown 8vo. 4s. 6d.

MACDONELL (John).—THE LAND QUESTION. 8vo. 10s. 6d.

MACFARLANE (Alexander).—PHYSICAL ARITHMETIC. Crown 8vo. 7s. 6d.

MACGREGOR (James Gordon).—An Elementary Treatise on Kinematics and Dynamics. Crown 8vo. 10s. 6d.

MACKENZIE (Sir Morell).—The Hygiene of the Vocal Organs. 7th Ed. Crn. 8vo. 6s.

MACKIE (Rev. Ellis).—Parallel Passages for Translation into Greek and English. Globe 8vo. 4s. 6d.

MACLAGAN (Dr. T.).—The Germ Theory. 8vo. 10s. 6d.

MACLAREN (Rev. Alexander).—Sermons preached at Manchester. 11th Edition. Fcp. 8vo. 4s. 6d.

—— A Second Series of Sermons. 7th Edition. Fcp. 8vo. 4s. 6d.

—— A Third Series. 6th Ed. Fcp. 8vo. 4s. 6d.

—— Week-day Evening Addresses. 4th Edition. Fcp. 8vo. 2s. 6d.

—— The Secret of Power, and other Sermons. Fcp. 8vo. 4s. 6d.

MACLAREN (Arch.).—The Fairy Family. A Series of Ballads and Metrical Tales. Crown 8vo, gilt. 5s.

MACLEAN (Surgeon-Gen. W. C.).—Diseases of Tropical Climates. Cr. 8vo. 10s. 6d.

MACLEAR (Rev. Canon).—A Class-Book of Old Testament History. With Four Maps. 18mo. 4s. 6d.

—— A Class-Book of New Testament History. Including the connection of the Old and New Testament. 18mo. 5s. 6d.

—— A Shilling Book of Old Testament History. 18mo. 1s.

—— A Shilling Book of New Testament History. 18mo. 1s.

—— A Class-Book of the Catechism of the Church of England. 18mo. 1s. 6d.

—— A First Class-Book of the Catechism of the Church of England, with Scripture Proofs for Junior Classes and Schools. 18mo. 6d.

—— A Manual of Instruction for Confirmation and First Communion, with Prayers and Devotions. 32mo. 2s.

—— First Communion, with Prayers and Devotions for the Newly Confirmed. 32mo. 6d.

—— The Order of Confirmation, with Prayers and Devotions. 32mo. 6d.

—— The Hour of Sorrow; or, The Office for the Burial of the Dead. 32mo. 2s.

—— Apostles of Mediæval Europe. Crn. 8vo. 4s. 6d.

—— An Introduction to the Creeds. 18mo. 2s. 6d.

—— An Introduction to the Thirty-nine Articles. 18mo.

M'LENNAN (J. F.).—The Patriarchal Theory. Edited and completed by Donald M'Lennan, M.A. 8vo. 14s.

—— Studies in Ancient History. Comprising a Reprint of "Primitive Marriage." New Edition. 8vo. 16s.

MACMILLAN (D.). Memoir of Daniel Macmillan. By Thomas Hughes, Q.C. With Portrait. Crown 8vo. 4s. 6d.
Cheap Edition. Crown 8vo, sewed. 1s.

MACMILLAN (Rev. Hugh).—Bible Teachings in Nature. 15th Ed. Gl. 8vo 6s.

—— Holidays on High Lands; or, Rambles and Incidents in Search of Alpine Plants. 2nd Edition. Globe 8vo. 6s.

—— The True Vine; or, The Analogies of our Lord's Allegory. 5th Edition. Globe 8vo. 6s.

—— The Ministry of Nature. 8th Edition. Globe 8vo. 6s.

—— The Sabbath of the Fields. 6th Edition. Globe 8vo. 6s.

—— The Marriage in Cana. Globe 8vo. 6s.

—— Two Worlds are Ours. 3rd Edition. Globe 8vo. 6s.

—— The Olive Leaf. Globe 8vo. 6s.

—— Roman Mosaics; or, Studies in Rome and its Neighbourhood. Globe 8vo. 6s.

MACMILLAN (M. C.)—First Latin Grammar. Extra fcp. 8vo. 1s. 6d.

MACMILLAN'S MAGAZINE. Published Monthly. 1s.—Vols. I.—LXII. 7s. 6d. each. [Cloth covers for binding, 1s. each.]

MACMILLAN'S SIX-SHILLING NOVELS. Crown 8vo. 6s. each volume.

By William Black.
A Princess of Thule.
Strange Adventures of a Phaeton
The Maid of Killeena, and other Tales.
Madcap Violet.
Green Pastures and Piccadilly.
The Beautiful Wretch; The Four MacNicols; The Pupil of Aurelius.
Macleod of Dare. Illustrated.
White Wings: A Yachting Romance.
Shandon Bells. | Yolande.
Judith Shakespeare.
The Wise Women of Inverness, a Tale: and other Miscellanies.
White Heather. | Sabina Zembra.

By J. H. Shorthouse.
John Inglesant. | Sir Percival.
A Teacher of the Violin, etc.
The Countess Eve.

By Rudyard Kipling.
Plain Tales from the Hills.
The Light that Failed.

By Henry James.
The American. | The Europeans.
Daisy Miller; An International Episode; Four Meetings.
The Madonna of the Future, and other Tales.
Roderick Hudson.
Washington Square; The Pension Beaurepas; A Bundle of Letters.
The Portrait of a Lady.
Stories Revived. Two Series. 6s. each.
The Bostonians.
The Reverberator.

A Doubting Heart. By Annie Keary.
Realmah. By the Author of "Friends in Council."
Old Sir Douglas. By Hon. Mrs. Norton.
Virgin Soil. By Tourgenief.
The Harbour Bar.
Bengal Peasant Life. By Lal Behari Day.

LIST OF PUBLICATIONS.

MACMILLAN'S SIX-SHILLING NO-VELS—*continued*.

VIDA: STUDY OF A GIRL. By AMY DUNSMUIR.
JILL. By E. A. DILLWYN.
NEÆRA: A TALE OF ANCIENT ROME. By J. W. GRAHAM.
THE NEW ANTIGONE: A ROMANCE.
A LOVER OF THE BEAUTIFUL. By the MARCHIONESS OF CARMARTHEN.
A SOUTH SEA LOVER. By A. ST. JOHNSTON.
A CIGARETTE MAKER'S ROMANCE. By F. MARION CRAWFORD.

MACMILLAN'S THREE-AND-SIX-PENNY SERIES. Cr. 8vo. 3s. 6d. each

By Rolf Boldrewood.
ROBBERY UNDER ARMS: A Story of Life and Adventure in the Bush and in the Goldfields of Australia.
THE MINER'S RIGHT.
THE SQUATTER'S DREAM.

By Mrs. Craik, Author of "John Halifax, Gentleman."
OLIVE. | THE OGILVIES.
AGATHA'S HUSBAND.
THE HEAD OF THE FAMILY.
TWO MARRIAGES. | THE LAUREL BUSH.
MY MOTHER AND I.
MISS TOMMY: A MEDIÆVAL ROMANCE.
KING ARTHUR: NOT A LOVE STORY.

By F. Marion Crawford.
MR. ISAACS: A TALE OF MODERN INDIA.
DR. CLAUDIUS: A TRUE STORY.
A ROMAN SINGER. | ZOROASTER.
A TALE OF A LONELY PARISH.
MARZIO'S CRUCIFIX. | PAUL PATOFF.
WITH THE IMMORTALS.
GREIFENSTEIN. | SANT' ILARIO.

By Sir H. S. Cunningham.
THE CŒRULEANS: A VACATION IDYLL
THE HERIOTS. | WHEAT AND TARES.

By Thomas Hardy.
THE WOODLANDERS. | WESSEX TALES.

By Bret Harte.
CRESSY.
THE HERITAGE OF DEDLOW MARSH, AND OTHER TALES.

By Thomas Hughes. See p. 22.

By Henry James.
A LONDON LIFE. | THE ASPERN PAPERS, etc.
THE TRAGIC MUSE.

By Annie Keary.
CASTLE DALY. | JANET'S HOME.
A YORK AND A LANCASTER ROSE.
OLDBURY.

By Charles Kingsley. See p. 25.

By D. Christie Murray.
AUNT RACHEL. | SCHWARTZ.
THE WEAKER VESSEL.
JOHN VALE'S GUARDIAN.

By Mrs. Oliphant.
NEIGHBOURS ON THE GREEN.
JOYCE. | A BELEAGUERED CITY.
KIRSTEEN.

By Charlotte M. Yonge. See p. 54.

MACMILLAN'S THREE-AND-SIX-PENNY SERIES—*continued*.

FAITHFUL AND UNFAITHFUL. By M. LEE.
REUBEN SACHS. By AMY LEVY.
MISS BRETHERTON. By Mrs. H. WARD.
LOUISIANA, AND THAT LASS O' LOWRIE'S. By FRANCES HODGSON BURNETT.
THE RING OF AMASIS. By Lord LYTTON.
MAROONED. By W. CLARK RUSSELL.

Uniform with the above.

STORM WARRIORS; OR, LIFEBOAT WORK ON THE GOODWIN SANDS. By the Rev. JOHN GILMORE.
TALES OF OLD JAPAN. By A. B. MITFORD.
A YEAR WITH THE BIRDS. By W. WARDE FOWLER. Illustrated by BRYAN HOOK.
TALES OF THE BIRDS. By the same. Illustrated by BRYAN HOOK.
LEAVES OF A LIFE. By MONTAGU WILLIAMS, Q.C.
TRUE TALES FOR MY GRANDSONS. By Sir SAMUEL W. BAKER, F.R.S.
TALES OF OLD TRAVEL. By HENRY KINGSLEY.

MACMILLAN'S TWO-SHILLING NOVELS. Globe 8vo. 2s. each.

By Mrs. Craik, Author of "John Halifax, Gentleman."
TWO MARRIAGES. | AGATHA'S HUSBAND.
THE OGILVIES.

By Mrs. Oliphant.
THE CURATE IN CHARGE.
A SON OF THE SOIL. | YOUNG MUSGRAVE.
HE THAT WILL NOT WHEN HE MAY.
A COUNTRY GENTLEMAN.
HESTER. | SIR TOM.
THE SECOND SON. | THE WIZARD'S SON.

By the Author of "Hogan, M.P."
HOGAN, M.P.
THE HONOURABLE MISS FERRARD.
FLITTERS, TATTERS, AND THE COUNSELLOR, WEEDS, AND OTHER SKETCHES.
CHRISTY CAREW. | ISMAY'S CHILDREN.

By George Fleming.
A NILE NOVEL. | MIRAGE.
THE HEAD OF MEDUSA. | VESTIGIA.

By Mrs. Macquoid.
PATTY.

By Annie Keary.
JANET'S HOME. | OLDBURY.
CLEMENCY FRANKLYN.
A YORK AND A LANCASTER ROSE.

By W. E. Norris.
MY FRIEND JIM. | CHRIS.

By Henry James.
DAISY MILLER; AN INTERNATIONAL EPISODE; FOUR MEETINGS.
RODERICK HUDSON.
THE MADONNA OF THE FUTURE, AND OTHER TALES.
WASHINGTON SQUARE.
PRINCESS CASAMASSIMA.

By Frances Hodgson Burnett.
LOUISIANA, AND THAT LASS O' LOWRIE'S. Two Stories.
HAWORTH'S.

MACMILLAN'S TWO-SHILLING NOVELS—continued.

By Hugh Conway.
A FAMILY AFFAIR. | LIVING OR DEAD.

By D. Christie Murray.
AUNT RACHEL.

By Helen Jackson.
RAMONA: A STORY.

A SLIP IN THE FENS.

MACMILLAN'S HALF-CROWN SERIES OF JUVENILE BOOKS. Globe 8vo, cloth, extra. 2s. 6d. each.

OUR YEAR. By the Author of "[John Halifax, Gentleman."

LITTLE SUNSHINE'S HOLIDAY. By the Author of "John Halifax, Gentleman."

WHEN I WAS A LITTLE GIRL. By the Author of "St. Olave's."

NINE YEARS OLD. By the Author of "When I was a Little Girl," etc.

A STOREHOUSE OF STORIES. Edited by CHARLOTTE M. YONGE. 2 vols.

AGNES HOPETOUN'S SCHOOLS AND HOLIDAYS. By Mrs. OLIPHANT.

THE STORY OF A FELLOW SOLDIER. By FRANCES AWDRY. (A Life of Bishop Patteson for the Young.)

RUTH AND HER FRIENDS: A STORY FOR GIRLS.

THE HEROES OF ASGARD: TALES FROM SCANDINAVIAN MYTHOLOGY. By A. and E. KEARY.

THE RUNAWAY. By the Author of "Mrs. Jerningham's Journal."

WANDERING WILLIE. By the Author of "Conrad the Squirrel."

PANSIE'S FLOUR BIN. Illustrated by ADRIAN STOKES.

MILLY AND OLLY. By Mrs. T. H. WARD. Illustrated by Mrs. ALMA TADEMA.

THE POPULATION OF AN OLD PEAR TREE; OR, STORIES OF INSECT LIFE. From the French of E. VAN BRUYSSEL. Edited by CHARLOTTE M. YONGE. Illustrated.

HANNAH TARNE. By MARY E. HULLAH. Illustrated by W. J. HENNESSY.

By Mrs. Molesworth. *Illustrated by Walter Crane. See* p. 37.

MACMILLAN'S READING BOOKS.
Adapted to the English and Scotch Codes.
Primer . . . . . . (48 pp.) 18mo, 2d.
Book I. for Standard I. (96 pp.) 18mo, 4d.
Book II. for Standard II. (144 pp.) 18mo, 5d.
Book III. for Standard III. (160 pp.) 18mo, 6d.
Book IV. for Standard IV. (176 pp.) 18mo, 8d.
Book V. for Standard V. (380 pp.) 18mo, 1s.
Book VI. for Standard VI. (430 pp.) Cr. 8vo, 2s.

MACMILLAN'S COPY-BOOKS.
*1. Initiatory Exercises and Short Letters.
*2. Words consisting of Short Letters.
*3. Long Letters, with words containing Long Letters. Figures.
*4. Words containing Long Letters.
4A. Practising and Revising Copybook for Nos. 1 to 4.

MACMILLAN'S COPY-BOOKS—contd.
*5. Capitals, and Short Half-text Words beginning with a Capital.
*6. Half-text Words beginning with a Capital. Figures.
*7. Small-hand and Half-text, with Capitals and Figures.
*8. Small-hand and Half-text, with Capitals and Figures.
8A. Practising and Revising Copybook for Nos. 5 to 8.
*9. Small-hand Single Head Lines. Figures.
10. Small-hand Single Head Lines. Figures.
*11. Small-hand Double Head Lines. Figures.
12. Commercial and Arithmetical Examples, etc.
12A. Practising and Revising Copybook for Nos. 8 to 12.

The Copybooks may be had in two sizes:
(1) Large Post 4to, 4d. each;
(2) Post oblong, 2d. each.

The numbers marked * may also be had in Large Post 4to, with GOODMAN'S PATENT SLIDING COPIES. 6d. each.

MACMILLAN'S LATIN COURSE. Part I.
By A. M. COOK, M.A. 2nd Edition, enlarged. Globe 8vo. 3s. 6d.
Part II. By the same. Gl. 8vo. 2s. 6d.

MACMILLAN'S SHORTER LATIN COURSE.
By A. M. COOK, M.A. Being an Abridgment of "Macmillan's Latin Course, Part I." Globe 8vo. 1s. 6d.

MACMILLAN'S LATIN READER.
A Latin Reader for the Lower Forms in Schools. By H. J. HARDY. Gl. 8vo. 2s. 6d.

MACMILLAN'S GREEK COURSE.
Edit. by Rev. W. G. RUTHERFORD, LL.D. Gl. 8vo.
I. FIRST GREEK GRAMMAR. By the Rev. W. G. RUTHERFORD, M.A. Part I. Accidence, 2s.; Part II. Syntax, 2s.; or in 1 vol. 3s. 6d.
II. EASY EXERCISES IN GREEK ACCIDENCE. By H. G. UNDERHILL, M.A. 2s.
III. SECOND GREEK EXERCISE BOOK. By Rev. W. A. HEARD, M.A. 2s. 6d.

MACMILLAN'S GREEK READER.
Stories and Legends. A First Greek Reader. With Notes, Vocabulary, and Exercises, by F. H. COLSON, M.A. Globe 8vo. 3s.

MACMILLAN'S ELEMENTARY CLASSICS. 18mo. 1s. 6d. each.
This Series falls into two classes:—
(1) First Reading Books for Beginners, provided not only with *Introductions and Notes*, but with *Vocabularies*, and in some cases with *Exercises* based upon the Text.
(2) Stepping-stones to the study of particular authors, intended for more advanced students, who are beginning to read such authors as Terence, Plato, the Attic Dramatists, and the harder parts of Cicero, Horace, Virgil, and Thucydides.

These are provided with Introductions and Notes, but no *Vocabulary*. The Publishers have been led to provide the more strictly Elementary Books with Vocabularies by the representations of many teachers, who hold that beginners do not understand the use of a Dictionary, and of others who, in the case of middle-class schools where the cost of books is a serious consideration, advocate the Vocabulary system on grounds of economy.

MACMILLAN'S ELEMENTARY CLASSICS—*continued.*

It is hoped that the two parts of the Series, fitting into one another, may together fulfil all the requirements of Elementary and Preparatory Schools, and the Lower Forms of Public Schools.

The following Elementary Books, *with Introductions, Notes, and Vocabularies,* and in some cases with *Exercises,* are either ready or in preparation:

LATIN ACCIDENCE AND EXERCISES ARRANGED FOR BEGINNERS. By WILLIAM WELCH, M.A., and C. G. DUFFIELD, M.A.

ÆSCHYLUS.—PROMETHEUS VINCTUS. Edit. by Rev. H. M. STEPHENSON, M.A.

ARRIAN.—SELECTIONS. Edited by JOHN BOND, M.A., and A. S. WALPOLE, M.A.

AULUS GELLIUS, STORIES FROM. By Rev. G. H. NALL, M.A.

CÆSAR. — THE INVASION OF BRITAIN. Being Selections from Books IV. and V. of the "De Bello Gallico." Adapted for Beginners by W. WELCH, and C. G. DUFFIELD.

— THE HELVETIAN WAR. Selected from Book I. of "The Gallic War," arranged for the use of Beginners by W. WELCH, M.A., and C. G. DUFFIELD, M.A.

— THE GALLIC WAR. Scenes from Books V. and VI. Edited by C. COLBECK, M.A.

— THE GALLIC WAR. Book I. Edited by Rev. A. S. WALPOLE, M.A.

— THE GALLIC WAR. Books II. and III. Ed. by Rev. W. G. RUTHERFORD, LL.D.

— THE GALLIC WAR. Book IV. Edited by C. BRYANS, M.A.

— THE GALLIC WAR. Books V. and VI. (separately). By the same Editor.

— THE GALLIC WAR. Book VII. Ed. by J. BOND, M.A., and A. S. WALPOLE, M.A.

CICERO.—DE SENECTUTE. Edited by E. S. SHUCKBURGH, M.A.

— DE AMICITIA. Ed. by E. S. SHUCKBURGH.

— STORIES OF ROMAN HISTORY. Edited by Rev. G. E. JEANS and A. V. JONES.

EURIPIDES.—ALCESTIS. By the Rev. M. A. BAYFIELD, M.A.

— HECUBA. Edited by Rev. J. BOND, M.A., and A. S. WALPOLE, M.A.

— MEDEA. Edited by A. W. VERRALL, Litt.D., and Rev. M. A. BAYFIELD, M.A.

EUTROPIUS. Adapted for the use of Beginners by W. WELCH and C. G. DUFFIELD.

HOMER.—ILIAD. Book I. Ed. by Rev. J. BOND, M.A., and A. S. WALPOLE, M.A.

— ILIAD. Book XVIII. THE ARMS OF ACHILLES. Edited by S. R. JAMES, M.A.

— ODYSSEY. Book I. Edited by Rev. J. BOND, M.A., and A. S. WALPOLE, M.A.

HORACE.—ODES. Books I.—IV. Edited by T. E. PAGE, M.A. 1s. 6d. each.

LIVY. Book I. Ed. by H. M. STEPHENSON.

— THE HANNIBALIAN WAR. Being part of the 21st and 22nd Books of Livy. Adapted for Beginners by G. C. MACAULAY, M.A.

MACMILLAN'S ELEMENTARY CLASSICS—*continued.*

LIVY.—THE SIEGE OF SYRACUSE. Being part of the 24th and 25th Books of Livy. Adapted for Beginners by G. RICHARDS, M.A., and Rev. A. S. WALPOLE, M.A.

— Book XXI. With Notes adapted from Mr. Capes' Edition for Junior Students, by Rev. W. W. CAPES, M.A., and J. E. MELHUISH, M.A.

— Book XXII. By the same Editors.

— LEGENDS OF ANCIENT ROME, FROM LIVY. Adapted for Beginners. With Notes, by H. WILKINSON, M.A.

LUCIAN, EXTRACTS FROM. Edited by J. BOND, M.A., and A. S. WALPOLE, M.A.

NEPOS.—SELECTIONS ILLUSTRATIVE OF GREEK AND ROMAN HISTORY. Edited by G. S. FARNELL, B.A.

OVID.—SELECTIONS. Edited by E. S. SHUCKBURGH, M.A.

— EASY SELECTIONS FROM OVID IN ELEGIAC VERSE. Arranged for the use of Beginners by H. WILKINSON, M.A.

— STORIES FROM THE METAMORPHOSES. Arranged for the use of Beginners by J. BOND, M.A., and A. S. WALPOLE, M.A.

PHÆDRUS.—SELECT FABLES. Adapted for use of Beginners by Rev. A. S. WALPOLE, M.A.

THUCYDIDES.—THE RISE OF THE ATHENIAN EMPIRE. Book I. Ch. 89—117 and 128—138. Edited by F. H. COLSON, M.A.

VIRGIL.—GEORGICS. Book I. Edited by T. E. PAGE, M.A.

— GEORGICS. Book II. Edited by Rev. J. H. SKRINE, M.A.

— ÆNEID. Book I. Edited by Rev. A. S. WALPOLE, M.A.

— ÆNEID. Book II. Ed. by T. E. PAGE.

— ÆNEID. Book III. Edited by T. E. PAGE, M.A.

— ÆNEID. Book IV. Edit. by Rev. H. M. STEPHENSON, M.A.

— ÆNEID. Book V. Edited by Rev. A. CALVERT, M.A.

— ÆNEID. Book VI. Ed. by T. E. PAGE.

— ÆNEID. Book VII. THE WRATH OF TURNUS. Edited by A. CALVERT, M.A.

— ÆNEID. Book VIII. Edited by Rev. A. CALVERT, M.A.

— ÆNEID. Book IX. Edited by Rev. H. M. STEPHENSON, M.A.

— ÆNEID. Book X. Ed. by S. G. OWEN, M.A.

— SELECTIONS. Edited by E. S. SHUCKBURGH, M.A.

XENOPHON.—ANABASIS: Selections. Edit. by W. WELCH, M.A., and C. G. DUFFIELD, M.A.

— ANABASIS. Book I., Chaps. i.—viii. Edited by E. A. WELLS, M.A.

— ANABASIS. Book I. Edited by Rev. A. S. WALPOLE, M.A.

— ANABASIS. Book II. Edited by Rev. A. S. WALPOLE, M.A.

MACMILLAN'S ELEMENTARY CLASSICS—*continued.*

XENOPHON.—ANABASIS. Book III. Edit. by Rev. G. H. NALL, M.A.
— ANABASIS. Book IV. Edited by Rev. E. D. STONE, M.A.
— SELECTIONS FROM BOOK IV. OF "THE ANABASIS." Edit. by Rev. E. D. STONE.
— SELECTIONS FROM "THE CYROPAEDIA." Edited by Rev. A. H. COOKE, M.A.

The following more advanced books have *Introductions, Notes,* but no *Vocabularies:*

CICERO.—SELECT LETTERS. Edit. by Rev. G. E. JEANS, M.A.
HERODOTUS.—SELECTIONS FROM BOOKS VII. AND VIII. THE EXPEDITION OF XERXES. Edited by A. H. COOKE, M.A.
HORACE.—SELECTIONS FROM THE SATIRES AND EPISTLES. Edited by Rev. W. J. V. BAKER, M.A.
— SELECT EPODES AND ARS POETICA. Edited by H. A. DALTON, M.A.
PLATO.—EUTHYPHRO AND MENEXENUS. Edited by C. E. GRAVES, M.A.
TERENCE.—SCENES FROM THE ANDRIA. Edited by F. W. CORNISH, M.A.
THE GREEK ELEGIAC POETS, FROM CALLINUS TO CALLIMACHUS. Selected and Edited by Rev. H. KYNASTON.
THUCYDIDES. Book IV., Chaps. i.—lxi. THE CAPTURE OF SPHACTERIA. Edited by C. E. GRAVES, M.A.

Other Volumes to follow.

MACMILLAN'S CLASSICAL SERIES FOR COLLEGES AND SCHOOLS.

Fcp. 8vo. Being select portions of Greek and Latin authors, edited, with Introductions and Notes, for the use of Middle and Upper Forms of Schools, or of Candidates for Public Examinations at the Universities and elsewhere.

ÆSCHINES.—IN CTESIPHONTA. Edited by Rev. T. GWATKIN, M.A., and E. S. SHUCKBURGH, M.A. 5s.
ÆSCHYLUS.—PERSÆ. Edited by A. O. PRICKARD, M.A. With Map. 2s. 6d.
— THE "SEVEN AGAINST THEBES." Edit. by A. W. VERRALL, Litt.D., and M. A. BAYFIELD, M.A. 2s. 6d.
ANDOCIDES.—DE MYSTERIIS. Edited by W. J. HICKIE, M.A. 2s. 6d.
ATTIC ORATORS, SELECTIONS FROM THE. Antiphon, Andocides, Lysias, Isocrates, and Isæus. Ed. by R. C. JEBB, Litt.D. 5s.
CÆSAR.—THE GALLIC WAR. Edited after Kraner by Rev. J. BOND, M.A., and Rev. A. S. WALPOLE, M.A. With Maps. 4s. 6d.
CATULLUS.—SELECT POEMS. Edited by F. P. SIMPSON, B.A. 3s. 6d. [The Text of this Edition is carefully adapted to School use.]
CICERO.—THE CATILINE ORATIONS. From the German of Karl Halm. Edited by A. S. WILKINS, Litt.D. 2s. 6d.
— PRO LEGE MANILIA. Edited, after Halm, by Prof. A. S. WILKINS, Litt.D. 2s. 6d.

MACMILLAN'S CLASSICAL SERIES—*continued.*

CICERO.—THE SECOND PHILIPPIC ORATION. From the German of Karl Halm. Edited, with Corrections and Additions, by Prof. J. E. B. MAYOR. 3s. 6d.
— PRO ROSCIO AMERINO. Edited, after Halm, by E. H. DONKIN, M.A. 2s. 6d.
— PRO P. SESTIO. Edited by Rev. H. A. HOLDEN, M.A. 3s. 6d.
— SELECT LETTERS. Edited by Prof. R. Y. TYRRELL, M.A.
DEMOSTHENES.—DE CORONA. Edited by B. DRAKE, M.A. Revised by E. S. SHUCKBURGH, M.A. 3s. 6d.
— ADVERSUS LEPTINEM. Edited by Rev. J. R. KING, M.A. 2s. 6d.
— THE FIRST PHILIPPIC. Edited, after C. Rehdantz, by Rev. T. GWATKIN. 2s. 6d.
EURIPIDES.—HIPPOLYTUS. Edited by Prof. J. P. MAHAFFY and J. B. BURY. 2s. 6d.
— MEDEA. Edited by A. W. VERRALL, Litt.D. 2s. 6d.
— IPHIGENIA IN TAURIS. Edited by E. B. ENGLAND, M.A. 3s.
— ION. Ed. by M. A. BAYFIELD, M.A. 2s. 6d.
HERODOTUS. Book III. Edited by G. C. MACAULAY, M.A. 2s. 6d.
— Book VI. Edited by Prof. J. STRACHAN, M.A. 3s. 6d.
— Book VII. Edited by Mrs. MONTAGU BUTLER. 3s. 6d.
HOMER.—ILIAD. Books I. IX. XI. XVI.-XXIV. THE STORY OF ACHILLES. Ed. by J. H. PRATT, M.A., and W. LEAF, Litt.D. 5s.
— ODYSSEY. Book IX. Edited by Prof. J. E. B. MAYOR, M.A. 2s. 6d.
— ODYSSEY. Books XXI.-XXIV. THE TRIUMPH OF ODYSSEUS. Edited by S. G. HAMILTON, B.A. 2s. 6d.
HORACE.—THE ODES. Edited by T. E. PAGE, M.A. 5s. (Books I. II. III. and IV. separately, 2s. each.)
— THE SATIRES. Edited by Prof. A. PALMER, M.A. 5s.
— THE EPISTLES AND ARS POETICA. Edit. by Prof. A. S. WILKINS, Litt.D. 5s.
JUVENAL.—THIRTEEN SATIRES. Edited, for the use of Schools, by E. G. HARDY, M.A. 5s. [The Text of this Edition is carefully adapted to School use.]
— SELECT SATIRES. Edited by Prof. J. E. B. MAYOR. X. XI. 3s. 6d.; XII.-XVI. 4s. 6d.
LIVY. Books II. and III. Edited by Rev. H. M. STEPHENSON, M.A. 3s. 6d.
— Books XXI. and XXII. Edited by Rev. W. W. CAPES, M.A. 4s. 6d.
— Books XXIII. and XXIV. Ed. by G. C. MACAULAY. With Maps. 3s. 6d.
— THE LAST TWO KINGS OF MACEDON. Extracts from the Fourth and Fifth Decades of Livy. Selected and Edit. by F. H. RAWLINS, M.A. With Maps. 2s. 6d.
LUCRETIUS. Books I.—III. Edited by J. H. WARBURTON LEE, M.A. 3s. 6d.

LIST OF PUBLICATIONS.

MACMILLAN'S CLASSICAL SERIES—*continued.*

LYSIAS.—SELECT ORATIONS. Edited by E. S. SHUCKBURGH, M.A. 5s.

MARTIAL.—SELECT EPIGRAMS. Edited by Rev. H. M. STEPHENSON, M.A. 5s.

OVID.—FASTI. Edited by G. H. HALLAM, M.A. With Maps. 3s. 6d.

— HEROIDUM EPISTULÆ XIII. Edited by E. S. SHUCKBURGH, M.A. 3s. 6d.

— METAMORPHOSES. Books XIII. and XIV. Edited by C. SIMMONS, M.A. 3s. 6d.

PLATO.—THE REPUBLIC. Books I.—V. Edited by T. H. WARREN, M.A. 5s.

— LACHES. Edited by M. T. TATHAM, M.A. 2s. 6d.

PLAUTUS.—MILES GLORIOSUS. Edited by Prof. R. Y. TYRRELL, M.A. 3s. 6d.

— AMPHITRUO. Edited by A. PALMER, M.A. 3s. 6d.

— CAPTIVI. Ed. by A. RHYS-SMITH, M.A.

PLINY.—LETTERS. Books I. and II. Edited by J. COWAN, M.A. 3s.

— LETTERS. Book III. Edited by Prof. J. E. B. MAYOR. With Life of Pliny by G. H. RENDALL. 3s. 6d.

PLUTARCH. — LIFE OF THEMISTOKLES. Edited by Rev. H. A. HOLDEN, M.A., LL.D. 3s. 6d.

— LIVES OF GALBA AND OTHO. Edited by E. G. HARDY, M.A. 5s.

POLYBIUS.—The History of the Achæan League as contained in the remains of Polybius. Edited by W. W. CAPES. 5s.

PROPERTIUS.—SELECT POEMS. Edited by Prof. J. P. POSTGATE, M.A. 5s.

SALLUST.—CATILINE AND JUGURTHA. Ed. by C. MERIVALE, D.D. 3s. 6d.—Or separately, 2s. each.

— BELLUM CATULINAE. Edited by A. M. COOK, M.A. 2s. 6d.

TACITUS.—AGRICOLA AND GERMANIA. Ed. by A. J. CHURCH, M.A., and W. J. BRODRIBB, M.A. 3s. 6d.—Or separately, 2s. each.

— THE ANNALS. Book VI. By the same Editors. 2s.

— THE HISTORIES. Books I. and II. Edited by A. D. GODLEY, M.A. 3s. 6d.

— THE HISTORIES. Books III.—V. By the same Editor. 3s. 6d.

TERENCE.—HAUTON TIMORUMENOS. Edit. by E. S. SHUCKBURGH, M.A. 2s. 6d.—With Translation, 3s. 6d.

— PHORMIO. Ed. by Rev. J. BOND, M.A., and Rev. A. S. WALPOLE, M.A. 2s. 6d.

THUCYDIDES. Book II. Edited by E. C. MARCHANT, M.A.

— Book IV. Ed. by C. E. GRAVES. 3s. 6d.

— Book V. By the same Editor.

— Books VI. and VII. THE SICILIAN EXPEDITION. Edited by Rev. P. FROST, M.A. With Map. 3s. 6d.

VIRGIL.—ÆNEID. Books II. and III. THE NARRATIVE OF ÆNEAS. Edited by E. W. HOWSON, M.A. 2s.

MACMILLAN'S CLASSICAL SERIES—*continued.*

XENOPHON.—HELLENICA. Books I. and II. Edited by H. HAILSTONE, M.A. 2s. 6d.

— CYROPÆDIA. Books VII. and VIII. Ed. by Prof. A. GOODWIN, M.A. 2s. 6d.

— MEMORABILIA SOCRATIS. Edited by A. R. CLUER, B.A. 5s.

— THE ANABASIS. Books I.—IV. Edited by Professors W. W. GOODWIN and J. W. WHITE. Adapted to Goodwin's Greek Grammar. With a Map. 3s. 6d.

— HIERO. Edited by Rev. H. A. HOLDEN, M.A., LL.D. 2s. 6d.

— OECONOMICUS. By the same Editor. With Introduction, Explanatory Notes Critical Appendix, and Lexicon. 5s.

The following are in preparation:

DEMOSTHENES.—IN MIDIAM. Edited by Prof. A. S. WILKINS, Litt.D., and HERMAN HAGER, Ph.D.

EURIPIDES.—BACCHAE. Edited by Prof. R. Y. TYRRELL, M.A.

HERODOTUS. Book V. Edited by Prof. J. STRACHAN, M.A.

ISÆOS.—THE ORATIONS. Edited by Prof WM. RIDGEWAY, M.A.

OVID.—METAMORPHOSES. Books I.—III. Edited by C. SIMMONS, M.A.

SALLUST.—JUGURTHA. Edited by A. M. COOK, M.A.

TACITUS.—THE ANNALS. Books I. and II. Edited by J. S. REID, Litt.D.

Other Volumes will follow.

MACMILLAN'S GEOGRAPHICAL SERIES. Edited by ARCHIBALD GEIKIE, F.R.S., Director-General of the Geological Survey of the United Kingdom.

THE TEACHING OF GEOGRAPHY. A Practical Handbook for the use of Teachers. Globe 8vo. 2s.

GEOGRAPHY OF THE BRITISH ISLES. By ARCHIBALD GEIKIE, F.R.S. 18mo. 1s.

THE ELEMENTARY SCHOOL ATLAS. 24 Maps in Colours. By JOHN BARTHOLOMEW, F.R.G.S. 4to. 1s.

AN ELEMENTARY CLASS-BOOK OF GENERAL GEOGRAPHY. By HUGH ROBERT MILL, D.Sc. Edin. Illustrated. Cr. 8vo. 3s. 6d.

MAPS AND MAP DRAWING. By W. A. ELDERTON. 18mo. 1s.

GEOGRAPHY OF EUROPE. By JAMES SIME, M.A. With Illustrations. Gl. 8vo. 3s.

ELEMENTARY GEOGRAPHY OF INDIA, BURMA, AND CEYLON. By H. F. BLANFORD, F.G.S. Globe 8vo. 2s. 6d.

MACMILLAN'S SCIENCE CLASS-BOOKS. Fcp. 8vo.

LESSONS IN APPLIED MECHANICS. By J. H. COTTERILL and J. H. SLADE. 5s. 6d.

LESSONS IN ELEMENTARY PHYSICS. By Prof. BALFOUR STEWART, F.R.S. New Edition. 4s. 6d. (Questions on, 2s.)

EXAMPLES IN PHYSICS. By Prof. D. E. JONES, B.Sc. 3s. 6d.

MACMILLAN'S SCIENCE CLASS-BOOKS *continued.*

ELEMENTARY LESSONS IN HEAT, LIGHT, AND SOUND. By Prof. D. E. JONES, B.Sc. Globe 8vo. 2s. 6d.

QUESTIONS AND EXAMPLES ON EXPERIMENTAL PHYSICS: Sound, Light, Heat, Electricity, and Magnetism. By B. LOEWY, F.R.A.S. 2s.

A GRADUATED COURSE OF NATURAL SCIENCE FOR ELEMENTARY AND TECHNICAL SCHOOLS AND COLLEGES. Part I. First Year's Course. By the same. Gl. 8vo. 2s.

ELEMENTARY LESSONS ON SOUND. By Dr. W. H. STONE. 3s. 6d.

ELECTRIC LIGHT ARITHMETIC. By R. E. DAY, M.A. 2s.

A COLLECTION OF EXAMPLES ON HEAT AND ELECTRICITY. By H. H. TURNER. 2s. 6d.

AN ELEMENTARY TREATISE ON STEAM. By Prof. J. PERRY, C.E. 4s. 6d.

ELECTRICITY AND MAGNETISM. By Prof. SILVANUS P. THOMPSON. 4s. 6d.

POPULAR ASTRONOMY. By Sir G. B. AIRY, K.C.B., late Astronomer-Royal. 4s. 6d.

ELEMENTARY LESSONS ON ASTRONOMY. By J. N. LOCKYER, F.R.S. New Edition. 5s. 6d. (Questions on 1s. 6d.)

LESSONS IN ELEMENTARY CHEMISTRY. By Sir H. ROSCOE, F.R.S. 4s. 6d.—Problems adapted to the same, by Prof. THORPE and W. TATE. With Key. 2s.

OWENS COLLEGE JUNIOR COURSE OF PRACTICAL CHEMISTRY. By F. JONES. With Preface by Sir H. ROSCOE, F.R.S. 2s. 6d.

QUESTIONS ON CHEMISTRY. A Series of Problems and Exercises in Inorganic and Organic Chemistry. By F. JONES. 3s.

OWENS COLLEGE COURSE OF PRACTICAL ORGANIC CHEMISTRY. By JULIUS B. COHEN, Ph.D. With Preface by Sir H. ROSCOE and Prof. SCHORLEMMER. 2s. 6d.

ELEMENTS OF CHEMISTRY. By Prof. IRA REMSEN. 2s. 6d.

EXPERIMENTAL PROOFS OF CHEMICAL THEORY FOR BEGINNERS. By WILLIAM RAMSAY, Ph.D. 2s. 6d.

NUMERICAL TABLES AND CONSTANTS IN ELEMENTARY SCIENCE. By SYDNEY LUPTON, M.A. 2s. 6d.

ELEMENTARY LESSONS IN PHYSICAL GEOGRAPHY. By ARCHIBALD GEIKIE, F.R.S. 4s. 6d. (Questions on, 1s. 6d.)

ELEMENTARY LESSONS IN PHYSIOLOGY. By T. H. HUXLEY, F.R.S. 4s. 6d. (Questions on, 1s. 6d.)

LESSONS IN ELEMENTARY ANATOMY. By St. G. MIVART, F.R.S. 6s. 6d.

LESSONS IN ELEMENTARY BOTANY. By Prof. D. OLIVER, F.R.S. 4s. 6d.

DISEASES OF FIELD AND GARDEN CROPS. By W. G. SMITH. 4s. 6d.

LESSONS IN LOGIC, INDUCTIVE AND DEDUCTIVE. By W. S. JEVONS, LL.D. 3s. 6d.

THE ECONOMICS OF INDUSTRY. By Prof. A. MARSHALL and M. P. MARSHALL. 2s. 6d.

MACMILLAN'S SCIENCE CLASS-BOOKS—*continued.*

POLITICAL ECONOMY FOR BEGINNERS. By Mrs. FAWCETT. With Questions. 2s. 6d.

ELEMENTARY LESSONS IN THE SCIENCE OF AGRICULTURAL PRACTICE. By Prof. H. TANNER. 3s. 6d.

CLASS-BOOK OF GEOGRAPHY. By C. B. CLARKE, F.R.S. 3s.; sewed, 2s. 6d.

SHORT GEOGRAPHY OF THE BRITISH ISLANDS. By J. R. GREEN and ALICE S. GREEN. With Maps. 3s. 6d.

MACMILLAN'S PROGRESSIVE FRENCH COURSE. By G. EUGÈNE FASNACHT. Extra fcp. 8vo.

I. FIRST YEAR, CONTAINING EASY LESSONS IN THE REGULAR ACCIDENCE. Thoroughly revised Edition. 1s.

II. SECOND YEAR, CONTAINING AN ELEMENTARY GRAMMAR. With copious Exercises, Notes, and Vocabularies. New Edition, enlarged. 2s.

III. THIRD YEAR, CONTAINING A SYSTEMATIC SYNTAX AND LESSONS IN COMPOSITION. 2s. 6d.

THE TEACHER'S COMPANION TO THE SAME. With copious Notes, Hints for different renderings, Synonyms, Philological Remarks, etc. 1st Year, 4s. 6d. 2nd Year, 4s. 6d. 3rd Year, 4s. 6d.

MACMILLAN'S PROGRESSIVE FRENCH READERS. By G. EUGÈNE FASNACHT. Extra fcp. 8vo.

I. FIRST YEAR, CONTAINING TALES, HISTORICAL EXTRACTS, LETTERS, DIALOGUES, FABLES, BALLADS, NURSERY SONGS, etc. With Two Vocabularies: (1) In the Order of Subjects; (2) In Alphabetical Order. 2s. 6d.

II. SECOND YEAR, CONTAINING FICTION IN PROSE AND VERSE, HISTORICAL AND DESCRIPTIVE EXTRACTS, ESSAYS, LETTERS, etc. 2s. 6d.

MACMILLAN'S FRENCH COMPOSITION. By G. EUGÈNE FASNACHT. Extra fcp. 8vo.—Part I. ELEMENTARY. 2s. 6d.—Part II. ADVANCED.

THE TEACHER'S COMPANION TO THE SAME. Part I. 4s. 6d.

MACMILLAN'S FRENCH READINGS FOR CHILDREN. By G. E. FASNACHT. Illustrated. Globe 8vo.

MACMILLAN'S PROGRESSIVE GERMAN COURSE. By G. EUGÈNE FASNACHT. Extra fcp. 8vo.

I. FIRST YEAR, CONTAINING EASY LESSONS ON THE REGULAR ACCIDENCE. 1s. 6d.

II. SECOND YEAR, CONTAINING CONVERSATIONAL LESSONS ON SYSTEMATIC ACCIDENCE AND ELEMENTARY SYNTAX, WITH PHILOLOGICAL ILLUSTRATIONS AND ETYMOLOGICAL VOCABULARY. New Edition, enlarged. 3s. 6d.

THE TEACHER'S COMPANION TO THE SAME. 1st Year, 4s. 6d.; 2nd Year, 4s. 6d.

LIST OF PUBLICATIONS. 35

MACMILLAN'S PROGRESSIVE GERMAN READERS. By G. EUGÈNE FASNACHT. Extra fcap. 8vo.

I. FIRST YEAR, CONTAINING AN INTRODUCTION TO THE GERMAN ORDER OF WORDS, WITH COPIOUS EXAMPLES, EXTRACTS FROM GERMAN AUTHORS IN PROSE AND POETRY, NOTES, VOCABULARIES. 2s. 6d.

MACMILLAN'S GERMAN COMPOSITION. By G. E. FASNACHT. Extra fcp. 8vo.—Part I. FIRST COURSE: PARALLEL GERMAN-ENGLISH EXTRACTS, PARALLEL ENGLISH-GERMAN SYNTAX. 2s. 6d.

THE TEACHER'S COMPANION TO THE SAME. Part I. 4s. 6d.

MACMILLAN'S SERIES OF FOREIGN SCHOOL CLASSICS. Edited by G. E. FASNACHT. 18mo.

Select works of the best foreign Authors, with suitable Notes and Introductions based on the latest researches of French and German Scholars by practical masters and teachers.

FRENCH.

CORNEILLE.—LE CID. Edited by G. E. FASNACHT. 1s.

DUMAS.—LES DEMOISELLES DE ST. CYR. Edited by VICTOR OGER. 1s. 6d.

FRENCH READINGS FROM ROMAN HISTORY. Selected from various Authors. Edited by C. COLBECK, M.A. 4s. 6d.

LA FONTAINE'S FABLES. Books I.—VI. Ed. by L. M. MORIARTY. [In preparation.

MOLIÈRE.—LES FEMMES SAVANTES. By G. E. FASNACHT. 1s.

— LE MISANTHROPE. By the same. 1s.

— LE MÉDECIN MALGRÉ LUI. By the same. 1s.

— LES PRECIEUSES RIDICULES. By the same. [In the Press.

— L'AVARE. Edited by L. M. MORIARTY. 1s.

— LE BOURGEOIS GENTILHOMME. By the same. 1s. 6d.

RACINE.- BRITANNICUS. Edited by EUGÈNE PELLISSIER. 2s.

SAND (George).—LA MARE AU DIABLE. Edited by W. E. RUSSELL, M.A. 1s.

SANDEAU (Jules).—MADEMOISELLE DE LA SEIGLIÈRE. Edit. by H. C. STEEL. 1s. 6d.

THIERS'S HISTORY OF THE EGYPTIAN EXPEDITION. Edited by Rev. H. A. BULL, M.A. [In preparation.

VOLTAIRE.—CHARLES XII. Edited by G. E. FASNACHT. 3s. 6d.

GERMAN.

FREYTAG.—DOKTOR LUTHER. Edited by FRANCIS STORR, M.A. [In preparation.

GOETHE.—GÖTZ VON BERLICHINGEN. Edit. by H. A. BULL, M.A. 2s.

— FAUST. Part I. Ed. by Miss J. LEE. 4s. 6d.

HEINE.—SELECTIONS FROM THE REISEBILDER AND OTHER PROSE WORKS. Edit. by C. COLBECK, M.A. 2s. 6d.

LESSING.—MINNA VON BARNHELM. Edited by J. SIME, M.A. [In preparation.

MACMILLAN'S FOREIGN SCHOOL CLASSICS—GERMAN—continued.]

SCHILLER.—DIE JUNGFRAU VON ORLEANS. Edited by JOSEPH GOSTWICK. 2s. 6d.

SCHILLER.—WALLENSTEIN. Part I. DAS LÄGER. Edited by H. B. COTTERILL, M.A. 2s.

— MARIA STUART. Edited by C. SHELDON, M.A., D.Lit. 2s. 6d.

— WILHELM TELL. Edited by G. E. FASNACHT 2s. 6d.

— SELECTIONS FROM SCHILLER'S LYRICAL POEMS. Edited by E. J. TURNER, M.A., and E. D. A. MORSHEAD, M.A. 2s. 6d.

UHLAND.—SELECT BALLADS. Adapted as a First Easy Reading Book for Beginners. Edited by G. E. FASNACHT. 1s.

MACMILLAN'S PRIMARY SERIES OF FRENCH AND GERMAN READING BOOKS. Edited by G. EUGÈNE FASNACHT. With Illustrations. Globe 8vo.

CORNAZ.—NOS ENFANTS ET LEURS AMIS. Edited by EDITH HARVEY. 1s. 6d.

DE MAISTRE.—LA JEUNE SIBÉRIENNE ET LE LÉPREUX DE LA CITÉ D'AOSTE. Edit. by S. BARLET, B.Sc. 1s. 6d.

FLORIAN.—SELECT FABLES. Edited by CHARLES YELD, M.A. 1s. 6d.

GRIMM.—KINDER- UND HAUSMÄRCHEN. Selected and Edited by G. E. FASNACHT. Illustrated. 2s. 6d.

HAUFF.—DIE KARAVANE. Edited by HERMAN HAGER, Ph.D. With Exercises by G. E. FASNACHT. 3s.

LA FONTAINE.—FABLES. A Selection, by L. M. MORIARTY, M.A. With Illustrations by RANDOLPH CALDECOTT. 2s. 6d.

LAMARTINE.—JEANNE D'ARC. Edited by M. DE G. VERRALL. [In the Press.

MOLESWORTH.—FRENCH LIFE IN LETTERS. By Mrs. MOLESWORTH. 1s. 6d.

PERRAULT.—CONTES DE FÉES. Edited by G. E. FASNACHT. 1s. 6d.

SCHMID.—HEINRICH VON EICHENFELS. Ed. by G. E. FASNACHT. 2s. 6d.

MACNAMARA (C.).—A HISTORY OF ASIATIC CHOLERA. Crown 8vo. 10s. 6d.

MADAGASCAR: AN HISTORICAL AND DESCRIPTIVE ACCOUNT OF THE ISLAND AND ITS FORMER DEPENDENCIES. By Captain S. OLIVER, F.S.A. 2 vols. Med. 8vo. 2l. 12s. 6d.

MADAME TABBY'S ESTABLISHMENT. By KARL. Illus. by L. WAIN. Cr. 8vo. 4s. 6d.

MADOC (Fayr).—THE STORY OF MELICENT. Crown 8vo. 4s. 6d.

MAHAFFY (Rev. Prof. J. P.).—SOCIAL LIFE IN GREECE, FROM HOMER TO MENANDER 6th Edition. Crown 8vo. 9s.

— GREEK LIFE AND THOUGHT FROM THE AGE OF ALEXANDER TO THE ROMAN CONQUEST. Crown 8vo. 12s. 6d.

— RAMBLES AND STUDIES IN GREECE. Illustrated. 3rd Edition. Crn. 8vo. 10s. 6d.

— A HISTORY OF CLASSICAL GREEK LITERATURE. Crown 8vo. Vol. I The Poets. With an Appendix on Homer by Prof. SAYCE. In 2 Parts.—Vol. II. The Prose Writers. In 2 Parts, 4s. 6d. each

MAHAFFY (Rev. Prof. J. P.).—THE GREEK WORLD UNDER ROMAN SWAY, FROM POLYBIUS TO PLUTARCH. Cr. 8vo. 10s. 6d.

—— GREEK ANTIQUITIES. Illust. 18mo. 1s.

—— EURIPIDES. 18mo. 1s. 6d.

—— THE DECAY OF MODERN PREACHING: AN ESSAY. Crown 8vo. 3s. 6d.

—— THE PRINCIPLES OF THE ART OF CONVERSATION. 2nd Ed. Crown 8vo. 4s. 6d.

MAHAFFY (Rev. Prof. J. P.) and ROGERS (J. E.).—SKETCHES FROM A TOUR THROUGH HOLLAND AND GERMANY. Illustrated by J. E. ROGERS. Extra crown 8vo. 10s. 6d.

MAHAFFY (Prof. J. P.) and BERNARD (J. H.).—*See* p. 24 *under* KANT.

MAITLAND (F. W.).—PLEAS OF THE CROWN FOR THE COUNTY OF GLOUCESTER, A.D. 1221. Edited by F. W. MAITLAND. 8vo. 7s. 6d.

—— JUSTICE AND POLICE. Cr. 8vo. 3s. 6d.

MALET (Lucas).—MRS. LORIMER: A SKETCH IN BLACK AND WHITE. Cr. 8vo. 4s. 6d.

MANCHESTER SCIENCE LECTURES FOR THE PEOPLE. Eighth Series, 1876—77. With Illustrations. Cr. 8vo. 2s.

MANSFIELD C. B.).—AERIAL NAVIGATION. Cr. 8vo. 10s. 6d.

MARCUS AURELIUS ANTONINUS.—BOOK IV. OF THE MEDITATIONS. The Greek Text Revised. With Translation and Commentary, by HASTINGS CROSSLEY, M.A. 8vo. 6s.

MARRIOTT (J. A. R.).—THE MAKERS OF MODERN ITALY: MAZZINI, CAVOUR, GARIBALDI. Three Oxford Lectures. Crown 8vo. 1s. 6d.

MARSHALL (Prof. Alfred).—PRINCIPLES OF ECONOMICS. 2 vols. 8vo. Vol. I. 12s. 6d. net.

MARSHALL (Prof. A. and Mary P.).—THE ECONOMICS OF INDUSTRY. Ex.fcp.8vo. 2s.6d.

MARSHALL (J. M.).—A TABLE OF IRREGULAR GREEK VERBS. 8vo. 1s.

MARTEL (Chas.). MILITARY ITALY. With Map. 8vo. 12s. 6d.

MARTIAL.—SELECT EPIGRAMS FOR ENGLISH READERS. Translated by W. T. WEBB, M.A. Ext. fcp. 8vo. 4s. 6d. —*See also* p. 33

MARTIN (Frances). THE POET'S HOUR. Poetry Selected and Arranged for Children. 12mo. 2s. 6d.

—— SPRING-TIME WITH THE POETS. Fcp. 8vo. 3s. 6d.

—— ANGELIQUE ARNAULD, Abbess of Port Royal. Crown 8vo. 4s. 6d.

MARTIN (Frederick).—THE HISTORY OF LLOYDS, AND OF MARINE INSURANCE IN GREAT BRITAIN. 8vo. 14s.

MARTINEAU (Miss C. A.).—EASY LESSONS ON HEAT. Globe 8vo. 2s. 6d.

MARTINEAU (Harriet). — BIOGRAPHICAL SKETCHES, 1852—75. Crown 8vo. 6s.

MARTINEAU (Dr. James). -SPINOZA. 2nd Edition. Crown 8vo. 6s.

MASSON (Prof. David).—RECENT BRITISH PHILOSOPHY. 3rd Edition. Cr. 8vo. 6s.

—— DRUMMOND OF HAWTHORNDEN. Crown 8vo. 10s. 6d.

MASSON (Prof. D.).—WORDSWORTH, SHELLEY, KEATS, AND OTHER ESSAYS. Crown 8vo. 5s.

—— CHATTERTON: A STORY OF THE YEAR 1770. Crown 8vo. 5s.

—— LIFE OF MILTON. See "Milton."

—— MILTON'S POEMS. See "Milton."

MASSON (Gustave).—A COMPENDIOUS DICTIONARY OF THE FRENCH LANGUAGE (FRENCH-ENGLISH AND ENGLISH-FRENCH). Crown 8vo. 6s.

MASSON (Mrs.).—THREE CENTURIES OF ENGLISH POETRY. Being Selections from Chaucer to Herrick. Globe 8vo. 3s. 6d.

MATTHEWS (G. F.).—MANUAL OF LOGARITHMS. 8vo. 5s. net.

MATURIN (Rev. W.).—THE BLESSEDNESS OF THE DEAD IN CHRIST. Cr. 8vo. 7s. 6d.

MAUDSLEY (Dr. Henry).—THE PHYSIOLOGY OF MIND. Crown 8vo. 10s. 6d.

—— THE PATHOLOGY OF MIND. 8vo. 18s.

—— BODY AND MIND. Crown 8vo. 6s. 6d.

MAURICE.—LIFE OF FREDERICK DENISON MAURICE. By his Son, FREDERICK MAURICE, Two Portraits. 3rd Ed. 2 vols. Demy 8vo. 36s. *Cheap Edition* (4th Thousand) 2 vols. Crown 8vo. 16s.

MAURICE (Frederick Denison).—THE KINGDOM OF CHRIST. 3rd Edition. 2 vols. Crn. 8vo. 12s.

—— LECTURES ON THE APOCALYPSE. 2nd Edition. Crown 8vo. 6s.

—— SOCIAL MORALITY. 3rd Ed. Cr. 8vo. 6s.

—— THE CONSCIENCE. Lectures on Casuistry. 3rd Edition. Crown 8vo. 4s. 6d.

—— DIALOGUES ON FAMILY WORSHIP. Crown 8vo. 4s. 6d.

—— THE PATRIARCHS AND LAWGIVERS OF THE OLD TESTAMENT. 7th Ed. Cr. 8vo. 4s. 6d.

—— THE PROPHETS AND KINGS OF THE OLD TESTAMENT. 5th Edition. Crn. 8vo. 6s.

—— THE GOSPEL OF THE KINGDOM OF HEAVEN. 3rd Edition. Crown 8vo. 6s.

—— THE GOSPEL OF ST. JOHN. 8th Edition. Crown 8vo. 6s.

—— THE EPISTLES OF ST. JOHN. 4th Edit. Crown 8vo. 6s.

—— EXPOSITORY SERMONS ON THE PRAYERBOOK; AND ON THE LORD'S PRAYER. New Edition. Crown 8vo. 6s.

—— THEOLOGICAL ESSAYS. 4th Edition. Crn. 8vo. 6s.

—— THE DOCTRINE OF SACRIFICE DEDUCED FROM THE SCRIPTURES. 2nd Edition. Crown 8vo. 6s.

—— MORAL AND METAPHYSICAL PHILOSOPHY. 4th Edition. 2 vols. 8vo. 16s.

—— THE RELIGIONS OF THE WORLD. 6th Edition. Crown 8vo. 4s. 6d.

—— ON THE SABBATH DAY; THE CHARACTER OF THE WARRIOR; AND ON THE INTERPRETATION OF HISTORY. Fcp. 8vo. 2s. 6d.

—— LEARNING AND WORKING. Crown 8vo. 4s. 6d.

—— THE LORD'S PRAYER, THE CREED, AND THE COMMANDMENTS. 18mo. 1s.

LIST OF PUBLICATIONS. 37

MAURICE (F. D.).—SERMONS PREACHED IN COUNTRY CHURCHES. 2nd Edition. Cr. 8vo. 6s.
—— THE FRIENDSHIP OF BOOKS, AND OTHER LECTURES. 3rd Edition. Cr. 8vo. 4s. 6d.
—— THE UNITY OF THE NEW TESTAMENT. 2nd Edition. 2 vols. Crown 8vo. 12s.
—— LESSONS OF HOPE. Readings from the Works of F. D. MAURICE. Selected by Rev. J. LL. DAVIES, M.A. Crown 8vo. 5s.
—— THE COMMUNION SERVICE FROM THE BOOK OF COMMON PRAYER, WITH SELECT READINGS FROM THE WRITINGS OF THE REV. F. D. MAURICE. Edited by Bishop COLENSO. 16mo. 2s. 6d.

MAURICE (Col. F.).—WAR. 8vo. 5s. net.

MAXWELL. PROFESSOR CLERK MAXWELL, A LIFE OF. By Prof. L. CAMPBELL, M.A., and W. GARNETT, M.A. 2nd Edition. Crown 8vo. 7s. 6d.

MAYER (Prof. A. M.).—SOUND. A Series of Simple, Entertaining, and Inexpensive Experiments in the Phenomena of Sound. With Illustrations. Crown 8vo. 3s. 6d.

MAYER (Prof. A. M.) and BARNARD (C.)—LIGHT. A Series of Simple, Entertaining, and Useful Experiments in the Phenomena of Light. Illustrated. Crown 8vo. 2s. 6d.

MAYOR (Prof. John E. B.).—A FIRST GREEK READER. New Edition. Fcp. 8vo. 4s. 6d.
—— AUTOBIOGRAPHY OF MATTHEW ROBINSON. Fcp. 8vo. 5s.
—— A BIBLIOGRAPHICAL CLUE TO LATIN LITERATURE. Crown 8vo. 10s. 6d. [See also under "Juvenal."]

MAYOR (Prof. Joseph B.).—GREEK FOR BEGINNERS. Fcp. 8vo. Part I. 1s. 6d.—Parts II. and III. 3s. 6d.—Complete, 4s. 6d.

MAZINI (Linda).—IN THE GOLDEN SHELL. With Illustrations. Globe 8vo. 4s. 6d.

MELDOLA (Prof. R.)—THE CHEMISTRY OF PHOTOGRAPHY. Crown 8vo. 6s.

MELDOLA (Prof. R.) and WHITE (Wm.).—REPORT ON THE EAST ANGLIAN EARTHQUAKE OF 22ND APRIL, 1884. 8vo. 3s. 6d.

MELEAGER: FIFTY POEMS OF. Translated by WALTER HEADLAM. Fcp. 4to. 7s. 6d.

MERCIER (Dr. C.).—THE NERVOUS SYSTEM AND THE MIND. 8vo. 12s. 6d.

MERCUR (Prof. J.).—ELEMENTS OF THE ART OF WAR. 8vo. 17s.

MEREDITH (George).—A READING OF EARTH. Extra fcp. 8vo. 5s.
—— POEMS AND LYRICS OF THE JOY OF EARTH. Extra fcp. 8vo. 6s.
—— BALLADS AND POEMS OF TRAGIC LIFE. Crown 8vo. 6s.

MEYER (Ernst von).—HISTORY OF CHEMISTRY. Trans. by G. MACGOWAN, Ph.D. 8vo. 14s. net.

MIALL.—LIFE OF EDWARD MIALL. By his Son, ARTHUR MIALL. 8vo. 10s. 6d.

MICHELET (M.).—A SUMMARY OF MODERN HISTORY. Translated by M. C. M. SIMPSON. Globe 8vo. 4s. 6d.

MILL (H. R.).—ELEMENTARY CLASS-BOOK OF GENERAL GEOGRAPHY. Cr. 8vo. 3s. 6d.

MILLAR (J. B.) -ELEMENTS OF DESCRIPTIVE GEOMETRY. 2nd Edition. Crown 8vo. 6s.

MILLER (R. Kalley).—THE ROMANCE OF ASTRONOMY. 2nd Ed. Cr. 8vo. 4s. 6d.

MILLIGAN (Rev. Prof. W.).—THE RESURRECTION OF OUR LORD. 2nd Ed. Cr. 8vo. 5s.
—— THE REVELATION OF ST. JOHN. 2nd Edition. Crown 8vo. 7s. 6d.

MILNE (Rev. John J.).—WEEKLY PROBLEM PAPERS. Fcp. 8vo. 4s. 6d.
—— COMPANION TO WEEKLY PROBLEMS. Cr. 8vo. 10s. 6d.
—— SOLUTIONS OF WEEKLY PROBLEM PAPERS. Crown 8vo. 10s. 6d.

MILNE (Rev. J. J.) and DAVIS (R. F.).—GEOMETRICAL CONICS. Part I. THE PARABOLA. Crown 8vo. 2s.

MILTON.—THE LIFE OF JOHN MILTON. By Prof. DAVID MASSON. Vol. I., 21s.; Vol. III., 18s.; Vols. IV. and V., 32s.; Vol. VI., with Portrait, 21s.
—— POETICAL WORKS. Edited, with Introductions and Notes, by Prof. DAVID MASSON, M.A. 3 vols. 8vo. 2l. 2s.
—— POETICAL WORKS. Ed. by Prof. MASSON. 3 vols. Fcp. 8vo. 15s.
—— POETICAL WORKS. (*Globe Edition*.) Ed. by Prof. MASSON. Globe 8vo. 3s. 6d.
See also ENGLISH CLASSICS, p. 12.

MINCHIN (Rev. Prof. G. M.).—NATURÆ VERITAS. Fcp. 8vo. 2s. 6d.

MINTO (W.).—THE MEDIATION OF RALPH HARDELOT. 3 vols. Crown 8vo. 31s. 6d.

MITFORD (A. B.).—TALES OF OLD JAPAN. With Illustrations. Crown 8vo. 3s. 6d.

MIVART (St. George).—LESSONS IN ELEMENTARY ANATOMY. Fcp. 8vo. 6s. 6d.

MIXTER (Prof. W. G.).—AN ELEMENTARY TEXT-BOOK OF CHEMISTRY. 2nd Edition. Crown 8vo. 7s. 6d.

MIZ MAZE (THE); OR, THE WINKWORTH PUZZLE. A Story in Letters by Nine Authors. Crown 8vo. 4s. 6d.

MOLESWORTH (Mrs.). Illustrated by WALTER CRANE.
HERR BABY. Globe 8vo. 2s. 6d.
GRANDMOTHER DEAR. Globe 8vo. 2s. 6d.
THE TAPESTRY ROOM. Globe 8vo. 2s. 6d.
A CHRISTMAS CHILD. Globe 8vo. 2s. 6d.
ROSY. Globe 8vo. 2s. 6d.
TWO LITTLE WAIFS. Globe 8vo. 2s. 6d.
CHRISTMAS TREE LAND. Gl. 8vo. 2s. 6d.
"US"; AN OLD-FASHIONED STORY. Globe 8vo. 2s. 6d.
"CARROTS," JUST A LITTLE BOY. Globe 8vo. 2s. 6d.
TELL ME A STORY. Globe 8vo. 2s. 6d.
THE CUCKOO CLOCK. Globe 8vo. 2s. 6d.
FOUR WINDS FARM. Globe 8vo. 2s. 6d.
LITTLE MISS PEGGY. Globe 8vo. 2s. 6d.
THE RECTORY CHILDREN. Gl. 8vo. 2s. 6d.
A CHRISTMAS POSY. Crown 8vo. 4s. 6d.

MOLESWORTH (Mrs.)—*continued*.

   The Children of the Castle. Crown 8vo. 4s. 6d.

   Summer Stories. Crown 8vo. 4s. 6d.

   Four Ghost Stories. Crown 8vo. 6s.

   French Life in Letters. With Notes on Idioms, etc. Globe 8vo. 1s. 6d.

MOLIÈRE.—Le Malade Imaginaire. Edit. by F. Tarver, M.A. Fcp. 8vo. 2s. 6d. *See also* p. 35.

MOLLOY (Rev. G.).—Gleanings in Science: A Series of Popular Lectures on Scientific Subjects. 8vo. 7s. 6d.

MONAHAN (James H.).—The Method of Law. Crown 8vo. 6s.

MONTELIUS—WOODS.—The Civilisation of Sweden in Heathen Times. By Prof. Oscar Montelius. Translated by Rev. F. H. Woods, B.D. With Illustrations. 8vo. 14s.

MOORE (Prof. C. H.).—The Development and Character of Gothic Architecture. Illustrated. Medium 8vo. 18s.

MOORHOUSE (Rt. Rev. Bishop).—Jacob: Three Sermons. Extra fcp. 8vo. 3s. 6d.

—— The Teaching of Christ. Crown 8vo. 3s. net.

MORISON (J. C.).—The Life and Times of Saint Bernard. 4th Edition. Crown 8vo. 6s.

MORISON (Jeanie).—The Purpose of the Ages. Crown 8vo. 9s.

MORLEY (John).—Works. Collected Edit. In 11 vols. Globe 8vo. 5s. each.

   Voltaire. 1 vol.—Rousseau. 2 vols.—Diderot and the Encyclopædists. 2 vols.—On Compromise. 1 vol.—Miscellanies. 3 vols.—Burke. 1 vol.—Studies in Literature. 1 vol.

MORRIS (Rev. Richard, LL.D.).—Historical Outlines of English Accidence. Fcp. 8vo. 6s.

—— Elementary Lessons in Historical English Grammar. 18mo. 2s. 6d.

—— Primer of English Grammar. 18mo, cloth. 1s.

MORRIS (R.) and BOWEN (H. C.).—English Grammar Exercises. 18mo. 1s.

MORRIS (R.) and KELLNER (L.).—Historical Outlines of English Syntax. Extra fcp. 8vo.

MORTE D'ARTHUR. The Edition of Caxton revised for Modern Use. By Sir Edward Strachey. Gl. 8vo. 3s. 6d.

MOULTON (Louise Chandler).—Swallow-Flights. Extra fcp. 8vo. 4s. 6d.

—— In the Garden of Dreams: Lyrics and Sonnets. Crown 8vo. 6s.

MUDIE (C. E.).—Stray Leaves: Poems. 4th Edition. Extra fcp. 8vo. 3s. 6d.

MUIR (T.).—The Theory of Determinants in the Historical Order of its Development. Part I. Determinants in General. Leibnitz (1693) to Cayley (1841). 8vo. 10s. 6d.

MUIR (M. M. Pattison).—Practical Chemistry for Medical Students. Fcp. 8vo. 1s. 6d.

MUIR (M. M. P.) and WILSON (D. M.).—The Elements of Thermal Chemistry. 8vo. 12s. 6d.

MÜLLER—THOMPSON.—The Fertilisation of Flowers. By Prof. Hermann Müller. Translated by D'Arcy W. Thompson. With a Preface by Charles Darwin, F.R.S. Medium 8vo. 21s.

MULLINGER (J. B.).—Cambridge Characteristics in the Seventeenth Century. Crown 8vo. 4s. 6d.

MURPHY (J. J.).—Habit and Intelligence. 2nd Ed. Illustrated. 8vo. 16s.

MURRAY (E. C. Grenville).—Round about France. Crown 8vo. 7s. 6d.

MURRAY (D. Christie).—*See* p. 29.

MURRAY (D. Christie) and HERMAN (Henry).—He Fell Among Thieves. 2 vols. Globe 8vo. 12s.

MUSIC.—A Dictionary of Music and Musicians, A.D. 1450—1889. Edited by Sir George Grove, D.C.L. In 4 vols. 8vo. 21s. each.—Parts I.—XIV., XIX.—XXII. 3s. 6d. each.—Parts XV. XVI. 7s.—Parts XVII. XVIII. 7s.—Parts XXIII.—XXV. Appendix. Ed. J. A. F. Maitland, M.A. 9s.

—— A Complete Index to the Above. By Mrs. E. Wodehouse. 8vo. 7s. 6d.

MYERS (E.).—The Puritans: A Poem. Extra fcap. 8vo. 2s. 6d.

—— Pindar's Odes. Translated, with Introduction and Notes. Crown 8vo. 5s.

—— Poems. Extra fcp. 8vo. 4s. 6d.

—— The Defence of Rome, and other Poems. Extra fcp. 8vo. 5s.

—— The Judgment of Prometheus, and other Poems. Extra fcp. 8vo. 3s. 6d.

MYERS (F. W. H.).—The Renewal of Youth, and other Poems. Crown 8vo. 7s. 6d.

—— St. Paul: A Poem. Ex. fcp. 8vo. 2s. 6d.

—— Essays. 2 vols.—I. Classical. II. Modern. Crown 8vo. 4s. 6d. each.

MYLNE (The Rt. Rev. Bishop).—Sermons Preached in St. Thomas's Cathedral, Bombay. Crown 8vo. 6s.

NADAL (E. S.).—Essays at Home and Elsewhere. Crown 8vo. 6s.

NAPOLEON I., HISTORY OF. By P. Lanfrey. 4 vols. Crown 8vo. 30s.

NATURAL RELIGION. By the Author of "Ecce Homo." 3rd Edit. Globe 8vo. 6s.

NATURE: A Weekly Illustrated Journal of Science. Published every Thursday. Price 6d. Monthly Parts, 2s. and 2s. 6d.; Current Half-yearly vols., 15s. each. Vols. I.—XLI. [Cases for binding vols. 1s. 6d. each.]

LIST OF PUBLICATIONS.

NATURE PORTRAITS. A Series of Portraits of Scientific Worthies engraved by JEENS and others in Portfolio. India Proofs, 5s. each. [Portfolio separately, 6s. net.]

NATURE SERIES. Crown 8vo:

THE ORIGIN AND METAMORPHOSES OF INSECTS. By Sir JOHN LUBBOCK, M.P., F.R.S. With Illustrations. 3s. 6d.

THE TRANSIT OF VENUS. By Prof. G. FORBES. With Illustrations. 3s. 6d.

POLARISATION OF LIGHT. By W. SPOTTISWOODE, LL.D. Illustrated. 3s. 6d.

ON BRITISH WILD FLOWERS CONSIDERED IN RELATION TO INSECTS. By Sir JOHN LUBBOCK, M.P., F.R.S. Illustrated. 4s. 6d.

FLOWERS, FRUITS, AND LEAVES. By Sir JOHN LUBBOCK. Illustrated. 4s. 6d.

HOW TO DRAW A STRAIGHT LINE: A LECTURE ON LINKAGES. By A. B. KEMPE, B.A. Illustrated. 1s. 6d.

LIGHT: A SERIES OF SIMPLE, ENTERTAINING, AND USEFUL EXPERIMENTS. By A. M. MAYER and C. BARNARD. Illustrated. 2s. 6d.

SOUND: A SERIES OF SIMPLE, ENTERTAINING, AND INEXPENSIVE EXPERIMENTS. By A. M. MAYER. 3s. 6d.

SEEING AND THINKING. By Prof. W. K. CLIFFORD, F.R.S. Diagrams. 3s. 6d.

CHARLES DARWIN. Memorial Notices reprinted from "Nature." By THOMAS H. HUXLEY, F.R.S., G. J. ROMANES, F.R.S., ARCHIBALD GEIKIE, F.R.S., and W. T. DYER, F.R.S. 2s. 6d.

ON THE COLOURS OF FLOWERS. By GRANT ALLEN. Illustrated. 3s. 6d.

THE CHEMISTRY OF THE SECONDARY BATTERIES OF PLANTÉ AND FAURE. By J. H. GLADSTONE and A. TRIBE. 2s. 6d.

A CENTURY OF ELECTRICITY. By T. C. MENDENHALL. 4s. 6d.

ON LIGHT. The Burnett Lectures. By Sir GEORGE GABRIEL STOKES, M.P., F.R.S. Three Courses: I. On the Nature of Light. II. On Light as a Means of Investigation. III. On Beneficial Effects of Light. 7s. 6d.

THE SCIENTIFIC EVIDENCES OF ORGANIC EVOLUTION. By GEORGE J. ROMANES, M.A., LL.D. 2s. 6d.

POPULAR LECTURES AND ADDRESSES. By Sir WM. THOMSON. In 3 vols. Vol. I. Constitution of Matter. Illustrated. 6s.—Vol. III. Navigation.

THE CHEMISTRY OF PHOTOGRAPHY. By Prof. R. MELDOLA, F.R.S. Illustrated. 6s.

MODERN VIEWS OF ELECTRICITY. By Prof. O. J. LODGE, LL.D. Illustrated. 6s. 6d.

TIMBER AND SOME OF ITS DISEASES. By Prof. H. M. WARD, M.A. Illustrated. 6s.

ARE THE EFFECTS OF USE AND DISUSE INHERITED? An Examination of the View held by Spencer and Darwin. By W. PLATT BALL. 3s. 6d.

NEW ANTIGONE (THE): A ROMANCE. Crown 8vo. 6s.

NEWCOMB (Prof. Simon).—POPULAR ASTRONOMY. With 112 Engravings and Maps of the Stars. 2nd Edition. 8vo. 18s.

NEWMAN (F. W.).—MATHEMATICAL TRACTS. 8vo. Part I. 5s.—Part II. 4s.

—— ELLIPTIC INTEGRALS. 8vo. 9s.

NEWTON (Sir C. T.).—ESSAYS ON ART AND ARCHÆOLOGY. 8vo. 12s. 6d.

NEWTON'S PRINCIPIA. Edited by Prof. Sir W. THOMSON and Prof. BLACKBURN. 4to. 31s. 6d.

—— FIRST BOOK. Sections I. II. III. With Notes, Illustrations, and Problems. By P. FROST, M.A. 3rd Edition. 8vo. 12s.

NIXON (J. E.).—PARALLEL EXTRACTS. Arranged for Translation into English and Latin, with Notes on Idioms. Part I. Historical and Epistolary. 2nd Ed. Cr. 8vo. 3s. 6d.

—— PROSE EXTRACTS. Arranged for Translation into English and Latin, with General and Special Prefaces on Style and Idiom. I. Oratorical. II. Historical. III. Philosophical. IV. Anecdotes and Letters. 2nd Edition, enlarged to 280 pages. Crown 8vo. 4s. 6d.—SELECTIONS FROM THE SAME. Globe 8vo. 3s.

NOEL (Lady Augusta).—WANDERING WILLIE. Globe 8vo. 2s. 6d.

—— HITHERSEA MERE. 3 vols. Cr. 8vo. 31s. 6d.

NORDENSKIÖLD.—VOYAGE OF THE "VEGA" ROUND ASIA AND EUROPE. By Baron A. E. VON NORDENSKIÖLD. Translated by ALEXANDER LESLIE. 400 Illustrations, Maps, etc. 2 vols. Medium 8vo. 45s.
Cheap Edition. With Portrait, Maps, and Illustrations. Crown 8vo. 6s.

NORGATE (Kate).—ENGLAND UNDER THE ANGEVIN KINGS. 2 vols. With Maps and Plans. 8vo. 32s.

NORRIS (W. E.).—MY FRIEND JIM. Globe 8vo. 2s.

—— CHRIS. Globe 8vo. 2s.

NORTON (the Hon. Mrs.).—THE LADY OF LA GARAYE. 9th Ed. Fcp. 8vo. 4s. 6d.

—— OLD SIR DOUGLAS. Crown 8vo. 6s.

OLD SONGS. With Drawings by E. A. ABBEY and A. PARSONS. 4to. Morocco gilt. 1l. 11s. 6d.

OLIPHANT (Mrs. M. O. W.).—FRANCIS OF ASSISI. Crown 8vo. 6s.

—— THE MAKERS OF VENICE: DOGES, CONQUERORS, PAINTERS, AND MEN OF LETTERS. Illustrated. Crown 8vo. 10s. 6d.

—— THE MAKERS OF FLORENCE: DANTE, GIOTTO, SAVONAROLA, AND THEIR CITY. Illustrated. Cr. 8vo. 10s. 6d.

—— ROYAL EDINBURGH: HER SAINTS, KINGS, PROPHETS, AND POETS. Illustrated by G. REID, R.S.A. Crn. 8vo. 10s 6d.

—— THE LITERARY HISTORY OF ENGLAND IN THE END OF THE XVIII. AND BEGINNING OF THE XIX. CENTURY. 3 vols. 8vo. 21s.
See also p. 29

OLIPHANT (T. L. Kington).—THE OLD AND MIDDLE ENGLISH. Globe 8vo. 9s.

OLIPHANT (T. L. Kington).—THE DUKE AND THE SCHOLAR, AND OTHER ESSAYS. 8vo. 7s. 6d.

—— THE NEW ENGLISH. 2 vols. Cr. 8vo. 21s.

OLIVER (Prof. Daniel).—LESSONS IN ELEMENTARY BOTANY. Illustr. Fcp. 8vo. 4s. 6d.

—— FIRST BOOK OF INDIAN BOTANY. Illustrated. Extra fcp. 8vo. 6s. 6d.

OLIVER (Capt. S. P.).—MADAGASCAR: AN HISTORICAL AND DESCRIPTIVE ACCOUNT OF THE ISLAND AND ITS FORMER DEPENDENCIES. 2 vols. Medium 8vo. 2l. 12s. 6d.

ORCHIDS: BEING THE REPORT ON THE ORCHID CONFERENCE HELD AT SOUTH KENSINGTON, 1885. 8vo. 2s. 6d. net.

OSTWALD (Prof. W.).—OUTLINES OF GENERAL CHEMISTRY. Translated by Dr. J. WALKER. 8vo. 10s. net.

OTTÉ (E. C.).—SCANDINAVIAN HISTORY. With Maps. Globe 8vo. 6s.

OVERING (H.).—TIM: A STORY OF SCHOOL LIFE. Crown 8vo.

OVID.—See pp. 31, 33.

OWENS COLLEGE CALENDAR, 1889—90. Crown 8vo. 3s. net.

OWENS COLLEGE ESSAYS AND ADDRESSES. By Professors and Lecturers of the College. 8vo. 14s.

OXFORD, A HISTORY OF THE UNIVERSITY OF. From the Earliest Times to the Year 1530. By H. C. MAXWELL LYTE, M.A. 8vo. 16s.

PALGRAVE (Sir Francis).—HISTORY OF NORMANDY AND OF ENGLAND. 4 vols. 8vo. 4l. 4s.

PALGRAVE (William Gifford).—A NARRATIVE OF A YEAR'S JOURNEY THROUGH CENTRAL AND EASTERN ARABIA, 1862—63. 9th Edition. Crown 8vo. 6s.

—— ESSAYS ON EASTERN QUESTIONS. 8vo. 10s. 6d.

—— DUTCH GUIANA. 8vo. 9s.

—— ULYSSES; OR, SCENES AND STUDIES IN MANY LANDS. 8vo. 12s. 6d.

PALGRAVE (Prof. Francis Turner).—THE FIVE DAYS' ENTERTAINMENTS AT WENTWORTH GRANGE. A Book for Children. Small 4to. 6s.

—— ESSAYS ON ART. Extra fcp. 8vo. 6s.

—— ORIGINAL HYMNS. 3rd Ed. 18mo. 1s. 6d.

—— LYRICAL POEMS. Extra fcp. 8vo. 6s.

—— VISIONS OF ENGLAND: A SERIES OF LYRICAL POEMS ON LEADING EVENTS AND PERSONS IN ENGLISH HISTORY. Crown 8vo. 7s. 6d.

—— THE GOLDEN TREASURY OF THE BEST SONGS AND LYRICAL POEMS IN THE ENGLISH LANGUAGE. 18mo. 2s. 6d. net. (Large Type) Crown 8vo. 10s. 6d.

—— THE CHILDREN'S TREASURY OF LYRICAL POETRY. 18mo. 2s. 6d.—Or in Two Parts, 1s. each.

PALGRAVE (Reginald F. D.).—THE HOUSE OF COMMONS: ILLUSTRATIONS OF ITS HISTORY AND PRACTICE. Crown 8vo. 2s. 6d.

PALGRAVE (R. H. Inglis).—DICTIONARY OF POLITICAL ECONOMY. Ed. by R. H. INGLIS PALGRAVE. 3s. 6d. each Part. [Part I. shortly.

PALMER (Lady Sophia).—MRS. PENICOTT'S LODGER, AND OTHER STORIES. Cr. 8vo. 2s. 6d.

PALMER (J. H.).—TEXT-BOOK OF PRACTICAL LOGARITHMS AND TRIGONOMETRY. Crown 8vo. 4s. 6d.

PANTIN (W. E. P.).—A FIRST LATIN VERSE BOOK. Globe 8vo. 1s. 6d.

PARADOXICAL PHILOSOPHY: A SEQUEL TO "THE UNSEEN UNIVERSE." Cr. 8vo. 7s. 6d.

PARKER (Prof. T. Jeffery).—A COURSE OF INSTRUCTION IN ZOOTOMY (VERTEBRATA). With 74 Illustrations. Crown 8vo. 8s. 6d.

—— LESSONS IN ELEMENTARY BIOLOGY. Illustrated. Crown 8vo. 10s. 6d.

PARKINSON (S.).—A TREATISE ON ELEMENTARY MECHANICS. Crown 8vo. 9s. 6d.

—— A TREATISE ON OPTICS. 4th Edition, revised. Crown 8vo. 10s. 6d.

PARKMAN (Francis). — MONTCALM AND WOLFE. Library Edition. Illustrated with Portraits and Maps. 2 vols. 8vo. 12s. 6d. each.

—— THE COLLECTED WORKS OF FRANCIS PARKMAN. Popular Edition. In 10 vols. Crown 8vo. 7s. 6d. each; or complete, 3l. 13s. 6d.—PIONEERS OF FRANCE IN THE NEW WORLD. 1 vol.—THE JESUITS IN NORTH AMERICA. 1 vol.—LA SALLE AND THE DISCOVERY OF THE GREAT WEST. 1 vol.—THE OREGON TRAIL. 1 vol.—THE OLD RÉGIME IN CANADA UNDER LOUIS XIV. 1 vol.—COUNT FRONTENAC AND NEW FRANCE under Louis XIV. 1 vol.—MONTCALM AND WOLFE. 2 vols.—THE CONSPIRACY OF PONTIAC. 2 vols.

PASTEUR — FAULKNER.—STUDIES ON FERMENTATION: THE DISEASES OF BEER, THEIR CAUSES, AND THE MEANS OF PREVENTING THEM. By L. PASTEUR. Translated by FRANK FAULKNER. 8vo. 21s.

PATER (W.).—THE RENAISSANCE: STUDIES IN ART AND POETRY. 4th Ed. Cr. 8vo. 10s. 6d.

—— MARIUS THE EPICUREAN: HIS SENSATIONS AND IDEAS. 3rd Edition. 2 vols. 8vo. 12s.

—— IMAGINARY PORTRAITS. 3rd Edition. Crown 8vo. 6s.

—— APPRECIATIONS. With an Essay on Style. 2nd Edition. Crown 8vo. 8s. 6d.

PATERSON (James).—COMMENTARIES ON THE LIBERTY OF THE SUBJECT, AND THE LAWS OF ENGLAND RELATING TO THE SECURITY OF THE PERSON. 2 vols. Cr. 8vo. 21s.

—— THE LIBERTY OF THE PRESS, SPEECH, AND PUBLIC WORSHIP. Crown 8vo. 12s.

PATMORE (C.).—THE CHILDREN'S GARLAND FROM THE BEST POETS. With a Vignette. 18mo. 2s. 6d. net.
Globe Readings Edition. For Schools. Globe 8vo. 2s.

LIST OF PUBLICATIONS. 41

PATTESON.—LIFE AND LETTERS OF JOHN COLERIDGE PATTESON, D.D., MISSIONARY BISHOP. By CHARLOTTE M. YONGE. 8th Edition. 2 vols. Crown 8vo. 12s.

PATTISON (Mark).—MEMOIRS. Crown 8vo. 8s. 6d.
—— SERMONS. Crown 8vo. 6s.

PAUL OF TARSUS. 8vo. 10s. 6d.

PEABODY (Prof. C. H.).—THERMODYNAMICS OF THE STEAM ENGINE AND OTHER HEAT-ENGINES. 8vo. 21s.

PEDLEY (S.).—EXERCISES IN ARITHMETIC. With upwards of 7000 Examples and Answers. Crown 8vo. 5s.—Also in Two Parts. 2s. 6d. each.

PELLISSIER (Eugène).—FRENCH ROOTS AND THEIR FAMILIES. Globe 8vo. 6s.

PENNELL (Joseph).—PEN DRAWING AND PEN DRAUGHTSMEN. With 158 Illustrations. 4to. 3l. 13s. 6d. net.

PENNINGTON (Rooke).—NOTES ON THE BARROWS AND BONE CAVES OF DERBYSHIRE. 8vo. 6s.

PENROSE (Francis).—ON A METHOD OF PREDICTING, BY GRAPHICAL CONSTRUCTION, OCCULTATIONS OF STARS BY THE MOON AND SOLAR ECLIPSES FOR ANY GIVEN PLACE. 4to. 12s.
—— AN INVESTIGATION OF THE PRINCIPLES OF ATHENIAN ARCHITECTURE. Illustrated. Folio. 7l. 7s. net.

PERRY (Prof. John).—AN ELEMENTARY TREATISE ON STEAM. 18mo. 4s. 6d.

PERSIA, EASTERN. AN ACCOUNT OF THE JOURNEYS OF THE PERSIAN BOUNDARY COMMISSION, 1870—71—72. 2 vols. 8vo. 42s.

PETTIGREW (J. Bell).—THE PHYSIOLOGY OF THE CIRCULATION. 8vo. 12s.

PHAEDRUS.—See p. 31.

PHILLIMORE (John G.).—PRIVATE LAW AMONG THE ROMANS. 8vo. 16s.

PHILLIPS (J. A.).—A TREATISE ON ORE DEPOSITS. Illustrated. Medium 8vo. 25s.

PHILOCHRISTUS.—MEMOIRS OF A DISCIPLE OF THE LORD. 3rd Ed. 8vo. 12s.

PHILOLOGY. THE JOURNAL OF SACRED AND CLASSICAL PHILOLOGY. 4 vols. 8vo. 12s. 6d. each net.
—— THE JOURNAL OF PHILOLOGY. New Series. Edited by W. A. WRIGHT, M.A., I. BYWATER, M.A., and H. JACKSON, M.A. 4s. 6d. each number (half-yearly) net.
—— THE AMERICAN JOURNAL OF PHILOLOGY. Edited by Prof. BASIL L. GILDERSLEEVE. 4s. 6d. each (quarterly) net.
—— TRANSACTIONS OF THE AMERICAN PHILOLOGICAL ASSOCIATION. Vols. I.—XX. 8s. 6d. per vol. net, except Vols. XV. and XX., which are 10s. 6d. net.

PHRYNICHUS. THE NEW PHRYNICHUS. A revised text of "The Ecloga" of the Grammarian PHRYNICHUS. With Introductions and Commentary. By W. GUNION RUTHERFORD, LL.D. 8vo. 18s.

PICKERING (Prof. Edward C.).—ELEMENTS OF PHYSICAL MANIPULATION. Medium 8vo. Part I., 12s. 6d.; Part II., 14s.

PICTON (J. A.).—THE MYSTERY OF MATTER, AND OTHER ESSAYS. Crown 8vo. 6s.

PINDAR'S EXTANT ODES. Translated by ERNEST MYERS. Crown 8vo. 5s.
—— THE OLYMPIAN AND PYTHIAN ODES. Edited, with Notes, by Prof. BASIL GILDERSLEEVE. Crown 8vo. 7s. 6d.
—— THE NEMEAN ODES. Edited by J. B. BURY, M.A. 8vo. 12s.

PIRIE (Prof. G.).—LESSONS ON RIGID DYNAMICS. Crown 8vo. 6s.

PLATO.—PHÆDO. Edited by R. D. ARCHER-HIND, M.A. 8vo. 8s. 6d.
—— TIMÆUS. With Introduction, Notes, and Translation, by the same Editor. 8vo. 16s.
—— PHÆDO. Ed. by Principal W. D. GEDDES, LL.D. 2nd Edition. 8vo. 8s. 6d.
See also pp. 17, 32, 33.

PLAUTUS. — THE MOSTELLARIA. With Notes, Prolegomena, and Excursus. By the late Prof. RAMSAY. Ed. by G. G. RAMSAY, M.A. 8vo. 14s. *See also* p. 33.

PLINY.—CORRESPONDENCE WITH TRAJAN. Edit. by E. G. HARDY, M.A. 8vo. 10s. 6d. *See also* p. 33.

PLUMPTRE (Very Rev. E. H.).—MOVEMENTS IN RELIGIOUS THOUGHT. Fcp. 8vo. 3s. 6d.

PLUTARCH. Being a Selection from the Lives in North's Plutarch which illustrate Shakespeare's Plays. Edited by Rev. W. W. SKEAT, M.A. Crn. 8vo. 6s. *See* p. 33.

POLLOCK (Prof. Sir F., Bart.).—ESSAYS IN JURISPRUDENCE AND ETHICS. 8vo. 10s. 6d.
—— THE LAND LAWS. 2nd Edition. Crown 8vo. 3s. 6d.
—— INTRODUCTION TO THE HISTORY OF THE SCIENCE OF POLITICS. Crown 8vo. 2s. 6d.
—— OXFORD LECTURES AND OTHER DISCOURSES. 8vo. 9s.

POLLOCK (Sir Frederick).—PERSONAL REMEMBRANCES. 2 vols. Crown 8vo. 16s.

POLYBIUS.—THE HISTORIES OF POLYBIUS. Translated by E. S. SHUCKBURGH. 2 vols. Crown 8vo. 24s. *See also* p. 33.

POOLE (M. E.).—PICTURES OF COTTAGE LIFE IN THE WEST OF ENGLAND. 2nd Ed. Crown 8vo. 3s. 6d.

POOLE (Reginald Lane).—A HISTORY OF THE HUGUENOTS OF THE DISPERSION AT THE RECALL OF THE EDICT OF NANTES. Crown 8vo. 6s.

POOLE, THOMAS, AND HIS FRIENDS. By Mrs. SANDFORD. 2 vols. Crn. 8vo. 15s.

POSTGATE (Prof. J. P.).—SERMO LATINUS. A Short Guide to Latin Prose Composition. Part I. Introduction. Part II. Selected Passages for Translation. Gl. 8vo. 2s. 6d.—Key to "Selected Passages." Crown 8vo. 3s. 6d.

POTTER (Louisa).—LANCASHIRE MEMORIES. Crown 8vo. 6s.

POTTER (R.).—THE RELATION OF ETHICS TO RELIGION. Crown 8vo. 2s. 6d.

POTTS (A. W.).—HINTS TOWARDS LATIN PROSE COMPOSITION. Globe 8vo. 3s.

—— PASSAGES FOR TRANSLATION INTO LATIN PROSE. 4th Ed. Extra fcp. 8vo. 2s. 6d.

—— LATIN VERSIONS OF PASSAGES FOR TRANSLATION INTO LATIN PROSE. Extra fcp. 8vo. 2s. 6d. (For Teachers only.)

PRACTICAL POLITICS. Published under the auspices of the National Liberal Federation. 8vo. 6s.

PRACTITIONER (THE): A MONTHLY JOURNAL OF THERAPEUTICS AND PUBLIC HEALTH. Edited by T. LAUDER BRUNTON, M.D., F.R.C.P., F.R.S., Assistant Physician to St. Bartholomew's Hospital, etc., etc.; DONALD MACALISTER, M.A., M.D., B.Sc., F.R.C.P., Fellow and Medical Lecturer, St. John's College, Cambridge, Physician to Addenbrooke's Hospital and University Lecturer in Medicine; and J. MITCHELL BRUCE, M.A., M.D., F.R.C.P., Physician and Lecturer on Therapeutics at Charing Cross Hospital. 1s. 6d. monthly. Vols. I.—XLIII. Half-yearly vols. 10s. 6d. [Cloth covers for binding, 1s. each.]

PRESTON (Rev. G.).—EXERCISES IN LATIN VERSE OF VARIOUS KINDS. Globe 8vo. 2s. 6d.—Key. Globe 8vo. 5s.

PRESTON (T.).—THE THEORY OF LIGHT. Illustrated. 8vo. 12s. 6d.

PRICE (L. L. F. R.)—INDUSTRIAL PEACE: ITS ADVANTAGES, METHODS, AND DIFFICULTIES. Medium 8vo. 6s.

PRICKARD (A. O.).—ARISTOTLE AND THE ART OF POETRY. Globe 8vo.

PRIMERS.—HISTORY. Edited by JOHN R. GREEN, Author of "A Short History of the English People," etc. 18mo. 1s. each:
EUROPE. By E. A. FREEMAN, M.A.
GREECE. By C. A. FYFFE, M.A.
ROME. By Bishop CREIGHTON.
GREEK ANTIQUITIES. By Prof. MAHAFFY.
ROMAN ANTIQUITIES. By Prof. WILKINS.
CLASSICAL GEOGRAPHY. By H. F. TOZER.
FRANCE. By CHARLOTTE M. YONGE.
GEOGRAPHY. By Sir GEO. GROVE, D.C.L.
INDIAN HISTORY, ASIATIC AND EUROPEAN. By J. TALBOYS WHEELER.
ANALYSIS OF ENGLISH HISTORY. By T. F. TOUT, M.A.

PRIMERS.—LITERATURE. Edited by JOHN R. GREEN, M.A., LL.D. 18mo. 1s. each:
ENGLISH GRAMMAR. By Rev. R. MORRIS.
ENGLISH GRAMMAR EXERCISES. By Rev. R. MORRIS and H. C. BOWEN.
EXERCISES ON MORRIS'S PRIMER OF ENGLISH GRAMMAR. By J. WETHERELL, M.A.
ENGLISH COMPOSITION. By Prof. NICHOL.
QUESTIONS AND EXERCISES IN ENGLISH COMPOSITION. By Prof. NICHOL and W. S. M'CORMICK.

PRIMERS (LITERATURE)—continued.
PHILOLOGY. By J. PEILE, M.A.
ENGLISH LITERATURE. By Rev. STOPFORD BROOKE, M.A.
CHILDREN'S TREASURY OF LYRICAL POETRY. Selected by Prof. F. T. PALGRAVE. In 2 parts. 1s. each.
SHAKSPERE. By Prof. DOWDEN.
GREEK LITERATURE. By Prof. JEBB.
HOMER. By Right Hon. W. E. GLADSTONE.
ROMAN LITERATURE. By A. S. WILKINS.

PRIMERS.—SCIENCE. Under the joint Editorship of Prof. HUXLEY, Sir H. E. ROSCOE, and Prof. BALFOUR STEWART. 18mo. 1s. each:
INTRODUCTORY. By Prof. HUXLEY.
CHEMISTRY. By Sir HENRY ROSCOE, F.R.S. With Illustrations, and Questions.
PHYSICS. By BALFOUR STEWART, F.R.S. With Illustrations, and Questions.
PHYSICAL GEOGRAPHY. By A. GEIKIE, F.R.S. With Illustrations, and Questions.
GEOLOGY. By ARCHIBALD GEIKIE, F.R.S.
PHYSIOLOGY. By MICHAEL FOSTER, F.R.S.
ASTRONOMY. By J. N. LOCKYER, F.R.S.
BOTANY. By Sir J. D. HOOKER, C.B.
LOGIC. By W. STANLEY JEVONS, F.R.S.
POLITICAL ECONOMY. By W. STANLEY JEVONS, LL.D., M.A., F.R.S.

Also Uniform with the above. 18mo. 1s. each.
ARNOLD (M.). — A BIBLE-READING FOR SCHOOLS: The Great Prophecy of Israel's Restoration (Isai. xl.-lxvi). Arranged and Edited for Young Beginners. 4th Edition.
BARKER (Lady).—FIRST LESSONS IN THE PRINCIPLES OF COOKING. 3rd Edition.
BERNERS (J.).—FIRST LESSONS ON HEALTH.
BETTANY (G. T.). — FIRST LESSONS IN PRACTICAL BOTANY.
BUCKLAND (Anna).—OUR NATIONAL INSTITUTIONS.
COLLIER (Hon. John).—A PRIMER OF ART.
ELDERTON (W. A.). — MAPS AND MAP DRAWING.
FIRST LESSONS IN BUSINESS MATTERS. By A BANKER'S DAUGHTER. 2nd Edition.
GASKOIN (Mrs. Herman). — CHILDREN'S TREASURY OF BIBLE STORIES.—Part I. Old Testament; II. New Testament; III. Three Apostles. 1s. each.
GEIKIE (A.).—GEOGRAPHY OF THE BRITISH ISLES.
GRAND'HOMME.—CUTTING OUT AND DRESSMAKING. From the French of Mdlle. GRAND'HOMME.
JEX-BLAKE (Dr. Sophia).—THE CARE OF INFANTS: A Manual for Mothers and Nurses.
MACLEAR (Rev. Canon). A SHILLING BOOK OF OLD TESTAMENT HISTORY.
—— A SHILLING BOOK OF NEW TESTAMENT HISTORY.

PRIMERS—*continued.*

TANNER (Prof. Henry).—FIRST PRINCIPLES OF AGRICULTURE.

TAYLOR (Franklin).—PRIMER OF PIANOFORTE PLAYING.

TEGETMEIER (W. B.).—HOUSEHOLD MANAGEMENT AND COOKERY.

THORNTON (J.). — PRIMER OF BOOK-KEEPING.

WRIGHT (Miss Guthrie). — THE SCHOOL COOKERY-BOOK.

PROCTER (Rev. F.).—A HISTORY OF THE BOOK OF COMMON PRAYER. 18th Edition. Crown 8vo. 10s. 6d.

PROCTER (Rev. F.) and MACLEAR (Rev. Canon).—AN ELEMENTARY INTRODUCTION TO THE BOOK OF COMMON PRAYER. 18mo. 2s. 6d.

PROPERT (J. Lumsden).—A HISTORY OF MINIATURE ART. With Illustrations. Super royal 4to. 3l. 13s. 6d.
Also bound in vellum. 4l. 14s. 6d.

PSALMS (THE). With Introductions and Critical Notes. By A. C. JENNINGS, M.A., and W. H. LOWE, M.A. In 2 vols. 2nd Edition. Crown 8vo. 10s. 6d. each.

PUCKLE (G. H.).—AN ELEMENTARY TREATISE ON CONIC SECTIONS AND ALGEBRAIC GEOMETRY. 6th Edit. Crn. 8vo. 7s. 6d.

PYLODET (L.).—NEW GUIDE TO GERMAN CONVERSATION. 18mo. 2s. 6d.

RADCLIFFE (Charles B.).—BEHIND THE TIDES. 8vo. 4s. 6d.

RAMSAY (Prof. William).—EXPERIMENTAL PROOFS OF CHEMICAL THEORY. 18mo. 2s. 6d.

RANSOME (Prof. Cyril).—SHORT STUDIES OF SHAKESPEARE'S PLOTS. Cr. 8vo. 3s. 6d.

RATHBONE (Wm.).—THE HISTORY AND PROGRESS OF DISTRICT NURSING, FROM ITS COMMENCEMENT IN THE YEAR 1859 TO THE PRESENT DATE. Crown 8vo. 2s. 6d.

RAWNSLEY (H. D.).—POEMS, BALLADS, AND BUCOLICS. Fcp. 8vo. 5s.

RAY (Prof. P. K.).—A TEXT-BOOK OF DEDUCTIVE LOGIC. 4th Ed. Globe 8vo. 4s. 6d.

RAYLEIGH (Lord).—THEORY OF SOUND. 8vo. Vol. I. 12s. 6d.—Vol. II. 12s. 6d.—Vol. III. (*in preparation.*)

RAYS OF SUNLIGHT FOR DARK DAYS. With a Preface by C. J. VAUGHAN, D.D. New Edition. 18mo. 3s. 6d.

REALMAH. By the Author of "Friends in Council." Crown 8vo. 6s.

REASONABLE FAITH: A SHORT RELIGIOUS ESSAY FOR THE TIMES. By "THREE FRIENDS." Crown 8vo. 1s.

RECOLLECTIONS OF A NURSE. By E. D. Crown 8vo. 2s.

REED.—MEMOIR OF SIR CHARLES REED. By his Son, CHARLES E. B. REED, M.A. With Portrait. Crown 8vo. 4s. 6d.

REICHEL (Rt. Rev. Bishop).—CATHEDRAL AND UNIVERSITY SERMONS. Crn. 8vo. 6s.

REMSEN (Prof. Ira).—AN INTRODUCTION TO THE STUDY OF ORGANIC CHEMISTRY. Crown 8vo. 6s. 6d.

—— AN INTRODUCTION TO THE STUDY OF CHEMISTRY (INORGANIC CHEMISTRY). Cr. 8vo. 6s. 6d.

—— THE ELEMENTS OF CHEMISTRY. A Text-Book for Beginners. Fcp. 8vo. 2s. 6d.

—— TEXT-BOOK OF INORGANIC CHEMISTRY. 8vo. 16s.

RENDALL (Rev. Frederic).—THE EPISTLE TO THE HEBREWS IN GREEK AND ENGLISH. With Notes. Crown 8vo. 6s.

—— THE THEOLOGY OF THE HEBREW CHRISTIANS. Crown 8vo. 5s.

—— THE EPISTLE TO THE HEBREWS. English Text, with Commentary. Crown 8vo. 7s. 6d.

RENDU—WILLS.—THE THEORY OF THE GLACIERS OF SAVOY. By M. LE CHANOINE RENDU. Translated by A. WILLS, Q.C. 8vo. 7s. 6d.

REULEAUX — KENNEDY. THE KINEMATICS OF MACHINERY. By Prof. F. REULEAUX. Translated by Prof. A. B. W. KENNEDY, F.R.S., C.E. Medium 8vo. 21s.

REYNOLDS (J. R.).—A SYSTEM OF MEDICINE. Edited by J. RUSSELL REYNOLDS, M.D., F.R.C.P. London. In 5 vols. Vols. I. II. III. and V. 8vo. 25s. each.—Vol. IV. 21s.

REYNOLDS (Prof. Osborne).—SEWER GAS, AND HOW TO KEEP IT OUT OF HOUSES. 3rd Edition. Crown 8vo. 1s. 6d.

RICE (Prof. J. M.) and JOHNSON (W. W.).—AN ELEMENTARY TREATISE ON THE DIFFERENTIAL CALCULUS. New Edition. 8vo. 18s. Abridged Edition. 9s.

RICHARDSON (A. T.).—THE "PROGRESSIVE" EUCLID. Books I. and II. Globe 8vo. 2s. 6d.

RICHARDSON (Dr. B. W.).—ON ALCOHOL. Crown 8vo. 1s.

—— DISEASES OF MODERN LIFE. Crown 8vo. (*Reprinting.*)

—— HYGEIA: A CITY OF HEALTH. Crown 8vo. 1s.

—— THE FUTURE OF SANITARY SCIENCE. Crown 8vo. 1s.

—— THE FIELD OF DISEASE. A Book of Preventive Medicine. 8vo. 25s.

RICHEY (Alex. G.).—THE IRISH LAND LAWS. Crown 8vo. 3s. 6d.

ROBINSON (Prebendary H. G.).—MAN IN THE IMAGE OF GOD, AND OTHER SERMONS. Crown 8vo. 7s. 6d.

ROBINSON (Rev. J. L.).—MARINE SURVEYING: AN ELEMENTARY TREATISE ON. Prepared for the Use of Younger Naval Officers. With Illustrations. Crown 8vo. 7s. 6d.

ROBY (H. J.).—A GRAMMAR OF THE LATIN LANGUAGE FROM PLAUTUS TO SUETONIUS. In Two Parts.—Part I. containing Sounds, Inflexions, Word Formation, Appendices, etc. 5th Edition. Crown 8vo. 9s.—Part II. Syntax, Prepositions, etc. 6th Edition. Crown 8vo. 10s. 6d.

—— A LATIN GRAMMAR FOR SCHOOLS. Cr. 8vo. 5s.

—— EXERCISES IN LATIN SYNTAX AND IDIOM. Arranged with reference to Roby's School Latin Grammar. By E. B. ENGLAND, M.A. Crown 8vo. 2s. 6d.—Key, 2s. 6d.

ROCKSTRO (W. S.).—LIFE OF GEORGE FREDERICK HANDEL. Crown 8vo. 10s. 6d.

ROGERS (Prof. J. E. T.).—HISTORICAL GLEANINGS.—First Series. Cr. 8vo. 4s. 6d. —Second Series. Crown 8vo. 6s.

—— COBDEN AND POLITICAL OPINION. 8vo. 10s. 6d.

ROMANES (George J.).—THE SCIENTIFIC EVIDENCES OF ORGANIC EVOLUTION. Cr. 8vo. 2s. 6d.

ROSCOE (Sir Henry E., M.P., F.R.S.).— LESSONS IN ELEMENTARY CHEMISTRY. With Illustrations. Fcp. 8vo. 4s. 6d.

—— PRIMER OF CHEMISTRY. With Illustrations. 18mo. With Questions. 1s.

ROSCOE (Sir H. E.) and SCHORLEMMER (C.).—A TREATISE ON CHEMISTRY. With Illustrations. 8vo.—Vols. I. and II. INORGANIC CHEMISTRY: Vol. I. THE NON-METALLIC ELEMENTS. With a Portrait of DALTON. 21s.—Vol. II. Part I. METALS. 18s.; Part II. METALS. 18s.—Vol. III. ORGANIC CHEMISTRY: Parts I. II. and IV. 21s. each; Parts III. and V. 18s. each.

ROSCOE—SCHUSTER.—SPECTRUM ANALYSIS. By Sir HENRY E. ROSCOE, LL.D., F.R.S. 4th Edition, revised by the Author and A. SCHUSTER, Ph.D., F.R.S. Medium 8vo. 21s.

ROSENBUSCH—IDDINGS.—MICROSCOPICAL PHYSIOGRAPHY OF THE ROCK-MAKING MINERALS. By Prof. H. ROSENBUSCH. Translated by J. P. IDDINGS. Illustrated. 8vo. 24s.

ROSS (Percy).—A MISGUIDIT LASSIE. Crown 8vo. 4s. 6d.

ROSSETTI (Dante Gabriel).—A RECORD AND A STUDY. By W. SHARP. Crown 8vo. 10s. 6d.

ROSSETTI (Christina).—POEMS. New and Enlarged Edition. Globe 8vo. 7s. 6d.

—— SPEAKING LIKENESSES. Illustrated by ARTHUR HUGHES. Crown 8vo. 4s. 6d.

ROUSSEAU. By JOHN MORLEY. 2 vols. Globe 8vo. 10s.

ROUTH E. J.).—A TREATISE ON THE DYNAMICS OF A SYSTEM OF RIGID BODIES. 8vo.—Part I. ELEMENTARY. 5th Edition. 14s.—Part II. ADVANCED. 4th Edit. 14s.

—— STABILITY OF A GIVEN STATE OF MOTION, PARTICULARLY STEADY MOTION. 8vo. 8s. 6d.

ROUTLEDGE (James).—POPULAR PROGRESS IN ENGLAND. 8vo. 16s.

RUMFORD (Count).—COMPLETE WORKS OF COUNT RUMFORD. With Memoir by GEORGE ELLIS, and Portrait. 5 vols. 8vo. 4l. 14s. 6d.

RUNAWAY (THE). By the Author of "Mrs. Jerningham's Journal." Gl. 8vo. 2s. 6d.

RUSH (Edward).—THE SYNTHETIC LATIN DELECTUS. A First Latin Construing Book. Extra fcp. 8vo. 2s. 6d.

RUSHBROOKE (W. G.).—SYNOPTICON: AN EXPOSITION OF THE COMMON MATTER OF THE SYNOPTIC GOSPELS. Printed in Colours. In Six Parts, and Appendix. 4to.—Part I. 3s. 6d.—Parts II. and III. 7s.—Parts IV. V. and VI., with Indices. 10s. 6d.—Appendices. 10s. 6d.—Complete in 1 vol. 35s.

RUSSELL (Sir Charles).—NEW VIEWS ON IRELAND. Crown 8vo. 2s. 6d.

—— THE PARNELL COMMISSION: THE OPENING SPEECH FOR THE DEFENCE. 8vo. 10s. 6d.—Cheap Edition. Sewed. 2s.

RUSSELL (Dean).—THE LIGHT THAT LIGHTETH EVERY MAN: Sermons. With an Introduction by Dean PLUMPTRE, D.D. Crown 8vo. 6s.

RUST (Rev. George).—FIRST STEPS TO LATIN PROSE COMPOSITION. 18mo. 1s. 6d.

—— A KEY TO RUST'S FIRST STEPS TO LATIN PROSE COMPOSITION. By W. YATES. 18mo. 3s. 6d.

RUTHERFORD (W. Gunion, M.A., LL.D.). —FIRST GREEK GRAMMAR. Part I. Accidence, 2s.; Part II. Syntax, 2s.; or in 1 vol. 3s. 6d.

—— THE NEW PHRYNICHUS. Being a revised Text of the Ecloga of the Grammarian Phrynichus, with Introduction and Commentary. 8vo. 18s.

—— BABRIUS. With Introductory Dissertations, Critical Notes, Commentary, and Lexicon. 8vo. 12s. 6d.

—— THUCYDIDES. Book IV. A Revision of the Text, illustrating the Principal Causes of Corruption in the Manuscripts of this Author. 8vo. 7s. 6d.

RYLAND (F.).—CHRONOLOGICAL OUTLINES OF ENGLISH LITERATURE. Crn. 8vo. 6s.

ST. JOHNSTON (A.).—CAMPING AMONG CANNIBALS. Crown 8vo. 4s. 6d.

—— A SOUTH SEA LOVER: A Romance. Cr. 8vo. 6s.

—— CHARLIE ASGARDE: THE STORY OF A FRIENDSHIP. Crown 8vo. 5s.

SAINTSBURY (George).—A HISTORY OF ELIZABETHAN LITERATURE. Cr. 8vo. 7s. 6d.

SALLUST.—THE CONSPIRACY OF CATILINE AND THE JUGURTHINE WAR. Translated by A. W. POLLARD, B.A. Crn. 8vo. 6s. CATILINE separately. Crown 8vo. 3s.

See also p. 33.

SALMON (Rev. Prof. George).—NON-MIRACULOUS CHRISTIANITY, AND OTHER SERMONS. 2nd Edition. Crown 8vo. 6s.

—— GNOSTICISM AND AGNOSTICISM, AND OTHER SERMONS. Crown 8vo. 7s. 6d.

LIST OF PUBLICATIONS.

SANDERSON (F. W.).—HYDROSTATICS FOR BEGINNERS. Globe 8vo. 4s. 6d.

SANDHURST MATHEMATICAL PAPERS, FOR ADMISSION INTO THE ROYAL MILITARY COLLEGE, 1881—89. Edited by E. J. BROOKSMITH, B.A. Cr. 8vo. 3s. 6d.

SANDYS (J. E.).—AN EASTER VACATION IN GREECE. Crown 8vo. 3s. 6d.

SAYCE (Prof. A. H.).—THE ANCIENT EMPIRES OF THE EAST. Crown 8vo. 6s.

—— HERODOTOS. Books I.—III. The Ancient Empires of the East. Edited, with Notes, and Introduction. 8vo. 16s.

SCHILLER.—See p. 35.

SCHILLER'S LIFE. By Prof. HEINRICH DÜNTZER. Translated by PERCY E. PINKERTON. Crown 8vo. 10s. 6d.

SCHMID.—HEINRICH VON EICHENFELS. Edited by G. E. FASNACHT. 2s. 6d.

SCHMIDT—WHITE.—AN INTRODUCTION TO THE RHYTHMIC AND METRIC OF THE CLASSICAL LANGUAGES. By Dr. J. H. HEINRICH SCHMIDT. Translated by JOHN WILLIAMS WHITE, Ph.D. 8vo. 10s. 6d.

SCIENCE LECTURES AT SOUTH KENSINGTON. With Illustrations.—Vol. I. Containing Lectures by Capt. ABNEY, R.E., F.R.S.; Prof. STOKES; Prof. A. B. W. KENNEDY, F.R.S., C.E.; F. J. BRAMWELL, C.E., F.R.S.; Prof. F. FORBES; H. C. SORBY, F.R.S.; J. T. BOTTOMLEY, F.R.S.E.; S. H. VINES, D.Sc.; Prof. CAREY FOSTER. Crown 8vo. 6s.

Vol. II. Containing Lectures by W. SPOTTISWOODE, F.R.S.; Prof. FORBES; H. W. CHISHOLM; Prof. T. F. PIGOT; W. FROUDE, LL.D., F.R.S.; Dr. SIEMENS; Prof. BARRETT; Dr. BURDON-SANDERSON; Dr. LAUDER BRUNTON, F.R.S.; Prof. MCLEOD; Sir H. E. ROSCOE, F.R.S. Illust. Cr.8vo. 6s.

SCOTCH SERMONS, 1880. By Principal CAIRD and others. 3rd Edit. 8vo. 10s. 6d.

SCOTT. See ENGLISH CLASSICS, p. 12, and GLOBE READINGS, p. 17.

SCRATCHLEY—KINLOCH COOKE.—AUSTRALIAN DEFENCES AND NEW GUINEA. Compiled from the Papers of the late Major-General Sir PETER SCRATCHLEY, R.E., by C. KINLOCH COOKE. 8vo. 14s.

SCULPTURE, SPECIMENS OF ANCIENT. Egyptian, Etruscan, Greek, and Roman. Selected from different Collections in Great Britain by the SOCIETY OF DILETTANTI. Vol. II. 5l. 5s.

SEATON (Dr. Edward C.).—A HANDBOOK OF VACCINATION. Extra fcp. 8vo. 8s. 6d.

SEELEY (Prof. J. R.)—LECTURES AND ESSAYS. 8vo. 10s. 6d.

—— THE EXPANSION OF ENGLAND. Two Courses of Lectures. Crown 8vo. 4s. 6d.

—— OUR COLONIAL EXPANSION. Extracts from "The Expansion of England." Crown 8vo. 1s.

SEILER (Carl, M.D.)—MICRO-PHOTOGRAPHS IN HISTOLOGY, NORMAL AND PATHOLOGICAL. 4to. 31s. 6d.

SELBORNE (Roundell, Earl of).—A DEFENCE OF THE CHURCH OF ENGLAND AGAINST DISESTABLISHMENT. Crown 8vo. 2s. 6d.

—— ANCIENT FACTS AND FICTIONS CONCERNING CHURCHES AND TITHES. Cr. 8vo. 7s. 6d.

—— THE BOOK OF PRAISE. From the Best English Hymn Writers. 18mo. 4s. 6d.

—— A HYMNAL. Chiefly from "The Book of Praise." In various sizes.—A. In Royal 32mo, cloth limp. 6d.—B. Small 18mo, larger type, cloth limp. 1s.—C. Same Edition, fine paper, cloth. 1s. 6d.—An Edition with Music, Selected, Harmonised, and Composed by JOHN HULLAH. Square 18mo. 3s. 6d.

SERVICE (Rev. John).—SERMONS. With Portrait. Crown 8vo. 6s.

—— PRAYERS FOR PUBLIC WORSHIP. Crown 8vo. 4s. 6d.

SHAIRP (John Campbell).—GLEN DESSERAY, AND OTHER POEMS, LYRICAL AND ELEGIAC. Ed. by F. T. PALGRAVE. Crown 8vo. 6s.

SHAKESPEARE.—THE WORKS OF WILLIAM SHAKESPEARE. Cambridge Edition. New and Revised Edition, by W. ALDIS WRIGHT, M.A. 9 vols. 8vo. 10s. 6d. each.—Vol. I. Jan. 1891.

—— SHAKESPEARE. Edited by W. G. CLARK and W. A. WRIGHT. Globe Edition. Globe 8vo. 3s. 6d.

—— THE WORKS OF WILLIAM SHAKESPEARE. Victoria Edition.—Vol. I. Comedies.—Vol. II. Histories.—Vol. III. Tragedies. In Three Vols. Crown 8vo. 6s. each.

—— CHARLES LAMB'S TALES FROM SHAKSPEARE. Edited, with Preface, by the Rev. A. AINGER, M.A. 18mo. 4s. 6d. Globe Readings Edition. For Schools. Globe 8vo. 2s.—Library Edition. Globe 8vo. 5s.

See also ENGLISH CLASSICS, p. 12.

SHANN (G.).—AN ELEMENTARY TREATISE ON HEAT IN RELATION TO STEAM AND THE STEAM-ENGINE. Illustrated. Crown 8vo. 4s. 6d.

SHELBURNE. LIFE OF WILLIAM, EARL OF SHELBURNE. By Lord EDMOND FITZMAURICE. In 3 vols.—Vol. I. 8vo. 12s.—Vol. II. 8vo. 12s.—Vol. III. 8vo. 16s.

SHELLEY. COMPLETE POETICAL WORKS. Edited by Prof. DOWDEN. With Portrait. Crown 8vo. 7s. 6d.

SHIRLEY (W. N.).—ELIJAH: FOUR UNIVERSITY SERMONS. Fcp. 8vo. 2s. 6d.

SHORTHOUSE (J. H.).—JOHN INGLESANT: A ROMANCE. Crown 8vo. 6s.

—— THE LITTLE SCHOOLMASTER MARK: A SPIRITUAL ROMANCE. Two Parts. Crown 8vo. 2s. 6d. each; complete, 4s. 6d.

—— SIR PERCIVAL: A STORY OF THE PAST AND OF THE PRESENT. Crown 8vo. 6s.

—— A TEACHER OF THE VIOLIN, AND OTHER TALES. Crown 8vo. 6s.

—— THE COUNTESS EVE. Crown 8vo. 6s.

SHORTLAND (Admiral).—NAUTICAL SURVEYING. 8vo. 21s.

SHUCKBURGH (E. S.).—PASSAGES FROM LATIN AUTHORS FOR TRANSLATION INTO ENGLISH. Crown 8vo. 2s.

SHUCHHARDT (Carl).—DR. SCHLIEMANN'S EXCAVATIONS AT TROY, TIRYNS, MYCENAE, ORCHOMENOS, ITHACA PRESENTED IN THE LIGHT OF RECENT KNOWLEDGE. Translated by EUGENIE SELLERS. With Introduction by WALTER LEAF, Litt.D. Illustrated. 8vo. [*In the Press.*]

SHUFELDT (R. W.).—THE MYOLOGY OF THE RAVEN (*Corvus corax Sinuatus*). A Guide to the Study of the Muscular System in Birds. Illustrated. 8vo. 13s. net.

SIBSON.—DR. FRANCIS SIBSON'S COLLECTED WORKS. Edited by W. M. ORD, M.D. Illustrated. 4 vols. 8vo. 3*l*. 3s.

SIDGWICK (Prof. Henry).—THE METHODS OF ETHICS. 4th Edit., revised. 8vo. 14s.

—— A SUPPLEMENT TO THE SECOND EDITION. Containing all the important Additions and Alterations in the 4th Edit. 8vo. 6s.

—— THE PRINCIPLES OF POLITICAL ECONOMY. 2nd Edition. 8vo. 16s.

—— OUTLINES OF THE HISTORY OF ETHICS FOR ENGLISH READERS. Cr. 8vo. 3s. 6d.

—— ELEMENTS OF POLITICS. 8vo.

SIMPSON (F. P.).—LATIN PROSE AFTER THE BEST AUTHORS.—Part I. CÆSARIAN PROSE. Extra fcp. 8vo. 2s. 6d. KEY (for Teachers only). Ex. fcp. 8vo. 5s.

SIMPSON (W.).—AN EPITOME OF THE HISTORY OF THE CHRISTIAN CHURCH. Fcp. 8vo. 3s. 6d.

SKRINE (J. H.).—UNDER TWO QUEENS. Crown 8vo. 3s.

—— A MEMORY OF EDWARD THRING. Crown 8vo. 6s.

SMALLEY (George W.).—LONDON LETTERS AND SOME OTHERS. 2 vols. 8vo. 32s.

SMITH (Barnard).—ARITHMETIC AND ALGEBRA. New Edition. Crown 8vo. 10s. 6d.

—— ARITHMETIC FOR THE USE OF SCHOOLS. New Edition. Crown 8vo. 4s. 6d.

—— KEY TO ARITHMETIC FOR SCHOOLS. New Edition. Crown 8vo. 8s. 6d.

—— EXERCISES IN ARITHMETIC. Crown 8vo, 2 parts, 1s. each, or complete, 2s.—With Answers, 2s. 6d.—Answers separately, 6d.

—— SCHOOL CLASS-BOOK OF ARITHMETIC. 18mo. 3s. 6d.—Or, sold separately, in Three Parts. 1s. each.

—— KEY TO SCHOOL CLASS-BOOK OF ARITHMETIC. In Parts, I. II. and III. 2s. 6d. each.

—— SHILLING BOOK OF ARITHMETIC FOR NATIONAL AND ELEMENTARY SCHOOLS. 18mo, cloth.—Or separately, Part I. 2d.; II. 3d.; III. 7d.—With Answers, 1s. 6d.

—— ANSWERS TO THE SHILLING BOOK OF ARITHMETIC. 18mo. 6d.

—— KEY TO THE SHILLING BOOK OF ARITHMETIC. 18mo. 4s. 6d.

SMITH (Barnard).—EXAMINATION PAPERS IN ARITHMETIC. In Four Parts. 18mo. 1s. 6d.—With Answers, 2s.—Answers, 6d.

—— KEY TO EXAMINATION PAPERS IN ARITHMETIC. 18mo. 4s. 6d.

—— THE METRIC SYSTEM OF ARITHMETIC. 3d.

—— A CHART OF THE METRIC SYSTEM OF ARITHMETIC. On a Sheet, size 42 by 34 in., on Roller mounted and varnished. 3s. 6d.

—— EASY LESSONS IN ARITHMETIC. Combining Exercises in Reading, Writing, Spelling, and Dictation. Part I. for Standard I. in National Schools. Crown 8vo. 9d.

—— EXAMINATION CARDS IN ARITHMETIC. With Answers and Hints. Standards I. and II. In box. 1s.—Standards III. IV. and V. In boxes. 1s. each.—Standard VI. in Two Parts. In boxes. 1s. each.

SMITH (Catherine Barnard).—POEMS. Fcp. 8vo. 5s.

SMITH (Charles).—AN ELEMENTARY TREATISE ON CONIC SECTIONS. 7th Edition. Crown 8vo. 7s. 6d.

—— SOLUTIONS OF THE EXAMPLES IN "AN ELEMENTARY TREATISE ON CONIC SECTIONS." Crown 8vo. 10s. 6d.

—— AN ELEMENTARY TREATISE ON SOLID GEOMETRY. 2nd Edition. Cr. 8vo. 9s. 6d.

—— ELEMENTARY ALGEBRA. 2nd Edition. Globe 8vo. 4s. 6d.

—— A TREATISE ON ALGEBRA. 2nd Edition. Crown 8vo. 7s. 6d.

—— SOLUTIONS OF THE EXAMPLES IN "A TREATISE ON ALGEBRA." Cr. 8vo. 10s. 6d.

SMITH (Goldwin).—THREE ENGLISH STATESMEN. New Edition. Crown 8vo. 5s.

—— CANADA AND THE CANADIAN QUESTION. 8vo. 8s net.

—— PROHIBITIONISM IN CANADA AND THE UNITED STATES. 8vo, sewed. 6d.

SMITH (Horace).—POEMS. Globe 8vo. 5s.

SMITH (J.).—ECONOMIC PLANTS, DICTIONARY OF POPULAR NAMES OF: THEIR HISTORY, PRODUCTS, AND USES. 8vo. 14s.

SMITH (Rev. Travers).—MAN'S KNOWLEDGE OF MAN AND OF GOD. Crown 8vo. 6s.

SMITH (W. G.).—DISEASES OF FIELD AND GARDEN CROPS, CHIEFLY SUCH AS ARE CAUSED BY FUNGI. With 143 new Illustrations. Fcp. 8vo. 4s. 6d.

SMITH (W. Saumarez).—THE BLOOD OF THE NEW COVENANT: A THEOLOGICAL ESSAY. Crown 8vo. 2s. 6d.

SNOWBALL (J. C.).—THE ELEMENTS OF PLANE AND SPHERICAL TRIGONOMETRY. 14th Edition. Crown 8vo. 7s. 6d.

SONNENSCHEIN (A.) and MEIKLEJOHN (J. M. D.). THE ENGLISH METHOD OF TEACHING TO READ. Fcp. 8vo. Comprising—

THE NURSERY BOOK, containing all the Two Letter Words in the Language. 1d.— Also in Large Type on Four Sheets, with Roller. 5s.

THE FIRST COURSE, consisting of Short Vowels with Single Consonants. 7d.

SONNENSCHEIN (A.) and MEIKLEJOHN (J. M. D.).—THE ENGLISH METHOD OF TEACHING TO READ: SECOND COURSE, with Combinations and Bridges consisting of Short Vowels with Double Consonants. 7*d*.
—— THE THIRD AND FOURTH COURSES, consisting of Long Vowels and all the Double Vowels in the Language. 7*d*.

SOPHOCLES.—ŒDIPUS THE KING. Translated from the Greek into English Verse by E. D. A. MORSHEAD, M.A. Fcp. 8vo. 3*s*. 6*d*.
—— ŒDIPUS TYRANNUS. A Record by L. SPEED and F. R. PRYOR of the performance at Cambridge. Illustr. Folio. 12*s*. 6*d*. net.

SPENDER (J. Kent).—THERAPEUTIC MEANS FOR THE RELIEF OF PAIN. 8vo. 8*s*. 6*d*.

SPINOZA: A STUDY OF. By JAMES MARTINEAU, LL.D. 2nd Ed. Cr. 8vo. 6*s*.

STANLEY (Very Rev. A. P.).—THE ATHANASIAN CREED. Crown 8vo. 2*s*.
—— THE NATIONAL THANKSGIVING. Sermons preached in Westminster Abbey. 2nd Ed. Crown 8vo. 2*s*. 6*d*.
—— ADDRESSES AND SERMONS DELIVERED AT ST. ANDREWS IN 1872-75 and 1877. Crown 8vo. 5*s*.
—— ADDRESSES AND SERMONS DELIVERED DURING A VISIT TO THE UNITED STATES AND CANADA IN 1878. Crown 8vo. 6*s*.

STANLEY (Hon. Maude).—CLUBS FOR WORKING GIRLS. Crown 8vo. 6*s*.

STATESMAN'S YEAR-BOOK (THE). A Statistical and Historical Annual of the States of the Civilised World for the year 1891. Twenty-seventh Annual Publication. Revised after Official Returns. Edited by J. SCOTT KELTIE. Crown 8vo. 10*s*. 6*d*.

STEPHEN (Caroline E.).—THE SERVICE OF THE POOR. Crown 8vo. 6*s*. 6*d*.

STEPHEN (Sir J. Fitzjames, K.C.S.I.).—A DIGEST OF THE LAW OF EVIDENCE. 5th Edition. Crown 8vo. 6*s*.
—— A DIGEST OF THE CRIMINAL LAW: CRIMES AND PUNISHMENTS. 4th Edition. 8vo. 16*s*.
—— A DIGEST OF THE LAW OF CRIMINAL PROCEDURE IN INDICTABLE OFFENCES. By Sir JAMES F. STEPHEN, K.C.S.I., etc., and HERBERT STEPHEN, LL.M. 8vo. 12*s*. 6*d*.
—— A HISTORY OF THE CRIMINAL LAW OF ENGLAND. 3 vols. 8vo. 48*s*.
—— THE STORY OF NUNCOMAR AND THE IMPEACHMENT OF SIR ELIJAH IMPEY. 2 vols. Crown 8vo. 15*s*.
—— A GENERAL VIEW OF THE CRIMINAL LAW OF ENGLAND. 2nd Edition. 8vo. 14*s*.

STEPHEN (J. K.).—INTERNATIONAL LAW AND INTERNATIONAL RELATIONS. Crown 8vo. 6*s*.

STEPHENS (J. B.).—CONVICT ONCE, AND OTHER POEMS. Crown 8vo. 7*s*. 6*d*.

STEVENSON (J. J.).—HOUSE ARCHITECTURE. With Illustrations. 2 vols. Royal 8vo. 18*s*. each. Vol. I. ARCHITECTURE. Vol. II. HOUSE PLANNING.

STEWART (Aubrey).—THE TALE OF TROY. Done into English. Globe 8vo. 3*s*. 6*d*.

STEWART (Prof. Balfour).—LESSONS IN ELEMENTARY PHYSICS. With Illustrations and Coloured Diagram. Fcp. 8vo. 4*s*. 6*d*.
—— PRIMER OF PHYSICS. Illustrated. New Edition, with Questions. 18mo. 1*s*.
—— QUESTIONS ON STEWART'S LESSONS ON ELEMENTARY PHYSICS. By T. H. CORE. 12mo. 2*s*.

STEWART (Prof. Balfour) and GEE (W. W. Haldane).—LESSONS IN ELEMENTARY PRACTICAL PHYSICS. Crown 8vo. Illustrated. Vol. I. GENERAL PHYSICAL PROCESSES. 6*s*.—Vol. II. ELECTRICITY AND MAGNETISM. Cr. 8vo. 7*s*. 6*d*.—Vol. III. OPTICS, HEAT, AND SOUND.
—— PRACTICAL PHYSICS FOR SCHOOLS AND THE JUNIOR STUDENTS OF COLLEGES. Globe 8vo. Vol. I. ELECTRICITY AND MAGNETISM. 2*s*. 6*d*.—Vol. II. HEAT, LIGHT, AND SOUND.

STEWART (Prof. Balfour) and TAIT (P. G.).—THE UNSEEN UNIVERSE; OR, PHYSICAL SPECULATIONS ON A FUTURE STATE. 15th Edition. Crown 8vo. 6*s*.

STEWART (S. A.) and CORRY (T. H.).—A FLORA OF THE NORTH-EAST OF IRELAND. Crown 8vo. 5*s*. 6*d*.

STOKES (Sir George G.).—ON LIGHT. The Burnett Lectures. Crown 8vo. 7*s*. 6*d*.

STONE (W. H.).—ELEMENTARY LESSONS ON SOUND. Illustrated. Fcap. 8vo. 3*s*. 6*d*.

STRACHAN (J. S.) and WILKINS (A. S.).—ANALECTA. Passages for Translation. Cr. 8vo. 5*s*.—KEY TO LATIN PASSAGES. Crn. 8vo. 6*d*.

STRACHEY (Lieut.-Gen. R.).—LECTURES ON GEOGRAPHY. Crown 8vo. 4*s*. 6*d*.

STRANGFORD (Viscountess). — EGYPTIAN SEPULCHRES AND SYRIAN SHRINES. New Edition. Crown 8vo. 7*s*. 6*d*.

STRETTELL (Alma).—SPANISH AND ITALIAN FOLK SONGS. Illustrated. Royal 16mo. 12*s*. 6*d*.

STUART, THE ROYAL HOUSE OF Illustrated by Forty Plates in Colours drawn from Relics of the Stuarts by WILLIAM GIBB. With Introduction by J. SKELTON, C.B., LL.D., and Descriptive Notes by W. ST. J. HOPE. Folio, half morocco, gilt edges. 7*l*. 7*s*. net.

STUBBS (Rev. C. W.).—FOR CHRIST AND CITY. Sermons and Addresses. Cr. 8vo. 6*s*.

SURGERY, THE INTERNATIONAL ENCYCLOPAEDIA OF. A Systematic Treatise on the Theory and Practice of Surgery by Authors of Various Nations. Edited by JOHN ASHHURST, Jun., M.D., Professor of Clinical Surgery in the University of Pennsylvania. 6 vols. Royal 8vo. 31*s*. 6*d*. each.

SYMONS (Arthur).—DAYS AND NIGHTS: POEMS. Globe 8vo. 6*s*.

TACITUS, THE WORKS OF. Transl. by A. J. CHURCH, M.A., and W. J. BRODRIBB, M.A.
—— THE HISTORY OF TACITUS. Translated. 4th Edition. Crown 8vo. 6*s*.
—— THE AGRICOLA AND GERMANIA. With the Dialogue on Oratory. Trans. Cr. 8vo. 4*s* 6*d*.

TACITUS ANNALS OF TACITUS. Translated. 5th Edition. Crown 8vo. 7s. 6d.
—— THE ANNALS. Edited by Prof. G. O. HOLBROOKE, M.A. 8vo. 16s.
—— THE HISTORIES. Edited, with Introduction and Commentary, by Rev. W. A. SPOONER, M.A. 8vo. 16s.
See also p. 33.

TAIT (Archbishop).—THE PRESENT POSITION OF THE CHURCH OF ENGLAND. Being the Charge delivered at his Primary Visitation. 3rd Edition. 8vo. 3s. 6d.
—— DUTIES OF THE CHURCH OF ENGLAND. Being Seven Addresses delivered at his Second Visitation. 8vo. 4s. 6d.
—— THE CHURCH OF THE FUTURE. Charges delivered at his Third Quadrennial Visitation. 2nd Edition. Crown 8vo. 3s. 6d.

TAIT.—THE LIFE OF ARCHIBALD CAMPBELL TAIT, ARCHBISHOP OF CANTERBURY. By the Rt. Rev. the BISHOP OF ROCHESTER and Rev. W. BENHAM. 2 vols 8vo. 30s. net.

TAIT.—CATHARINE AND CRAWFURD TAIT, WIFE AND SON OF ARCHIBALD CAMPBELL, ARCHBISHOP OF CANTERBURY: A MEMOIR. Edited by the Rev. W. BENHAM, B.D. Crown 8vo. 6s.
Popular Edition, abridged. Cr. 8vo. 2s. 6d.

TAIT (C. W. A.).—ANALYSIS OF ENGLISH HISTORY, BASED ON GREEN'S "SHORT HISTORY OF THE ENGLISH PEOPLE." Revised and Enlarged Edition. Crown 8vo. 4s. 6d.

TAIT (Prof. P. G.).—LECTURES ON SOME RECENT ADVANCES IN PHYSICAL SCIENCE. 3rd Edition. Crown 8vo. 9s.
—— HEAT. With Illustrations. Cr. 8vo. 6s.

TAIT (P. G.) and STEELE (W. J.).—A TREATISE ON DYNAMICS OF A PARTICLE. 6th Edition. Crown 8vo. 12s.

TANNER (Prof. Henry).—FIRST PRINCIPLES OF AGRICULTURE. 18mo. 1s.
—— THE ABBOTT'S FARM; OR, PRACTICE WITH SCIENCE. Crown 8vo. 3s. 6d.
—— THE ALPHABET OF THE PRINCIPLES OF AGRICULTURE. Extra fcp. 8vo. 6d.
—— FURTHER STEPS IN THE PRINCIPLES OF AGRICULTURE. Extra fcp. 8vo. 1s.
—— ELEMENTARY SCHOOL READINGS IN THE PRINCIPLES OF AGRICULTURE FOR THE THIRD STAGE. Extra fcp. 8vo. 1s.
—— ELEMENTARY LESSONS IN THE SCIENCE OF AGRICULTURAL PRACTICE. Fcp. 8vo. 3s. 6d.

TAVERNIER (Baron): TRAVELS IN INDIA OF JEAN BAPTISTE TAVERNIER, BARON OF AUBONNE. Translated by V. BALL, LL.D. Illustrated. 2 vols. 8vo. 2l. 2s.

TAYLOR (Franklin).—PRIMER OF PIANOFORTE PLAYING. 18mo. 1s.

TAYLOR (Isaac).—THE RESTORATION OF BELIEF. Crown 8vo. 8s. 6d.

TAYLOR (Isaac).—WORDS AND PLACES. 9th Edition. Maps. Globe 8vo. 6s.
—— ETRUSCAN RESEARCHES. With Woodcuts. 8vo. 14s.
—— GREEKS AND GOTHS: A STUDY OF THE RUNES. 8vo. 9s.

TAYLOR (Sedley).—SOUND AND MUSIC. 2nd Edition. Extra Crown 8vo. 8s. 6d.
—— A SYSTEM OF SIGHT-SINGING FROM THE ESTABLISHED MUSICAL NOTATION. 8vo. 5s. net.

TEBAY (S.).—ELEMENTARY MENSURATION FOR SCHOOLS. Extra fcp. 8vo. 3s. 6d.

TEGETMEIER (W. B.).—HOUSEHOLD MANAGEMENT AND COOKERY. 18mo. 1s.

TEMPLE (Right Rev. Frederick, D.D., Bishop of London).—SERMONS PREACHED IN THE CHAPEL OF RUGBY SCHOOL. 3rd and Cheaper Edition. Extra fcp. 8vo. 4s. 6d.
—— SECOND SERIES. 3rd Ed. Ex. fcp. 8vo. 6s.
—— THIRD SERIES. 4th Ed. Ex. fcp. 8vo. 6s.
—— THE RELATIONS BETWEEN RELIGION AND SCIENCE. Bampton Lectures, 1884. 7th and Cheaper Edition. Crown 8vo. 6s.

TENNYSON (Lord).—COMPLETE WORKS. New and enlarged Edition, with Portrait. Crown 8vo. 7s. 6d.
School Edition. In Four Parts. Crown 8vo. 2s. 6d. each.
—— POETICAL WORKS. *Pocket Edition.* 18mo, morocco, gilt edges. 7s. 6d. net.
—— WORKS. *Library Edition.* In 8 vols. Globe 8vo. 5s. each. Each volume may be had separately.—POEMS. 2 vols.—IDYLLS OF THE KING.—THE PRINCESS, AND MAUD.—ENOCH ARDEN, AND IN MEMORIAM.—BALLADS, AND OTHER POEMS.—QUEEN MARY, AND HAROLD.—BECKET, AND OTHER PLAYS.
—— WORKS. *Extra Fcp. 8vo. Edition,* on Hand-made Paper. In 7 volumes (supplied in sets only). 3l. 13s. 6d.
—— WORKS. *Miniature Edition,* in 14 vols., viz. THE POETICAL WORKS, 10 vols. in a box. 21s.—THE DRAMATIC WORKS, 4 vols. in a box. 10s. 6d.
—— *The Original Editions.* Fcp. 8vo.
POEMS. 6s.
MAUD, AND OTHER POEMS. 3s. 6d.
THE PRINCESS. 3s. 6d.
ENOCH ARDEN, etc. 3s. 6d.
THE HOLY GRAIL, AND OTHER POEMS. 4s. 6d.
BALLADS, AND OTHER POEMS. 5s.
HAROLD: A DRAMA. 6s.
QUEEN MARY: A DRAMA. 6s.
THE CUP, AND THE FALCON. 5s.
BECKET. 6s.
TIRESIAS, AND OTHER POEMS. 6s.
LOCKSLEY HALL SIXTY YEARS AFTER, etc. 6s.
DEMETER, AND OTHER POEMS. 6s.
—— LYRICAL POEMS. Selected and Annotated by Prof. F. T. PALGRAVE. 18mo. 4s. 6d. Large Paper Edition. 8vo. 9s.
—— IN MEMORIAM. 18mo. 4s. 6d. Large Paper Edition. 8vo. 9s.
—— THE TENNYSON BIRTHDAY BOOK. Edit. by EMILY SHAKESPEAR. 18mo. 2s. 6d.

LIST OF PUBLICATIONS. 49

TENNYSON (Lord).—THE BROOK. With 20 Illustrations by A. WOODRUFF. 32mo. 2s. 6d.

—— SELECTIONS FROM TENNYSON. With Introduction and Notes, by F. J. ROWE, M.A., and W. T. WEBB, M.A. Globe 8vo. 3s. 6d.

—— ENOCH ARDEN. By W. T. WEBB, M.A. Globe 8vo. [In the Press.

—— THE COMING OF ARTHUR, and THE PASSING OF ARTHUR. By F. J. ROWE, M.A. Globe 8vo. 2s.

—— A COMPANION TO "IN MEMORIAM." By ELIZABETH R. CHAPMAN. Globe 8vo. 2s.

—— *The Royal Edition.* 1 vol. 8vo. 16s.

—— SELECTIONS FROM TENNYSON'S WORKS. Square 8vo. 3s. 6d.

—— SONGS FROM TENNYSON'S WRITINGS. Square 8vo. 2s. 6d.

TENNYSON FOR THE YOUNG. Selections from Lord TENNYSON'S Poems. Edited with Notes, by the Rev. ALFRED AINGER, M.A. 18mo. 1s. net.

TENNYSON (Frederick).—THE ISLES OF GREECE: SAPPHO AND ALCAEUS. Crown 8vo. 7s. 6d.

TENNYSON (Hallam).—JACK AND THE BEAN-STALK. With 40 Illustrations by RANDOLPH CALDECOTT. Fcp. 4to. 3s. 6d.

TERENCE.—*See* pp. 32, 33.

TERESA (ST.): LIFE OF. By the Author of "Devotions before and after Holy Communion." Crown 8vo. 8s. 6d.

THEOCRITUS, BION, AND MOSCHUS. Rendered into English Prose, with Introductory Essay, by A. LANG, M.A. 18mo. 4s. 6d. Large Paper Edition. 8vo. 9s.

THOMPSON (Edith).—HISTORY OF ENGLAND. New Edit., with Maps. 18mo. 2s. 6d.

THOMPSON (Prof. Silvanus P.).—ELEMENTARY ELECTRICITY AND MAGNETISM. Illustrated. New Edition. Fcp. 8vo. 4s. 6d.

THOMSON (J. J.).—A TREATISE ON THE MOTION OF VORTEX RINGS. 8vo. 6s.

—— APPLICATIONS OF DYNAMICS TO PHYSICS AND CHEMISTRY. Crown 8vo. 7s. 6d.

THOMSON (Sir Wm.).—REPRINT OF PAPERS ON ELECTROSTATICS AND MAGNETISM. 2nd Edition. 8vo. 18s.

—— POPULAR LECTURES AND ADDRESSES. In 3 vols.—Vol. I. CONSTITUTION OF MATTER. Illustrated. Crown 8vo. 7s. 6d.—Vol. III. PAPERS ON NAVIGATION. 7s. 6d.

THOMSON (Sir C. Wyville). THE DEPTHS OF THE SEA. An Account of the General Results of the Dredging Cruises of H.M.SS. "Lightning" and "Porcupine" during the Summers of 1868-69-70. With Illustrations, Maps, and Plans. 2nd Edit. 8vo. 31s. 6d.

—— THE VOYAGE OF THE "CHALLENGER": THE ATLANTIC. With Illustrations, Coloured Maps, Charts, etc. 2 vols. 8vo. 45s.

THORNTON (J.).—FIRST LESSONS IN BOOK-KEEPING. New Edition. Crown 8vo. 2s. 6d.

—— KEY. Containing all the Exercises fully worked out, with brief Notes. Oblong 4to. 10s. 6d.

—— PRIMER OF BOOK-KEEPING. 18mo. 1s.

—— KEY. Demy 8vo. 2s. 6d.

THORPE (Prof. T. E.) and TATE (W.).—A SERIES OF CHEMICAL PROBLEMS, FOR USE IN COLLEGES AND SCHOOLS. New Edition, with Key. Fcap. 8vo. 2s.

THRING (Rev. Edward).—A CONSTRUING BOOK. Fcp. 8vo. 2s. 6d.

—— A LATIN GRADUAL. 2nd Ed. 18mo. 2s. 6d.

—— THE ELEMENTS OF GRAMMAR TAUGHT IN ENGLISH. 5th Edition. 18mo. 2s.

—— EDUCATION AND SCHOOL. 2nd Edition. Crown 8vo. 6s.

—— A MANUAL OF MOOD CONSTRUCTIONS. Extra fcp. 8vo. 1s. 6d.

—— THOUGHTS ON LIFE SCIENCE. 2nd Edit. Crown 8vo. 7s. 6d.

—— A MEMORY OF EDWARD THRING. By J. H. SKRINE. Portrait. Crown 8vo. 6s.

THROUGH THE RANKS TO A COMMISSION. New Edit. Cr. 8vo. 2s. 6d.

THRUPP (Rev. J. F.).—INTRODUCTION TO THE STUDY AND USE OF THE PSALMS. 2nd Edition. 2 vols. 8vo. 21s.

THUCYDIDES.—BOOK IV. A Revision of the Text, illustrating the Principal Causes of Corruption in the Manuscripts of this Author. By WILLIAM G. RUTHERFORD, M.A., LL.D. 8vo. 7s. 6d.

—— BOOK VIII. Edited, with Introduction and Commentary, by H. C. GOODHART, M.A. 8vo.

See also pp. 32, 33.

THUDICHUM (J. L. W.) and DUPRÉ (A.). —TREATISE ON THE ORIGIN, NATURE, AND VARIETIES OF WINE. Medium 8vo. 25s.

TODHUNTER (Isaac).—EUCLID FOR COLLEGES AND SCHOOLS. 18mo. 3s. 6d.

—— BOOKS I. AND II. 18mo. 1s.

—— KEY TO EXERCISES IN EUCLID. Crown 8vo. 6s. 6d.

—— MENSURATION FOR BEGINNERS. With Examples. 18mo. 2s. 6d.

—— KEY TO MENSURATION FOR BEGINNERS. By Rev. FR. L. MCCARTHY. Cr. 8vo. 7s. 6d.

—— ALGEBRA FOR BEGINNERS. With numerous Examples. 18mo. 2s. 6d.

—— KEY TO ALGEBRA FOR BEGINNERS. Cr. 8vo. 6s. 6d.

—— ALGEBRA FOR THE USE OF COLLEGES AND SCHOOLS. Crown 8vo. 7s. 6d.

—— KEY TO ALGEBRA FOR COLLEGES AND SCHOOLS. Crown 8vo. 10s. 6d.

—— TRIGONOMETRY FOR BEGINNERS. With numerous Examples. 18mo. 2s. 6d.

—— KEY TO TRIGONOMETRY FOR BEGINNERS. Crown 8vo. 8s. 6d.

—— PLANE TRIGONOMETRY FOR COLLEGES AND SCHOOLS. Crown 8vo. 5s.

TODHUNTER (Isaac).—KEY TO PLANE TRIGONOMETRY. Crown 8vo. 10s. 6d.

—— A TREATISE ON SPHERICAL TRIGONOMETRY FOR THE USE OF COLLEGES AND SCHOOLS. Crown 8vo. 4s. 6d.

—— MECHANICS FOR BEGINNERS. With numerous Examples. 18mo. 4s. 6d.

—— KEY TO MECHANICS FOR BEGINNERS. Crown 8vo. 6s. 6d.

—— A TREATISE ON THE THEORY OF EQUATIONS. Crown 8vo. 7s. 6d.

—— A TREATISE ON PLANE CO-ORDINATE GEOMETRY. Crown 8vo. 7s. 6d.

—— SOLUTIONS AND PROBLEMS CONTAINED IN A TREATISE ON PLANE CO-ORDINATE GEOMETRY. By C. W. BOURNE, M.A. Crown 8vo. 10s. 6d.

—— A TREATISE ON THE DIFFERENTIAL CALCULUS. Crown 8vo. 10s. 6d.

—— KEY TO TREATISE ON THE DIFFERENTIAL CALCULUS. By H. ST. J. HUNTER, M.A. Crown 8vo. 10s. 6d.

—— A TREATISE ON THE INTEGRAL CALCULUS. Crown 8vo. 10s. 6d.

—— KEY TO TREATISE ON THE INTEGRAL CALCULUS AND ITS APPLICATIONS. By H. ST. J. HUNTER, M.A. Cr. 8vo. 10s. 6d.

—— EXAMPLES OF ANALYTICAL GEOMETRY OF THREE DIMENSIONS. Crown 8vo. 4s.

—— THE CONFLICT OF STUDIES. 8vo. 10s. 6d.

—— AN ELEMENTARY TREATISE ON LAPLACE'S, LAMÉ'S, AND BESSEL'S FUNCTIONS. Crown 8vo. 10s. 6d.

—— A TREATISE ON ANALYTICAL STATICS. Edited by J. D. EVERETT, M.A., F.R.S. 5th Edition. Crown 8vo. 10s. 6d.

TOM BROWN'S SCHOOL DAYS. By AN OLD BOY.
Golden Treasury Edition. 18mo. 4s. 6d.
Illustrated Edition. Crown 8vo. 6s.
Uniform Edition. Crown 3vo. 3s. 6d.
People's Edition. 18mo. 2s.
People's Sixpenny Edition. Illustrated. Medium 4to. 6d.—Also uniform with the Sixpenny Edition of Charles Kingsley's Novels. Illustrated. Medium 8vo. 6d.

TOM BROWN AT OXFORD. By the Author of "Tom Brown's School Days." Illustrated. Crown 8vo. 6s.
Uniform Edition. Crown 8vo. 3s. 6d.

TRENCH (R. Chenevix).—HULSEAN LECTURES. 8vo. 7s. 6d.

TRENCH (Capt. F.).—THE RUSSO-INDIAN QUESTION. Crown 8vo. 7s. 6d.

TREVELYAN (Sir Geo. Otto).—CAWNPORE. Crown 8vo. 6s.

TRISTRAM (W. Outram).—COACHING DAYS AND COACHING WAYS. Illustrated by HERBERT RAILTON and HUGH THOMSON. Extra Crown 4to. 21s.

TRUMAN (Jos.).—AFTER-THOUGHTS: POEMS. Crown 8vo. 3s. 6d.

TULLOCH (Principal).—THE CHRIST OF THE GOSPELS AND THE CHRIST OF MODERN CRITICISM. Extra fcp. 8vo. 4s. 6d.

TURNER'S LIBER STUDIORUM. A Description and a Catalogue. By W. G. RAWLINSON. Medium 8vo. 12s. 6d.

TURNER (Charles Tennyson).—COLLECTED SONNETS, OLD AND NEW. Ex. fcp. 8vo. 7s. 6d.

TURNER (Rev. Geo.).—SAMOA, A HUNDRED YEARS AGO AND LONG BEFORE. Preface by E. B. TYLOR, F.R.S. Crown 8vo. 9s.

TURNER (H. H.).—A COLLECTION OF EXAMPLES ON HEAT AND ELECTRICITY. Cr. 8vo. 2s. 6d.

TYLOR (E. B.).—ANTHROPOLOGY. With Illustrations. Crown 8vo. 7s. 6d.

TYRWHITT (Rev. R. St. John).—OUR SKETCHING CLUB. 4th Ed. Cr. 8vo. 7s. 6d.

—— FREE FIELD. Lyrics, chiefly Descriptive. Globe 8vo. 3s. 6d.

—— BATTLE AND AFTER: Concerning Sergt. Thomas Atkins, Grenadier Guards; and other Verses. Globe 8vo. 3s. 6d.

UNDERHILL (H. G.).—EASY EXERCISES IN GREEK ACCIDENCE. Globe 8vo. 2s.

UPPINGHAM BY THE SEA. By J. H. S. Crown 8vo. 3s. 6d.

VAUGHAN (Very Rev. Charles J.).—NOTES FOR LECTURES ON CONFIRMATION. 14th Edition. Fcp. 8vo. 1s. 6d.

—— MEMORIALS OF HARROW SUNDAYS. 5th Edition. Crown 8vo. 10s. 6d.

—— LECTURES ON THE EPISTLE TO THE PHILIPPIANS. 4th Edition. Cr. 8vo. 7s. 6d.

—— LECTURES ON THE REVELATION OF ST. JOHN. 5th Edition. Crown 8vo. 10s. 6d.

—— EPIPHANY, LENT, AND EASTER. 3rd Edition. Crown 8vo. 10s. 6d.

—— HEROES OF FAITH. 2nd Ed. Cr. 8vo. 6s.

—— THE BOOK AND THE LIFE, AND OTHER SERMONS. 3rd Edition. Fcp. 8vo. 4s. 6d.

—— ST. PAUL'S EPISTLE TO THE ROMANS. The Greek Text with English Notes. 7th Edition. Crown 8vo. 7s. 6d.

—— TWELVE DISCOURSES ON SUBJECTS CONNECTED WITH THE LITURGY AND WORSHIP OF THE CHURCH OF ENGLAND. 4th Edition. Fcp. 8vo. 6s.

—— WORDS FROM THE GOSPELS. 3rd Edition. Fcp. 8vo. 4s. 6d.

—— THE EPISTLES OF ST. PAUL. For English Readers. Part I. containing the First Epistle to the Thessalonians. 2nd Ed. 8vo. 1s. 6d.

—— THE CHURCH OF THE FIRST DAYS. New Edition. Crown 8vo. 10s. 6d.

—— LIFE'S WORK AND GOD'S DISCIPLINE. 3rd Edition. Extra fcp. 8vo. 2s. 6d.

—— THE WHOLESOME WORDS OF JESUS CHRIST. 2nd Edition. Fcp. 8vo. 3s. 6d.

—— FOES OF FAITH. 2nd Ed. Fcp. 8vo. 3s. 6d.

VAUGHAN (Very Rev. Charles J.).—CHRIST SATISFYING THE INSTINCTS OF HUMANITY. 2nd Edition. Ext. fcp. 8vo. 3s. 6d.
—— COUNSELS FOR YOUNG STUDENTS. Fcp. 8vo. 2s. 6d.
—— THE TWO GREAT TEMPTATIONS. 2nd Edition. Fcp. 8vo. 3s. 6d.
—— ADDRESSES FOR YOUNG CLERGYMEN. Extra fcp. 8vo. 4s. 6d.
—— "MY SON, GIVE ME THINE HEART." Extra fcp. 8vo. 5s.
—— REST AWHILE. Addresses to Toilers in the Ministry. Extra fcp. 8vo. 5s.
—— TEMPLE SERMONS. Crown 8vo. 10s. 6d.
—— AUTHORISED OR REVISED? Sermons on some of the Texts in which the Revised Version differs from the Authorised. Crown 8vo. 7s. 6d.
—— ST. PAUL'S EPISTLE TO THE PHILIPPIANS. With Translation, Paraphrase, and Notes for English Readers. Crown 8vo. 5s.
—— LESSONS OF THE CROSS AND PASSION. WORDS FROM THE CROSS. THE REIGN OF SIN. THE LORD'S PRAYER. Four Courses of Lent Lectures. Crown 8vo. 10s. 6d.
—— UNIVERSITY SERMONS, NEW AND OLD. Crown 8vo. 10s. 6d.
—— THE EPISTLE TO THE HEBREWS. With Notes. Crown 8vo. 7s. 6d.

VAUGHAN (D. J.).—THE PRESENT TRIAL OF FAITH. Crown 8vo. 9s.

VAUGHAN (E. T.).—SOME REASONS OF OUR CHRISTIAN HOPE. Hulsean Lectures for 1875. Crown 8vo. 6s. 6d.

VAUGHAN (Robert).—STONES FROM THE QUARRY: Sermons. Crown 8vo. 5s.

VELEY (Marg.).—A GARDEN OF MEMORIES; MRS. AUSTIN; LIZZIE'S BARGAIN. Three Stories. 2 vols. Globe 8vo. 12s.

VENN (John).—ON SOME CHARACTERISTICS OF BELIEF, SCIENTIFIC AND RELIGIOUS. Hulsean Lectures, 1869. 8vo. 6s. 6d.
—— THE LOGIC OF CHANCE. 2nd Edition. Crown 8vo. 10s. 6d.
—— SYMBOLIC LOGIC. Crown 8vo. 10s. 6d.
—— THE PRINCIPLES OF EMPIRICAL OR INDUCTIVE LOGIC. 8vo. 18s.

VERRALL (A. W.).—STUDIES, LITERARY AND HISTORICAL, IN THE ODES OF HORACE. 8vo. 8s. 6d.

VERRALL (Mrs. M. de G.) and HARRISON (Miss Jane E.).—MYTHOLOGY AND MONUMENTS OF ANCIENT ATHENS. Illustrated. Crown 8vo. 16s.

VICTORIA UNIVERSITY CALENDAR, 1891. Crown 8vo. 1s. net.

VICTOR EMMANUEL II., FIRST KING OF ITALY. By G. S. GODKIN. 2nd Edition. Crown 8vo. 6s.

VIDA: STUDY OF A GIRL. By AMY DUNSMUIR. 3rd Edition. Crown 8vo. 6s.

VINCENT (Sir E.) and DICKSON (T. G.).—HANDBOOK TO MODERN GREEK. 3rd Ed. Crown 8vo. 6s.

VIRGIL.—THE WORKS OF VIRGIL RENDERED INTO ENGLISH PROSE. By JAS. LONSDALE, M.A., and S. LEE, M.A. Globe 8vo. 3s. 6d.
—— THE ÆNEID. Transl. into English Prose by J. W. MACKAIL, M.A. Cr. 8vo. 7s. 6d.
See also pp. 31, 33.

VOICES CRYING IN THE WILDERNESS. A Novel. Crown 8vo. 7s. 6d.

WALDSTEIN (C.).—CATALOGUE OF CASTS IN THE MUSEUM OF CLASSICAL ARCHÆOLOGY, CAMBRIDGE. Crown 8vo. 1s. 6d.
Large Paper Edition. Small 4to. 5s.

WALKER (Prof. Francis A.).—THE WAGES QUESTION. 8vo. 14s.
—— MONEY. 8vo. 16s.
—— MONEY IN ITS RELATION TO TRADE AND INDUSTRY. Crown 8vo. 7s. 6d.
—— POLITICAL ECONOMY. 2nd Edition. 8vo. 12s. 6d.
—— A BRIEF TEXT-BOOK OF POLITICAL ECONOMY. Crown 8vo. 6s. 6d.
—— LAND AND ITS RENT. Fcp. 8vo. 3s. 6d.
—— FIRST LESSONS IN POLITICAL ECONOMY. Crown 8vo. 5s.

WALLACE (Alfred Russel).—THE MALAY ARCHIPELAGO: THE LAND OF THE ORANG UTANG AND THE BIRD OF PARADISE. Maps and Illustrations. 10th Edition. Crown 8vo. 6s.
—— THE GEOGRAPHICAL DISTRIBUTION OF ANIMALS. With Illustrations and Maps. 2 vols. Medium 8vo. 42s.
—— ISLAND LIFE. With Illustrations and Maps. Crown 8vo. 6s.
—— BAD TIMES. An Essay on the present Depression of Trade. Crown 8vo. 2s. 6d.
—— DARWINISM. An Exposition of the Theory of Natural Selection, with some of its Applications. Illustrated. 3rd Edition. Crown 8vo. 9s.
—— CONTRIBUTIONS TO THE THEORY OF NATURAL SELECTION; AND TROPICAL NATURE AND OTHER ESSAYS. New Edition. Crown 8vo. 6s.

WALLACE (Sir D. Mackenzie).—EGYPT AND THE EGYPTIAN QUESTION. 8vo. 14s.

WALTON and COTTON—LOWELL.—THE COMPLETE ANGLER. With an Introduction by JAS. RUSSELL LOWELL. Illustrated. Extra crown 8vo. 2l. 12s. 6d. net.
Also an Edition on large paper, Proofs on Japanese paper. 3l. 13s. 6d. net.

WARD (Prof. A. W.).—A HISTORY OF ENGLISH DRAMATIC LITERATURE, TO THE DEATH OF QUEEN ANNE. 2 vols. 8vo. 32s.

WARD (Prof. H. M.).—TIMBER AND SOME OF ITS DISEASES. Illustrated. Cr. 8vo. 6s.

WARD (John).—EXPERIENCES OF A DIPLOMATIST. 8vo. 10s. 6d.

WARD (T. H.).—ENGLISH POETS. Selections, with Critical Introductions by various Writers, and a General Introduction by MATTHEW ARNOLD. Edited by T. H. WARD, M.A. 4 vols. 2nd Ed. Crown 8vo. 7s. 6d. each.—Vol. I. CHAUCER TO DONNE. — II. BEN JONSON TO DRYDEN. — III. ADDISON TO BLAKE. — IV. WORDSWORTH TO ROSSETTI.

WARD (Mrs. T. Humphry).—MILLY AND OLLY. With Illustrations by Mrs. ALMA TADEMA. Globe 8vo. 2s. 6d.

—— MISS BRETHERTON. Crown 8vo. 3s. 6d.

—— THE JOURNAL INTIME OF HENRI-FRÉDÉRIC AMIEL. Translated, with an Introduction and Notes. 2nd Ed. Cr. 8vo. 6s.

WARD (W.).—WILLIAM GEORGE WARD AND THE OXFORD MOVEMENT. Portrait. 8vo. 14s.

WATERTON (Charles).—WANDERINGS IN SOUTH AMERICA, THE NORTH-WEST OF THE UNITED STATES, AND THE ANTILLES. Edited by Rev. J. G. WOOD. With 100 Illustrations. Crown 8vo. 6s.
People's Edition. With 100 Illustrations. Medium 4to. 6d.

WATSON. A RECORD OF ELLEN WATSON. By ANNA BUCKLAND. Crown 8vo. 6s.

WATSON (R. Spence).—A VISIT TO WAZAN, THE SACRED CITY OF MOROCCO. 8vo. 10s. 6d.

WEBSTER (Augusta).—DAFFODIL AND THE CROAXAXICANS. Crown 8vo. 6s.

WELBY-GREGORY (The Hon. Lady).—LINKS AND CLUES. 2nd Edition. Crown 8vo. 6s.

WELCH (Wm.) and DUFFIELD (C. G.).—LATIN ACCIDENCE AND EXERCISES ARRANGED FOR BEGINNERS. 18mo. 1s. 6d.

WELLDON (Rev. J. E. C.).—THE SPIRITUAL LIFE, AND OTHER SERMONS. Cr. 8vo. 6s.

WESTCOTT (The Rt. Rev. Bishop.)—A GENERAL SURVEY OF THE HISTORY OF THE CANON OF THE NEW TESTAMENT DURING THE FIRST FOUR CENTURIES. 6th Edition. Crown 8vo. 10s. 6d.

—— INTRODUCTION TO THE STUDY OF THE FOUR GOSPELS. 7th Ed. Cr. 8vo. 10s. 6d.

—— THE GOSPEL OF THE RESURRECTION. 6th Edition. Crown 8vo. 6s.

—— THE BIBLE IN THE CHURCH. 10th Edit. 18mo. 4s. 6d.

—— THE CHRISTIAN LIFE, MANIFOLD AND ONE. Crown 8vo. 2s. 6d.

—— ON THE RELIGIOUS OFFICE OF THE UNIVERSITIES. Sermons. Cr. 8vo. 4s. 6d.

—— THE REVELATION OF THE RISEN LORD. 4th Edition. Crown 8vo. 6s.

—— THE HISTORIC FAITH. 3rd Edition. Cr. 8vo. 6s.

—— THE EPISTLES OF ST. JOHN. The Greek Text, with Notes. 2nd Edition. 8vo. 12s. 6d.

—— THE REVELATION OF THE FATHER. Cr. 8vo. 6s.

WESTCOTT (Bishop).—CHRISTUS CONSUMMATOR. 2nd Edition. Crown 8vo. 6s.

—— SOME THOUGHTS FROM THE ORDINAL. Crown 8vo. 1s. 6d.

—— SOCIAL ASPECTS OF CHRISTIANITY. Cr. 8vo. 6s.

—— GIFTS FOR MINISTRY. Addresses to Candidates for Ordination. Crown 8vo. 1s. 6d.

—— THE EPISTLE TO THE HEBREWS. The Greek Text, with Notes and Essays. 8vo. 14s.

—— THE VICTORY OF THE CROSS. Sermons preached during Holy Week, 1888, in Hereford Cathedral. Crown 8vo. 3s. 6d.

—— FROM STRENGTH TO STRENGTH. Three Sermons (In Memoriam J. B. D.) Crown 8vo. 2s.

—— ESSAYS IN THE HISTORY OF RELIGIOUS THOUGHT IN THE WEST. Globe 8vo. 6s.

—— THOUGHTS ON REVELATION AND LIFE. Selections from the Writings of Bp. WESTCOTT. Edited by Rev. S. PHILLIPS. Crown 8vo. 6s.

WESTCOTT (Bishop) and HORT (Prof.).—THE NEW TESTAMENT IN THE ORIGINAL GREEK. Revised Text. 2 vols. Crown 8vo. 10s. 6d. each.—Vol. I. Text.—Vol. II. The Introduction and Appendix.

—— THE NEW TESTAMENT IN THE ORIGINAL GREEK. An Edition for Schools. The Text revised by Bishop WESTCOTT and Dr. HORT. 18mo. 4s. 6d.; roan, 5s. 6d.; morocco, 6s. 6d.

WESTERMARCK (E.).—THE HISTORY OF HUMAN MARRIAGE. 8vo.

WHEELER (J. Talboys).—A SHORT HISTORY OF INDIA. With Maps. Crown 8vo. 12s.

—— INDIA UNDER BRITISH RULE. 8vo. 12s. 6d.

—— COLLEGE HISTORY OF INDIA. Asiatic and European. Crown 8vo. 3s.; sewed, 2s. 6d.

—— PRIMER OF INDIAN HISTORY, ASIATIC AND EUROPEAN. 18mo. 1s.

WHEN PAPA COMES HOME. By the Author of "When I was a Little Girl." With Illustrations. Globe 8vo. 4s. 6d.

WHEWELL. DR. WILLIAM WHEWELL, late Master of Trinity College, Cambridge. An Account of his Writings, with Selections from his Literary and Scientific Correspondence. By I. TODHUNTER, M.A. 2 vols. 8vo. 25s.

WHITE (Gilbert).—NATURAL HISTORY AND ANTIQUITIES OF SELBORNE. Edited by FRANK BUCKLAND. With a Chapter on Antiquities by Lord SELBORNE. Cr. 8vo. 6s.

WHITE (John Williams).—A SERIES OF FIRST LESSONS IN GREEK. Adapted to GOODWIN'S Greek Grammar. Crown 8vo. 3s. 6d.

WHITE (Dr. W. Hale).—A TEXT-BOOK OF GENERAL THERAPEUTICS. Illustrated. Cr. 8vo. 8s. 6d.

WHITHAM (Prof. J. M.).—STEAM ENGINE DESIGN. Illustrated. 8vo. 25s.

WHITNEY (Prof. W. D.).—A Compendious German Grammar. Crown 8vo. 4s. 6d.

—— A German Reader in Prose and Verse. With Notes and Vocabulary. Cr. 8vo. 5s.

—— A Compendious German and English Dictionary. Crown 8vo. 7s. 6d.—German-English Part separately. 5s.

WHITTIER.—Complete Poetical Works of John Greenleaf Whittier. With Portrait. 18mo. 4s. 6d.

—— The Complete Works of John Greenleaf Whittier. 7 vols. Crown 8vo. 6s. each.—Vol. I. Narrative and Legendary Poems.—II. Poems of Nature; Poems Subjective and Reminiscent; Religious Poems.—III. Anti-Slavery Poems; Songs of Labour and Reform.—IV. Personal Poems; Occasional Poems; The Tent on the Beach; with the Poems of Elizabeth H. Whittier, and an Appendix containing Early and Uncollected Verses.—V. Margaret Smith's Journal; Tales and Sketches.—VI. Old Portraits and Modern Sketches; Personal Sketches and Tributes; Historical Papers.—VII. The Conflict with Slavery, Politics and Reform: The Inner Life, Criticism.

WICKHAM (Rev. E. C.)—Wellington College Sermons. Crown 8vo. 6s.

WICKSTEED (Philip H.).—Alphabet of Economic Science.—I. Elements of the Theory of Value or Worth. Globe 8vo. 2s. 6d.

WIEDERSHEIM—PARKER.—Elements of the Comparative Anatomy of Vertebrates. Adapted from the German of Prof. Robert Wiedersheim, by Prof. W. Newton Parker. Illustrated. Medium 8vo. 12s. 6d.

WILBRAHAM (Frances M.).—In the Sere and Yellow Leaf: Thoughts and Recollections for Old and Young. Globe 8vo. 3s. 6d.

WILKINS (Prof. A. S.).—The Light of the World: An Essay. 2nd Edition. Crown 8vo. 3s. 6d.

—— Roman Antiquities. Illustr. 18mo. 1s.

—— Roman Literature. 18mo. 1s.

WILKINSON (S.).—The Brain of an Army. A Popular Account of the German General Staff. Crown 8vo. 2s. 6d.

WILLIAMS (G. H.).—Elements of Crystallography for Students of Chemistry, Physics, and Mineralogy. Crown 8vo. 6s.

WILLIAMS (Montagu).—Leaves of a Life. 15th Thousand. Cr. 8vo. 3s. 6d.; swd. 2s. 6d.

—— Later Leaves. 8vo. 15s.

WILLOUGHBY (F.).—Fairy Guardians. Illustrated by Townley Green. Crown 8vo. 5s.

WILSON (Dr. George).—Religio Chemici. Crown 8vo. 8s. 6d.

—— The Five Gateways of Knowledge. 9th Edition. Extra fcp. 8vo. 2s. 6d.

WILSON. Memoir of Prof. George Wilson, M.D. By His Sister. With Portrait. 2nd Edition. Crown 8vo. 6s.

WILSON (Rev. Canon).—The Bible Student's Guide. 2nd Edition. 4to. 25s.

WILSON (Sir Daniel, LL.D.).—Prehistoric Annals of Scotland. With Illustrations. 2 vols. Demy 8vo. 36s.

—— Prehistoric Man: Researches into the Origin of Civilisation in the Old and New World. 3rd Edition. With Illustrations. 2 vols. Medium 8vo. 36s.

—— Chatterton: A Biographical Study. Crown 8vo. 6s. 6d.

—— Caliban: A Critique on Shakespeare's "Tempest" and "A Midsummer Night's Dream." 8vo. 10s. 6d.

WILSON (Ven. Archdeacon).—Sermons Preached in Clifton College Chapel, 1879—83. Crown 8vo. 6s.

—— Clifton College Sermons. Second Series. 1888—90. Crown 8vo. 6s.

—— Essays and Addresses. Cr. 8vo. 4s. 6d.

—— Some Contributions to the Religious Thought of our Time. Crown 8vo. 6s.

—— Elementary Geometry. Books I.—V. Containing the Subjects of Euclid's First Six Books, following the Syllabus of Geometry prepared by the Geometrical Association. Extra fcp. 8vo. 4s. 6d.

—— Solid Geometry and Conic Sections. Extra fcp. 8vo. 3s. 6d.

WINGATE (Major F. R.).—Mahdiism and the Soudan. Being an Account of the Rise and Progress of Mahdiism, and of subsequent Events in the Soudan to the Present Time. With 10 Maps. 8vo.

WINKWORTH (Catherine).—Christian Singers of Germany. Crown 8vo. 4s. 6d.

WOLSELEY (General Viscount).—The Soldier's Pocket-Book for Field Service. 5th Edition. 16mo, roan. 5s.

—— Field Pocket-Book for the Auxiliary Forces. 16mo. 1s. 6d.

WOLSTENHOLME (Joseph).—Mathematical Problems on Subjects included in the First and Second Division of the Schedule of Subjects for the Cambridge Mathematical Tripos Examination. 2nd Edition. 8vo. 18s.

—— Examples for Practice in the Use of Seven-Figure Logarithms. 8vo. 5s.

WOOD (Andrew Goldie).—The Isles of the Blest, and other Poems. Globe 8vo. 5s.

WOOD (Rev. E. G.).—The Regal Power of the Church. 8vo. 4s. 6d.

WOODS (Miss M. A.).—A First Poetry Book. Fcp. 8vo. 2s. 6d.

—— A Second Poetry Book. 2 Parts. Fcp. 8vo. 2s. 6d. each

WOODS (Miss M. A.).—A Third Poetry Book. Fcp. 8vo. 4s. 6d.

—— Hymns for School Worship. 18mo. 1s. 6d.

WOODWARD (C. M.).—A History of the St. Louis Bridge. 4to. 2l. 2s. net.

WOOLNER (Thomas).—My Beautiful Lady. 3rd Edition. Fcp. 8vo. 5s.

—— Pygmalion: A Poem. Cr. 8vo. 7s. 6d.

—— Silenus: A Poem. Crown 8vo. 6s.

WOOLWICH MATHEMATICAL PAPERS. For Admission in the Royal Military Academy for the Years 1880—88. Edit. by E. J. Brooksmith, B.A. Cr. 8vo. 6s.

WORDS FROM THE POETS. With a Vignette and Frontispiece. 12th Edition. 18mo. 1s.

WORDSWORTH.—The Recluse: A Poem. Fcp. 8vo. 2s. 6d.

Large Paper Edition. 8vo. 10s. 6d. net.

—— The Complete Poetical Works. Copyright Edition. With an Introduction by John Morley, and Portrait. Cr. 8vo. 7s. 6d.

WORDSWORTHIANA: A Selection of Papers read to the Wordsworth Society. Edited by W. Knight. Crown 8vo. 7s. 6d.

WORSHIP (THE) OF GOD, AND FELLOWSHIP AMONG MEN. By Prof. Maurice and others. Fcp. 8vo. 3s. 6d.

WORTHEY (Mrs.).—The New Continent: A Novel. 2 vols. Globe 8vo. 12s.

WRIGHT (Rev. Arthur).—The Composition of the Four Gospels. Crown 8vo. 5s.

WRIGHT (Miss Guthrie).—The School Cookery-Book. 18mo. 1s.

WRIGHT (Rev. Josiah).—The Seven Kings of Rome. Abridged from the First Book of Livy. 8th Edition. Fcp. 8vo. 3s. 6d.

—— First Latin Steps. Crown 8vo. 3s.

—— Attic Primer. Crown 8vo. 2s. 6d.

—— A Complete Latin Course. Crown 8vo. 2s. 6d.

WRIGHT (Lewis).—Light. A Course of Experimental Optics, chiefly with the Lantern. With Illustrations and Coloured Plates. Crown 8vo. 7s. 6d.

WRIGHT (Miss Romley).—Middle-Class Cookery Book. Fcp. 8vo. 1s. 6d.

WRIGHT (W. Aldis).—The Bible Word-Book. 2nd Edition. Crown 8vo. 7s. 6d.

WURTZ. A History of Chemical Theory. By Ad. Wurtz. Translated by Henry Watts, F.R.S. Crown 8vo. 6s.

WYATT (Sir M. Digby).—Fine Art: A Sketch of its History, Theory, Practice, and Application to Industry. 8vo. 5s.

XENOPHON.—The Complete Works. Translated by H. G. Dakyns, M.A. 4 vols. Crown 8vo. Vol. I. The Anabasis and Books I. and II. of The Hellenica. 10s. 6d. Vol. II. Hellenica III.—VII., and the two Polities—Athenian and Laconian, the Agesilaus, and Tract on Revenues. With Maps and Plans.

See also pp. 31, 33.

YONGE (Charlotte M.).—Novels and Tales. Crown 8vo. 3s. 6d. each.

1. The Heir of Redclyffe.
2. Heartsease.
3. Hopes and Fears.
4. Dynevor Terrace.
5. The Daisy Chain.
6. The Trial: More Links of the Daisy Chain.
7. Pillars of the House. Vol. I.
8. Pillars of the House. Vol. II.
9. The Young Stepmother.
10. Clever Woman of the Family.
11. The Three Brides.
12. My Young Alcides.
13. The Caged Lion.
14. The Dove in the Eagle's Nest.
15. The Chaplet of Pearls.
16. Lady Hester: and the Danvers Papers.
17. Magnum Bonum.
18. Love and Life.
19. Unknown to History.
20. Stray Pearls.
21. The Armourer's Prentices.
22. The Two Sides of the Shield.
23. Nuttie's Father.
24. Scenes and Characters.
25. Chantry House.
26. A Modern Telemachus.
27. Bywords.
28. Beechcroft at Rockstone.
29. More Bywords.
30. A Reputed Changeling.
31. The Little Duke.
32. The Lances of Lynwood.
33. The Prince and the Page.
34. P's and Q's.
35. Little Lucy's Wonderful Globe.

—— A Book of Golden Deeds. 18mo. 4s. 6d.
Cheap Edition. 18mo. 1s.
Globe Readings Edition. Globe 8vo. 2s.

—— Cameos from English History. Extra fcp. 8vo. 5s. each. Vol. I. From Rollo to Edward II.—Vol. II. The Wars in France.—Vol. III. The Wars of the Roses.—Vol. IV. Reformation Times.—Vol. V. England and Spain. Vol. VI. Forty Years of Stuart Rule (1603—1643).—Vol. VII. The Rebellion and Restoration (1642—78).

LIST OF PUBLICATIONS.

YONGE (Charlotte M.) Scripture Readings for Schools and Families. Globe 8vo. 1s. 6d. each; also with Comments, 3s. 6d. each.—Genesis to Deuteronomy.—Second Series: Joshua to Solomon.—Third Series: Kings and the Prophets.—Fourth Series: The Gospel Times.— Fifth Series: Apostolic Times.

——— The Life of John Coleridge Patteson. 2 vols. Crown 8vo. 12s.

——— The Pupils of St. John. Illustrated. Crown 8vo. 6s.

——— Pioneers and Founders; or, Recent Workers in the Mission Field. Crown 8vo. 6s.

——— History of Christian Names. New Edition, revised. Crown 8vo. 7s. 6d.

——— Two Penniless Princesses. 2 vols. Crown 8vo. 12s.

YONGE (Charlotte M.).—The Victorian Half-Century. Crn. 8vo. 1s. 6d.; swd 1s.

——— The Herb of the Field. A New Edition, revised. Crown 8vo. 5s.

YOUNG (E. W.).—Simple Practical Methods of Calculating Strains on Girders, Arches, and Trusses. 8vo. 7s. 6d.

ZECHARIAH. The Hebrew Student's Commentary on Zechariah, Hebrew and LXX. By W. H. Lowe, M.A. 8vo. 10s. 6d.

ZIEGLER.—A Text-Book of Pathological Anatomy and Pathogenesis. By Ernst Ziegler. Translated and Edited for English Students by Donald MacAlister, M.A., M.D. With Illustrations. 8vo.— Part I. General Pathological Anatomy. 2nd Edition. 12s. 6d.—Part II Special Pathological Anatomy. Sections I.—VIII. 2nd Edition. 12s. 6d. Sections IX.—XII. 8vo. 12s. 6d.

MACMILLAN AND CO., LONDON.

———, PRINTER, ALEXANDRA STREET, CAMBRIDGE.

www.ingramcontent.com/pod-product-compliance
Lightning Source LLC
Chambersburg PA
CBHW030348230426
43664CB00007BB/579